THE APOCALYPSE
IN THE LIGHT OF THE TEMPLE

For Tony,
   May the Lord enlighten us all,
in the understanding of this
wonderful text,
      John & Gloria
                  Jerusalem

THE APOCALYPSE IN THE LIGHT OF THE TEMPLE

a new approach to the Book of Revelation

by John and Gloria Ben-Daniel

Beit Yochanan
Jerusalem

© 2003 by John and Gloria Ben-Daniel

Beit Yochanan,
P.O. Box 1106, Jerusalem 91000, Israel
Further information can be obtained at
www.newtorah.org

All rights reserved. Published 2003
Printed in Israel

ISBN 965–555–134–2

British Library Cataloguing-in-Publication Data.
A catalogue record for this book is available
from the British Library.

The cover presents the text of Ap 10,8 – 11,5 in Hebrew.
It has been adapted from the Hebrew-English Bible
of the Bible Society in Israel.

To "those who follow the Lamb
wherever he may go"
(Ap 14,4)

CONTENTS

Contents

PREFACE

Qué nos trató de decir San Juan con todo esto? was the question which occurred to one of us after listening to a reading from the Apocalypse more than 20 years ago—what on earth was St. John trying to tell us with all this? The present work is an attempt to explain the answer that has emerged, little by little, from the study and contemplation of this sacred text. The writing was completed in two stages: the initial draft, which was written in Rome and Milan (1992–1994), was later revised and expanded in Jerusalem (2001–2003). In these places and at all times, we have received help and encouragement from many generous and devoted persons, without whom this book would not yet have come to the light. Without mentioning any names, we remember them all with great affection, and thank them sincerely for their contribution. We also wish to express our thanks for the use of a number of libraries, especially the University Library in Cambridge, the library of the Gregorian University in Rome, and the libraries of the Hebrew University, the Ecole Biblique, the Studium Biblicum Franciscanum and the Caspari Centre in Jerusalem. Above all, we thank the Lord God for giving us the desire and the grace to come to know his Revelation.

This book is sent out with the conviction that it offers a new way of 'seeing' the Revelation recorded by St. John in the Apocalypse—a way that leads to an understanding of its visions *as a whole*, and an awareness of the divine unity in which they were originally experienced. It is written for any reader with an active interest in the Scriptures, and no specialist knowledge is required. However, a prior acquaintance with the Apocalypse is indeed necessary, and can easily be obtained by reading the entire text (only 15–20 pages in length) at least once or twice before embarking on its interpretation 'in the light of the Temple'.

Since the findings of this work challenge modern views about the origin and significance of the Apocalypse, our book is submitted to the Church with special concern for her approval: "For, of course, all that has been said about the manner of interpreting Scripture is ultimately subject to the judgement of the Church, which exercises the divinely conferred commission and ministry of watching over and interpreting the Word of God" (*Catechism of the Catholic Church*, no. 119, citing the conciliar document "Dei Verbum", 12.3).

The biblical quotations in this study have been translated by us from the original languages. For quotations from the New Testament we have used the 'critical' Greek text of Nestle-Aland, 'Novum Testamentum Graece', and for those of the Old Testament we have referred to the Masoretic Hebrew text reproduced in the Hebrew-English Bible of the Bible Society in Israel. The characteristic style of the Apocalypse in the original Greek text has been retained as far as possible, and can be recognized by frequent repetition of the conjunction 'and', as well as a strange mixing of past, present and future tenses.

The numerous biblical references given in parentheses, but not quoted, indicate passages in Scripture that support the statements and assertions expressed in this investigation; there is no need to consult them except when it is desired to check the argument in view. On the other hand the reader is strongly recommended to look at the footnotes, as a lot of extra information and explanation has been placed there to avoid interrupting the flow and overcrowding the main body of this work. For the same reason, the footnotes also contain the unavoidable interaction with scholarly opinions and other interpretations of the Apocalypse. As shortened references have been used throughout the book, the reader is referred to the complete bibliography at the end for full details of cited works and other sources.

The biblical abbreviations in this study are the same as those used in the New Revised Standard Version (NRSV) of the Holy Bible, with the exception of the Books of Kings and Revelation (Apocalypse), where 'Kings' and 'Rev' have been replaced by 'Kgs' and 'Ap' respectively.

THE APOCALYPSE IN THE LIGHT OF THE TEMPLE

INTRODUCTION

This book proposes a new approach to the interpretation of the Apocalypse, or Revelation, of St. John, by applying the traditional method of interpreting Scripture by means of Scripture.[1] The resulting interpretation differs from the one that is presented by the majority of modern scholars, and is called 'preterist'. Whilst these scholars interpret the Apocalypse in the light of the history of the Early Church, the interpretation in this book has been developed in the light of religious traditions concerning the ancient Temple of the Jews in Jerusalem. Whereas the 'preterist' interpretation is founded on the assumption that the greater part of the text is referring to the historical struggles of the Early Church,[2] this

---

[1] The rudiments of this form of interpretation are set out in the *Catechism of the Catholic Church*, nos. 128–130, 140, 111–114 and are summarized in St. Augustine's observation that "the New Testament lies hidden in the Old and the Old Testament is unveiled in the New". In order to carry out the final step in the interpretation of a text, i.e., its application to the present situation of the people of God, or 'actualization', "the most sure and promising method…is the interpretation of Scripture by Scripture, especially in the case of the texts of the Old Testament which have been reread in the Old Testament itself and/or in the New Testament" (Pontifical Biblical Commission, *Interpretation of the Bible in the Church*, IV, A.2). Since the Apocalypse is fundamentally a re-reading of Old Testament prophecies in the light of Christ's coming, this method would seem to be well suited to its interpretation for today.

[2] Perhaps the strongest objection to the preterist interpretation is that the Early Church did not regard the greater part of the text (i.e., chs. 6–18) to refer to her own experiences—as the proponents of this interpretation claim. The exclusion of the Apocalypse from the Canon of the Eastern Church, until the 6th or 7th centuries AD, can be cited as historical confirmation of this, along with statements of contemporary scholars (esp. St. Jerome and St. Dionysius of Alexandria) indicating the prevailing lack of insight into the Book at that time. Furthermore, L. Thompson has recently shown that in the late 1st century, the Early Church did not live in a world of conflict, tension and crisis, and did not experience the widespread persecutions and oppression that it was supposed to have experienced, according to the preterist interpretation (Thompson, *Apocalypse and Empire*, 15–17, 171–72,

interpretation proceeds from the hypothesis that the theme of the Temple is of such great importance in the Apocalypse, that it could be termed the 'organizing principle' of the text as a whole.[3]
This hypothesis is based on the following observations:

1. The various parts, furnishings, objects and actions associated specifically with the ancient Temple in Jerusalem are recalled with great frequency throughout the text. For example the central part of the Temple, the Sanctuary (ναός),[4] is mentioned 16 times

---

chs. 6–9). "It would be a mistake to interpret the Book of Revelation as a response to Domitian's supposed excessive claims to divinity or to a reign of terror at the end of Domitian's rule" (ibid., 116). By attributing to the text a meaning which was clearly not apparent at the time of its composition, the preterist interpretation proves itself to be a form of eisegesis (accommodation), rather than a product of sound exegesis.

[3] This hypothesis implies that the real background to the Apocalypse is not the Roman persecution of the Early Christian Church (as assumed in the preterist interpretation), but the destruction of the second Temple in AD 70 and the subsequent reformation of Judaism at Jamnia. The Apocalypse, then, can be understood as the divine response to the destruction of the Temple. In this preoccupation with the Temple, the Apocalypse is indeed representative of the entire apocalyptic tradition. As noted by J. J. Collins: "Much of Jewish apocalyptic literature was inspired by three major crises that befell Jerusalem and its temple. The first was the destruction of city and temple in the Babylonian era. While the literature of this period is prophetic rather than apocalyptic, it develops already many of the themes and motifs that appear again in the apocalyptic literature of the Hellenistic and Roman periods. The second was the crisis of the Maccabean era, when the temple was defiled, first by the Hellenizing High Priests and then by the Syrian soldiers of Antiochus Epiphanes. This upheaval was the occasion for the first great outpouring of apocalyptic literature in the books of Daniel and Enoch, and also initiated the course of events that led to the formation of the sect that we know from the Dead Sea Scrolls. The third was the destruction of Jerusalem by the Romans in 70 CE. This too was the occasion of several apocalyptic visions, including the New Testament Book of Revelation. The Jewish apocalypses of 4Ezra, 2Baruch and 3Baruch were all written near the end of the first century CE, and expressed reactions to the great disaster that had befallen the Jewish people" (Collins, *Jerusalem and the Temple in Jewish Apocalyptic Literature of the Second Temple Period*, 4).

[4] Most of the current translations of the Apocalypse translate the Greek word ναός by the word 'temple'. In the NT, however, ναός almost invariably refers to the central and most sacred part of the Temple, most appropriately translated by the

(Ap 3,12; 7,15; 11,1.2.19; 14,15.17; 15,5.6.8; 16,1.17; 21,22).
Also mentioned are the outer court (11,2) and altar (11,1), the
altar of incense (6,9; 8,3.5; 9,13; 14,18; 16,7), the golden
lampstand (1,12.13.20; 2,1.5; 11,4), as well as the harps (5,8;
14,2; 15,2), trumpets (chs. 8–11) and libation bowls (chs. 15–
16), which were all used in the liturgical activities of the former
Temple. Certain liturgical activities such as the offering of
incense, divine worship, thanksgiving and singing Psalms[5] are
described with considerable emphasis in this sacred setting,
whilst other liturgical actions are subtly alluded to. Despite this
profusion of Temple imagery in St. John's visions, it should be
noted that the Greek word for the Temple complex as a whole
(ἱερόν) does not appear in the text.

2. Most of these elements of the ancient Temple in Jerusalem are
   recalled in the visions of God's Throne in heaven and its
   immediate surroundings, in a context that indicates the dominant
   and controlling role of this theme in the Apocalypse. In technical
   terms, the theme of the Temple embraces both the spatial and
   temporal aspects of St. John's apocalyptic visions.[6]

---

word 'sanctuary'. This confusion over terminology has probably helped to obscure
the significance of the Temple theme in the Apocalypse.

[5] For a review of the liturgical language in the Apocalypse and its importance, see
ch. 4, 'Unity through the Language of Worship', in Thompson, *Apocalypse and
Empire*, 53–73.

[6] The most useful working definition of an apocalypse is the one proposed in 1979,
by J. J. Collins and other members of the Society of Biblical Literature: " 'Apocalypse' is a genre of revelatory literature with a narrative framework, in which a
revelation is mediated by an otherworldly being to a human recipient, disclosing a
transcendent reality which is both temporal, insofar as it envisages eschatological
salvation, and spatial, insofar as it involves another, supernatural world" (Collins,
"Introduction: Towards the Morphology of a Genre", *Semeia*, 14, 9). Thompson
helpfully notes that "scenes of heavenly worship express the spatial dimension of
transcendent reality in this apocalypse" (Thompson, *Apocalypse and Empire*, 63),
but he does not go far enough. The present study aims to show that these scenes also
underlie the temporal dimension of the visions, up to and including eschatological
salvation.

Given the importance of the theme of the Temple, the immediate aim of this study has been to collect and review information on the subject and apply this knowledge methodically to the relevant parts of the Apocalypse, with a view to understanding its sacred and liturgical setting in greater depth. The ultimate aim of the present study is to apply these findings to the interpretation of the Apocalypse as a whole, in order to clarify the meaning of its prophecy.

For the purposes of this work, the principle source of information about the Temple is taken to be the Catholic Bible, which comprises the Old and New Testaments (these will be referred to as OT and NT respectively) as well as certain apocryphal books. For information that is not available in the Bible, reference is made to other primary sources, such as the first Book of Enoch, the Mishnah, the writings of Josephus, and also to some of the secondary literature on ancient religious practices in Israel.[7] Only a few studies have concentrated on the theme of the Temple in the New Testament,[8] and most of these do not include a detailed examination of their subject in the Apocalypse. There are even fewer investigations that specifically address the theme of the Temple in the Apocalypse,[9] and none of the major commentaries on this Book

---

[7] In this area, the main works consulted for our study are the following: de Vaux, *Ancient Israel: Its Life and Institutions*; Castelot and Cody, "Religious Institutions", in *The New Jerome Biblical Commentary*; Haran, *Temples and Temple-Service in Ancient Israel*; Schürer, *History of the Jewish People in the Age of Jesus Christ*; Pedersen, *Israel: Its Life and Culture*; Clements, *God and Temple*; *The Encyclopaedia Judaica*.

[8] Reference has been made to the following studies: Congar, *The Mystery of the Temple*; McKelvey, *The New Temple: The Church in the New Testament*; Bissoli, *Il Tempio nella Letteratura Giudaica e Neotestamentaria*; Dunn, *The Partings of the Ways*; Walker, *Jesus and the Holy City*.

[9] E.g., *From the Temple of God to God as the Temple* by A. Spatafora and *Jewish Temple Imagery in the Book of Revelation* by Robert Briggs. Following an investigation of background and sources, both these works confirm the importance of the Temple theme in the Apocalypse, which is the starting point of the present study. Margaret Baker also provides a wealth of information on the subject in her recent book (*The Revelation of Jesus Christ*). However, instead of using this information to interpret the Apocalypse, she uses the Apocalypse 'to illuminate the

provides more than a superficial treatment of the subject.[10]

References to the Temple in Jerusalem are found throughout the Bible and reflect its growing importance as the centre of worship for the Israelites and one of the main pillars of their Faith.[11] This first Israelite Temple in Jerusalem was built by King Solomon (1Kgs chs.5–8; 2Chr chs.2–7) in the 10th century BC, on a site that had been chosen by King David (1Chr chs.21–22) on the rocky mount to the north of the ancient city. In the 6th century BC it was destroyed by the Babylonians, and a second Temple was built in the same place by the Jews a few decades later, on their return from exile in Babylon (Ezra chs.5–6). From 169 to 164 BC this Temple was pillaged and desecrated by agents of the Syrian king Antiochus Epiphanes, before being retaken and rededicated by Judas Maccabee, and fortified by the Hasmoneans at a later date (1Macc 1,33; 4,60; 13,52). Starting in 20 BC, the second Temple was impressively rebuilt by King Herod, and its outer court extended, but this work had barely been completed when, in 70 AD, it was demolished by Roman armies in response to the first Jewish rebellion.

---

social, religious and political situation of 1st century Palestine'. She therefore misses the fact that the horizon of the Apocalypse stretches well beyond 1st century Palestine.

[10] On the treatment of the Temple theme in the commentaries on the Apocalypse, Spatafora writes: "The verses containing the word ναός are treated in the commentaries. At times, the commentary amounts to little more than a repetition of the verse itself or to a few OT references. In many cases, the temple is simply understood to be God's abode in heaven. The temple in 11,1–2 is instead a metaphor for the Church....

"All other studies and commentaries appear to analyse the individual recurrences, but they fail to see a relationship between them. At the most they recognize that, in the eschaton, the heavenly temple is replaced by the New Jerusalem. They fail to comment on the development in the theme and the connections between the different references to the temple" (Spatafora, *From the Temple of God*, 7–9).

[11] For a helpful summary of the importance of the Temple in NT times, see Dunn, *Partings*, 31–35.

With the destruction of this holy site, the subject of the Temple has not by any means disappeared from history. In fact, under the question of sovereignty over the Temple Mount, the subject has received international attention recently as one of the obstacles to 'Peace', in the negotiations between the predominantly Muslim Palestinian Authority and the Jewish State of Israel. In their liturgical life and popular expectations, the Orthodox Jewish community has never ceased to insist on the continued sanctity of the Temple Mount and, for almost 2000 years, has kept alive the hope of returning to Jerusalem and rebuilding the Temple in its original place.[12] They are presently being restrained from completely realizing these hopes by the Islamic presence on the Temple Mount.[13]

Throughout the long history of the Temple, and despite its various reconstructions, its original form and situation changed very little. It consisted of an imposing central structure, the Sanctuary, situated within a sacred enclosure or inner court (1Kgs 6,36), which was in turn surrounded by an outer court (the 'great court' in 1Kgs 7,12). The inner court was later extended, and divided into an upper and a lower part linked by a gate.[14]

The Sanctuary itself was composed of three sections:

❖ the inner sanctum or Debir (דביר), which was the most sacred part of the whole Temple, since it contained the Ark of the Covenant and the mercy seat. It later came to be known as the Holy of Holies.

❖ The outer sanctum or Hekal (היכל), which contained the altar of incense, the lampstand and the table for the bread offering. This part later came to be called the Holy Place.

---

[12] According to the Jewish Law, the fulfilment of this expectation is the main criterion for identifying the Messiah (see Maimonides, *The Code [Mishneh Torah]*, Book 14: Judges, Treatise five: Kings and Wars, chs. 11–12, 238–42).

[13] The situation readily evokes St. Paul's prophecy for those who thought the Day of the Lord had already arrived (2Thess 2,3–12).

[14] For more details on the division of the inner court, see de Vaux, *Ancient Israel*, 316–17, and Haran, *Temples and Temple-Service*, 192–93.

❖ The Porch or Ulam (אולם), which connected the entrance of the Hekal with the inner court.

This inner court contained two fixed items of great importance for the cult: the bronze altar on which sacrifices were offered, and also the bronze 'sea' or reservoir containing water for the ritual purification of the priests. The outer court separated the sacred enclosure from the surrounding city and the hill on which it was situated came to be known as Mount Zion. While the inner court was strictly reserved for Jews, the outer court was open to people from the gentile nations, and for this reason came to be called 'the court of the gentiles'.

Excluding the outer court, the Temple was remarkably similar to the description of the Tent (אהל מועד) or Dwelling (משכן) that accompanied the Israelites during their journey from Sinai to Canaan across the desert. In fact, the description in the Pentateuch (Ex chs.25–31; 35–40) presents the Tent as a working model (exactly half the size), or forerunner, of the Temple that was later built in Jerusalem.[15] According to the same text, Moses was given divine instructions concerning the construction of this Tent, and specific laws and regulations governing its administration. The Temple was therefore understood to be the direct successor of the divinely ordained form of worship that was revealed to Moses on Mt. Sinai with the following words: "And they [the Israelites] shall make me a Sanctuary, so that I may dwell among them. According to the pattern of the Dwelling and its furnishings that I am showing you, so you shall make them" (Ex 25,8–9).

Implicit in this remark is the belief, which later became widespread, that the Tent and its successor, the Temple in Jerusalem, were copies of God's Dwelling in heaven, and that there was a close correspondence between the earthly and heavenly forms of worship.[16] The form of the Tent and Temple and their liturgical

---

[15] As indicated by de Vaux, in *Ancient Israel*, IV 2.2, 296.

[16] Studies on this theme include: Hamerton-Kelly, "The Temple and the Origins of Jewish Apocalyptic" in *Vetus Testamentum*, 20, 1–15; McKelvey, *The New Temple*, 25–41; Bissoli, *Il Tempio*.

activity were considered so faithful to the heavenly original that they could later be described as "a copy and a shadow of the heavenly realities" (Heb 8,5) that were revealed to Moses. The heavenly realities that were shown to Moses were, at different times, also revealed to other OT prophets[17](1Kgs 22,19; Is 6,1–6; Ezek ch.1; Dan 7,9–10), and after Jesus had entered the Tent "not made with human hands" (Heb 9,11–12), he revealed these realities to John, who described "all that he saw" in the Book of Apocalypse (Ap 1,1–2).

The principle underlying the present study is thereby confirmed, that the Temple that was revealed to John and is described in the Apocalypse is the same heavenly Dwelling that was revealed to Moses with the purpose of building the Tent or Dwelling of God on earth. There is therefore a close correspondence between the Temple described in the Apocalypse, the Tent that Moses built and the ancient Temple derived from it.

However, this correspondence is not one of simple identity or resemblance between an original or 'archetypal' form in heaven and its copies or 'types' on earth. A fundamental difference has been introduced by the advent of the Messiah. Reflecting the 'typological' relationship between the OT and the NT,[18] the Tent and Temple described in the OT represent provisional and preparative forms of worship, which find their messianic fulfilment in the Temple

---

[17] As a result, the subject of the heavenly Temple became a prominant feature in the apocalyptic tradition. In all of the following non-canonical writings the author ascends to heaven and proceeds to give a description of the Temple there: the Book of Watchers (1Enoch chs. 1–36), the Testament of Levi, 2Enoch, the Similitudes of Enoch (1Enoch chs. 37–71), the Apocalypse of Zephaniah, the Apocalypse of Abraham, the Ascension of Isaiah and 3Baruch (see Himmelfarb, *Ascent to Heaven in Jewish and Christian Apocalypses*, and Bissoli, *Il Tempio*). On this subject, however, the conclusions of the recent study by Briggs should be mentioned: "In short, the belief that John was appreciably influenced by non-scriptural Jewish literature, however true or untrue it may be regarding other themes in Revelation, is to be rejected regarding the temple. The sanctuary strains of the OT testimony alone were apparently more than adequate for John to have built his temple scenes and symbolisms upon" (Briggs, *Jewish Temple Imagery*, 217–18).

[18] As explained in the *Catechism of the Catholic Church*, nos. 128–130 and 140.

described in the NT Book of the Apocalypse. Interpreted with faith in Christ, then, passages describing the Temple in the Apocalypse are found to contain similarities as well as differences, when compared with related passages in the OT. Discussion of these similarities and differences is therefore an essential part of the interpretation, and an integral part of this study. Taking this into account, the method followed in this study is simply to compare, in a systematic way, references or allusions to the Temple in the Apocalypse with references to the Tent and Temple in the OT, or in other primary sources, when information is lacking.

According to the various stages of the comparison, this work is divided into three parts: the first part investigates references to the Sanctuary in heaven with the purpose of defining and identifying the liturgical activity which is taking place there (The Heavenly Liturgy). The second part examines the role of the prophet and prophecy in the construction of a new Temple on earth, whose Sanctuary is the Sanctuary in heaven (The Role of Prophet and Prophecy). The third part considers the prophecy itself, focusing on the culmination of the liturgical activity and the completion of the new Temple, before going on to consider the way in which the Holy City will be established on earth (The Fulfilment of the Mystery of God).

Given that the method used is comparative, continuous reference is made to corresponding passages in the OT. So profound is the relationship between the Apocalypse and the OT that it seems to be the author's intention that they should be compared. The Apocalypse is a short but dense document; it is expressed in the style and with the images of the OT and includes innumerable references, direct and indirect, to its Scriptures. By means of these references, the OT provides a very special resource for the interpretation of the Apocalypse.[19]

---

[19] This point is emphasized and applied effectively by Bauckham, *Climax of Prophecy*, xi.

Just as 'the Law and the Prophets'[20] gave their witness to Jesus Christ (Jn 1,45; Rom 3,21–22; Mk 9,2–8), so also 'the Law and the Prophets' are witnesses to his Revelation.[21] Reciprocally, Jesus reveals himself fulfilling 'the Law and the Prophets' through, and by means of, this Revelation.

---

[20] The 'Law and the Prophets' is a term which refers to the greater part of the Old Testament, i.e., the Pentateuch and the prophetic books. In New Testament times it was frequently used as an expression to denote the whole of the Old Testament.

[21] his Revelation: since 'Revelation' is the true meaning of the Greek word 'ἀποκάλυψις', from which the word 'Apocalypse' is derived, the Book of Apocalypse begins with the words 'the Revelation of Jesus Christ'. These words represent the authentic title of the book, according to an ancient Jewish tradition in which a book takes its title from the first word or words. In fact, 'The Revelation of Jesus Christ' would be a very suitable title for the Apocalypse, since this Revelation forms the source and contents of the Book (Ap 1,1–2).

Plan of the Ancient Temple in the Days of Jesus Christ

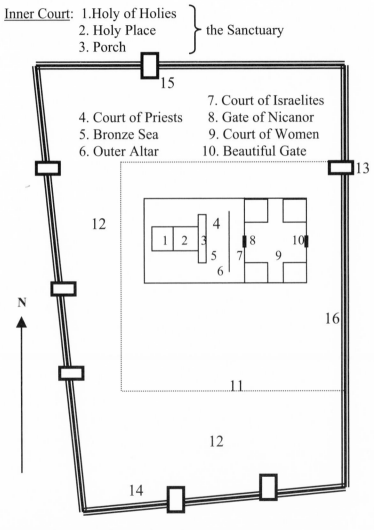

Inner Court: 1.Holy of Holies
2. Holy Place } the Sanctuary
3. Porch

15

7. Court of Israelites
4. Court of Priests   8. Gate of Nicanor
5. Bronze Sea   9. Court of Women
6. Outer Altar   10. Beautiful Gate

13

12

4
1 2 3
5 7 8 9 10
6

16

N

11

12

14

Outer Court: 11 Boundary   14. Royal Portico
(Court of Gentiles)   12. Outer Court   15. Sheep Gate
                13. Golden Gate   16. Portico of Solomon

Schematic Plans of the Temple

A. The Ancient Temple in Jerusalem:

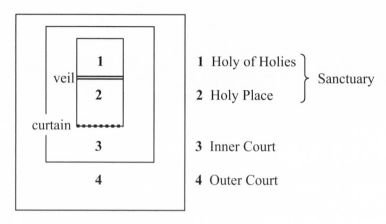

1 Holy of Holies ⎫
                  ⎬ Sanctuary
2 Holy Place   ⎭

3 Inner Court

4 Outer Court

N.B. Excluding the outer court (4), the Tent that
Moses supervised had the same plan.

B. The Temple represented in the Apocalypse:

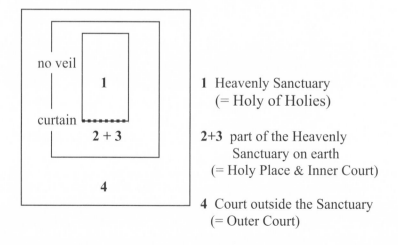

1 Heavenly Sanctuary
  (= Holy of Holies)

2+3 part of the Heavenly
    Sanctuary on earth
    (= Holy Place & Inner Court)

4 Court outside the Sanctuary
  (= Outer Court)

PART I

THE HEAVENLY LITURGY

Chapter 1

The Sanctuary of God

Like many prophets before him, St. John was granted a vision[22] of the Throne of God in heaven (Ap chs.4–5) and of the features 'around' and 'before' it. In the text of the Apocalypse, John uses the term 'sanctuary' (ναός) to designate this heavenly setting (Ap 7,9.15).

It is surprising with what detail the Sanctuary in heaven is described as a place—as a building with an open door (Ap 4,1), to which the prophet ascends and enters 'in spirit' at the command of a voice from inside. On entering, he finds himself in front of the Throne and the One seated there (Ap 4,2–3).

He then sees 'before' the Throne two features that confirm the correspondence between the interior of the heavenly Sanctuary and the interior of the Tent where God spoke face to face with Moses (Ex 25,22; 33,7–11):

a) The seven flames of fire burning before the Throne (Ap 4,5)

---

[22] St. John was granted a vision: the literary origin of the Apocalypse is much debated. In this study, the view is taken that the text is based on a true account of the visions granted to the author through mystical experience. This view finds ample support in the text itself. The saint was fully conscious, but totally passive ("like a dead man", Ap 1,17) under divine instruction. There are visions, locutions and sensations that stimulate all five senses in a spiritual way (sight, hearing, touch, smell and taste). There is ecstasy, spiritual transport and revelation of the entire universe—from the Throne of God in heaven to the depths of the Abyss—and the subject of the revelation concerns the whole earth and its inhabitants up to and beyond the end of the present era. St. John wrote the Apocalypse in obedience to a command from the Lord (Ap 1,11.19) and he recorded all that was revealed to him (Ap 1,2). This revelation comes from God and is "the Word of God and the witness of Jesus Christ" (Ap 1,1–2). Its words are trustworthy and true (Ap 19,9; 21,5; 22,6); they constitute a prophecy (Ap 1,3; 22,7.10) of events in the future (Ap 1,19; 4,1), which are coming quickly (Ap 1,1; 22,6).

correspond to the flames of the seven lamps kept alight before God, on the seven-branched lampstand, in front of the veil that divided the Tent (Lev 24,1–4; Ex 27,20–21).

b) The golden altar on which incense is offered (Ap 8,3–5) corresponds precisely with the golden altar ordered by Moses for the same purpose, and placed beside the seven-branched lampstand, in front of the veil that divided the Tent (Ex 40,26–27).

The fact that St. John did not describe a veil dividing the Sanctuary in heaven, as there used to be in the Tent (Ex 40,1–3; Mk 15,38), indicates that the entire heavenly Sanctuary corresponds to the area behind the veil in the Tent. In the Sanctuary of the ancient Temple, this area was the most sacred of all and was called 'the Holy of Holies' (see plan A, p.14).

However, before John was taken up 'in spirit' to the heavenly Sanctuary (Ap 4,1–2), he found himself 'in spirit on the day of the Lord' and saw 'one like a son of man' walking in the midst of seven golden lampstands (Ap 1,10–20). Since John had to *ascend* and *enter* the Sanctuary in heaven to receive his next vision (Ap 4,1), it can be inferred that the 'place' where he received this vision is *below* and *outside* the heavenly Sanctuary. In the cultic institution that Moses established, this 'place' corresponds to the court that surrounded the Tent, where the outer altar and washbasins were situated (Ex 40,29–33). The corresponding place in the former Temple, which was indeed below the level of the Sanctuary, was called the 'inner court' because it was the inner of two courts.

In St. John's vision, then, there is a form of separation between the 'place' where he sees the seven lampstands and the interior of the heavenly Sanctuary. This separation impedes the direct vision of the Throne and corresponds to the curtain that used to hang at the entrance of the Tent that Moses made (Ex 26,36; 40,28). In the former Temple in Jerusalem, this separation not only corresponds to the curtain over the entrance, but also to the steps that went up to the Sanctuary from the inner court.

As noted previously, the absence of a veil dividing the heavenly Sanctuary in John's vision indicates that the entire Sanctuary in heaven corresponds to only one part of the Sanctuary in the ancient Temple, the most sacred part known as 'the Holy of Holies'. Since the place beside 'the Holy of Holies' was called 'the Holy Place', it follows that the 'place' beside the heavenly Sanctuary, where John sees the seven golden lampstands, can be identified with this 'Holy Place'. So while 'the Holy Place' was enclosed within the Sanctuary of the ancient Temple, in the vision of John the corresponding area is outside and below the heavenly Sanctuary, and corresponds to the inner court. Representing the area closest to the heavenly Sanctuary, but below it, this 'holy place' can be understood as part of the Sanctuary on earth (see plan B, p.14). In the text of the Apocalypse, the two parts together, superior and inferior, come to be called simply 'the Sanctuary of God' (Ap 3,12; 11,1).

Chapter 2

The Spirit of God

John describes his entry to the 'holy place', now identified as the lower part of the Sanctuary of God, saying that he found himself "in spirit on the day of the Lord" (Ap 1,10), the day on which the local Christian communities assemble. Therefore, it can be expected that the assembly of these communities forms the subject of the introductory vision.

The seven golden lampstands that form the subject of this vision are clearly related to the seven-branched lampstand (the Menorah), on which, in the ancient cult, the flames were kept alight before God.[23] However, the seven branches of that lampstand were united at their base, whereas in St. John's vision the seven lampstands are separated from each other. They are no longer united by their base, but through the right hand of the 'one like a son of man', which is interposed between the lampstands and their flames, here represented as stars. In fact, his right hand is in the position of a lamp, and it is precisely a lamp (λύχνος) that symbolizes the role of the Lamb in the New Jerusalem (Ap 21,23).

The mystery that characterizes the introductory vision is explained in the text as follows: "the seven stars are angels of the

---

[23] This vision also recalls a vision of the prophet Zechariah (Zech 4,1–6a.10b–14) in which he saw two olive trees on either side of a lampstand. Oil from a branch on each tree (the two 'sons of oil', Zech 4,14) was channelled into a bowl on the lampstand, and fuelled seven flames that symbolized the Presence of God (the 'eyes of the Lord', Zech 4,10b). In St. John's vision (Ap 1,10–20) the 'one like a son of man' substitutes the two olive branches as the source of oil, as well as the tubes and the bowl seen by Zechariah. The lampstand is represented by the seven separate lampstands and its flames are represented by the seven stars. The two olive trees are identified with the two witnesses, whose prophetic ministry is described in another part of the text (Ap 11,3–13).

seven churches, and the seven lampstands are seven churches"[24](Ap 1,20).

The right hand of the 'one like a son of man' not only acts as a source of unity for all the churches, but also unites every church on earth with its angel in heaven. Just as the seven-branched lampstand was placed in front of the veil in the Tent, and provided a base for the eternal flame, so also each of the churches on earth is situated before the heavenly Sanctuary and provides a base for its light, that is, its angel in heaven. Thus, by means of the local churches, the light of heaven is witnessed to all people on earth.

When the prophet is taken up and enters the heavenly Sanctuary (Ap 4,1–2), that is to say into the upper part of the Sanctuary of God, the mystery is revealed in greater depth. By analogy with the seven-branched lampstand, the seven flames of fire that John sees burning before the Throne (Ap 4,5) represent the lights of the seven golden lampstands. However, in the introductory vision, the stars or angels of the churches also represent the lights of these seven golden lampstands. The seven flames of fire that burn *before the Throne* can therefore be identified with the stars and with the seven angels of the churches.

The fact that the seven angels of the churches are *before the Throne* suggests that they are the same as the seven angels that stand before God,[25] and are later given seven trumpets to sound (Ap 8,2)

---

[24] the seven lampstands are seven churches: even though the seven lampstands are identified with seven specific churches in Asia Minor (Ap 1,4.11), the choosing of seven suggests that they should be considered as representative of the whole Church, since 'seven' is a number which signifies the 'totality' or 'completeness' of a thing (Vanni, *L'Apocalisse*, 53, 184–88; Bauckham, *Climax of Prophecy*, 405). The universal character of the messages to the churches is confirmed by their closing refrain: "The one who has ears, let him hear what the Spirit says to the churches" (Ap 2,7.11.17.29; 3,6.13.22).

[25] seven angels that stand before God: in other contexts these angels are called 'the angels of the Presence' (Tob 12,15), 'the angels standing before God' (Lk 1,19), or simply 'archangels'. According to the biblical tradition, one of the archangels, Michael, was considered to be the guardian angel of the people of God (Dan 10,21; 12,1), identified at that time with the people of Israel. According to the interpetation presented here, not one, but all seven archangels act as the guardian angels of the

and seven libation bowls to pour out (Ap 15,5–8). Their representation as flames of fire recalls the class of angels that are called 'seraphim' in the Old Testament, from the Hebrew word meaning 'the burning ones' (שרפים, Is 6,2).

Furthermore, these seven angels, or flames of fire, are called the seven Spirits of God (Ap 1,4; 4,5) and can therefore be identified, in another part of the text, with the seven Spirits of God sent out into all the earth, which in turn are symbolized by the seven horns and seven eyes of the Lamb (Ap 5,6). Given that the number 'seven' signifies 'totality' or 'completeness',[26] the seven stars, angels, flames, Spirits, horns and eyes, all represent the Holy Spirit of God in his various operations and characteristics.

In summary, the seven angels of the churches can be identified with:

a) the seven stars in the right hand of the 'one like a son of man' (Ap 1,20);
b) the seven angels that stand before the Lord (Ap 8,2; 15,5–8);
c) the seven flames of fire before the Throne (Ap 4,5);
d) the seven Spirits of God before the Throne (Ap 1,4; 4,5);
e) the seven Spirits of God sent out into all the earth (Ap 5,6);
f) the seven Spirits of the 'one like a son of man' (Ap 3,1);
g) the seven horns and the seven eyes of the Lamb (Ap 5,6).

The activity that is represented in this introductory vision can be interpreted with the help of the instructions that were given to Moses, concerning the trimming and refuelling of the lampstand: "Command the people of Israel to bring you pure oil of crushed olives for the lamp, so that a light may be kept burning continually. In front of the veil of the testimony[27] inside the Tent of the meeting,

---

people of God, now identified with the total number of local churches (the Universal Church).

[26] See n. 24 above.

[27] testimony: is the translation of the Hebrew word עדות and signifies the written witness to the ancient Covenant with God. It therefore refers specifically to the Decalogue engraved on tablets of stone, frequently called the 'tablets of the testimony' (Ex 31.18; 32,15; 34,29) or simply the 'testimony' (Ex 16,34). As a

Aaron shall look after it from evening to morning, before the Lord continually, as a perpetual statute throughout the generations" (Lev 24,2–3).

In the Apocalypse, the figure of 'one like a son of man' corresponds to Aaron, the high priest; the sword projecting from his mouth[28](Ap 1,16) is the instrument with which he trims the lampstands, and the Spirit that speaks through him (Ap 2,7.11.17.29; 3,6.13.22) is the heavenly oil.[29] By trimming and refuelling the lampstands, which represent the local churches on earth, he keeps them firmly united to their flames, or angels, in heaven.

Not only does this vision of the trimming and refuelling of the lamps accurately represent the reproof and encouragement transmitted to the churches in the subsequent letters dictated to John (Ap chs.2–3), but it also introduces the liturgical character of this vision of God's Sanctuary.

---

result, both the Ark of the Covenant and the Tent, in which the tablets were kept, were sometimes called 'the Ark of the testimony' (Ex 25,22; 26,33; 40,21) or 'the Tent of the testimony' (Num 9,15; 17,22; 18,2) respectively.

[28] the sword projecting from his mouth: revealing the spiritual sense of the sword employed by God and by his servants in the OT (e.g., Is 49,2; Ps 45,4–5; 149,6–9; 1Chr 21,11–17; Hos 6,5–6; Wis 18,15), the sword in the NT is a symbol of the Word of God (Heb 4,12; Eph 6,17; Mt 10,34–36). In the present context it is used to separate and remove from the churches all that is wicked (Ap 2,4–5.16.21–23; 3,3.19), i.e., it cleans and purifies.

[29] the heavenly oil: the reference to 'oil' as a symbol of God's Spirit derives from the OT practice of consecrating kings (e.g., 1Sam 10,1–7; 16,13) and priests (Ex 30,22–33; Ps 89,21) by anointing them with sacred oil. In the NT the Holy Spirit fulfils and replaces the role of sacred oil in the traditional understanding of anointing (e.g., Lk 4,18; Acts 10,38; 1Jn 2,20.27). Similarly, in the present context, the Spirit which speaks through the 'one like a son of man' replaces the function of the oil in the vision of the seven lampstands: just as oil is needed to keep the lampstands united to their flames, so the Spirit is needed to keep the churches united with their angels before God. This function contrasts with that of the divine sword: while the divine sword separates and divides, the spiritual oil unites and edifies.

Chapter 3

The Priest

After identifying the 'one like a son of man' with the priest who used to service the lampstand in the Tent of Meeting, and later in the Sanctuary of the Temple in Jerusalem, it is entirely consistent that his long tunic, high girding and bare feet all describe the costume of a priest on duty (Ap 1,13.15).

However, besides being a priest, the 'one like a son of man' performs a role of extraordinary importance in the visions of the Apocalypse. He comes on a cloud to harvest the grain (Ap 14,14–15), before returning to the earth to tread the grapes in the winepress of God's anger (Ap 19,15; 14,20), defeat his enemies (Ap 19,19–21) and then repay each man according to his deeds (Ap 22,12).

Furthermore, he displays an authority that is greater than that of any man or angel (Heb 1,4) and can be identified with that of God himself: the description of his head and hair recalls the appearance of the 'Ancient of Days' seen by the prophet Daniel (Ap 1,14; cf. Dan 7,9); he carries the seven angels on his right hand (Ap 1,16.20) and has the seven Spirits of God (Ap 3,1). He shares the titles of Almighty God (Ap 22,13; 1,8; 1,17–18; 21,5–6), whose son he is (Ap 2,18.28; 3,5). Although he has a new name, he has been called the Word of God (Ap 19,13).

Even though the 'one like a son of man' clearly represents the risen and ascended Lord Jesus Christ, and is closely identified with the Spirit and with Almighty God, he also presents the typical appearance of an angel, as described in the Old Testament (Dan 10,5–6; Ezek 8,1–3) and in other parts of the Apocalypse (Ap 10,1–3; 15,6).

This manifestation of the divinity as an angel recalls the occasions in the Old Testament, where the appearance of the 'angel of the Lord' is indistinguishable from the manifestation of God himself.[30] In these situations, the angel of the Lord is merely the visible form by means of which God reveals himself, before proceeding to communicate directly. In the Apocalypse the situation is very similar: the 'one like a son of man' is the visible form through whom the Lord reveals himself in order to speak directly to John. He is therefore the angel of the Lord, sent to John, to show the servants of God (Ap 1,1; 22,6) in the churches (Ap 22,16) what must happen soon.

Being a manifestation of the Lord, the highest authority in heaven and on earth, the 'one like a son of man' represents no ordinary priest in the service of the heavenly Sanctuary, but rather the one with the greatest authority: the high priest. Nevertheless, the plainness of his clothing is striking. He is not wearing any of the ceremonial clothes that used to distinguish the high priest from his fellow priests, such as the ephod, breastplate, robe or mitre (Ex 28,1–39). In fact, he is dressed in the same way as the seven angels who are given the bowls full of the seven last plagues (Ap 15,6).

These angels are wearing ordinary linen,[31] clean and bright, and it is of great significance that the high priest appears to be wearing garments of ordinary linen on this occasion. In the former

---

[30] For example: when the angel of God appeared to Hagar (Gen 16,7–13) and to Abraham (Gen ch.18; 22,15–18); to Moses (Acts 7,30–34; cf. Ex 3,2–6; Acts 7,38; cf. Ex 24,16–18); and to the Israelites (Ex 14,19–31; Judg 2,1–4). In the Apocalypse, the question arises as to whether the angel comes from God or from Jesus. If, from the preceeding analysis of the angel's features, it is not already clear that God and Jesus are One, there is confirmation in the text itself: the angel who transmits the revelation to St. John (Ap 1,1) was sent by Jesus (Ap 22,16) and by the Lord, God of the Spirits of the prophets (Ap 22,6).

[31] ordinary linen: is the type of linen specified in the text by the Greek word λίνον (Ap 15,6). The particular kind of linen is important because, in both the ancient mediterranean society and in the Apocalypse, it was distinguished from a softer and much more expensive variety called 'fine linen' (βύσσος). In the Old Testament, fine linen was the material that was used to make the hangings for God's Dwelling (Ex 26,31.36; 27,9), and the garments worn by the high priest and his colleagues every day (Ex 28,4–5; 39,27–29). In the Apocalypse, both Babylon (Ap 18,12.16) and the bride of the Lamb (Ap 19,8.14) are dressed in fine linen (βύσσινος), with the difference that, in the case of the Lamb's bride, the fine linen represents the good deeds of the saints.

Temple, garments made of ordinary linen were worn by the high priest only once a year, on the great Day of Atonement, in order to enter the 'Holy of Holies' within the Sanctuary (Lev 16,4). These garments were considered too sacred for routine use, even more sacred than the regular vestments of the high priest, which were woven from threads of gold, wool and fine linen.[32]

Besides fulfilling the role of the high priest in the heavenly liturgy, the 'one like a son of man' can also be identified in the text as the victim of a ritual sacrifice, the 'Lamb that was slain' (Ap 5,6.12), whose appearance in the visions of the Apocalypse recall, and eternally represent, the death and Resurrection of Jesus Christ:

a) The 'one like a son of man' (Ap 19,16) and the Lamb (Ap 17,14) have the same unique title: 'King of kings and Lord of lords'. This title corresponds to the description of Jesus Christ as the 'highest of the kings of the earth' (Ap 1,5; Ps 89,28).

b) The 'one like a son of man' (Ap 22,12.16) and the Lamb (Ap 5,5) are both attributed the titles of the Messiah,[33] that is, of Jesus Christ.

c) The 'one like a son of man' (Ap 2,28; 3,21) and the Lamb (Ap 14,1) have the same relationship to God as Father, the same as Jesus (Ap 1,6).

d) The 'one like a son of man' (Ap 3,21) and the Lamb (Ap 7,17) are both at the centre of the Throne.

e) The 'one like a son of man' (Ap 3,1) and the Lamb (Ap 5,6) both have the seven Spirits of God.

f) The 'one like a son of man' (Ap 1,18; 2,8) and the Lamb (Ap 5,6) have both died and are now alive forever.

---

[32] *Encyclopaedia Judaica*, s.v. 'Priestly Vestments' (cols. 1068–69).

[33] the titles of the Messiah: those that are mentioned in the Apocalypse indicate the fulfilment of the most celebrated messianic prophecies in the OT: 'the lion of the tribe of Judah' (Gen 49,9–10); 'the bright morning star' (Num 24,17–19); 'the root and the offspring of David' (Is 11,1–10). The prophecy about the anointed descendant, or 'shoot', of David also appears in other prophetic books of the OT (Jer 23,5–6; 33,15; Zech 3,8; 6,12). The problem of how the Messiah can be the descendant and, at the same time, the root of David, was explained by Jesus when he was confronted by the Pharisees (Mt 22,42–46).

The 'one like a son of man' and the 'Lamb that was slain' both represent Jesus Christ, each corresponding to one of his two natures: divine and human respectively. In other words, Jesus Christ is not only represented in the Apocalypse as the high priest, but also as the sacrificial victim (cf. Heb 7,26–28), in a context which strongly suggests that this sacrifice constitutes the initial and central act in the heavenly liturgy.

Chapter 4

The Sacrificial Victim

In order to clarify the role of the Lamb as a sacrificial victim in the Sanctuary of God, it is necessary to refer to the regulations concerning sacrifices at the former Temple in Jerusalem. According to these rules, a lamb was the appropriate offering in a variety of situations: an ordinary person could offer a lamb as a sin offering (Lev 4,32–35) or as part of a ritual for purification (Lev 12,1–8; 14,10–32), or as a communion offering (Lev 3,7–10). The lamb that was slaughtered at the Feast of Passover was a special kind of communion sacrifice (Ex 12,1–12.21–28). In the other writings of the New Testament, the sacrifice of Jesus Christ is associated with one or other of these classes of sacrifice.

However, there was another class of sacrifice for which a lamb used to be offered—the whole burnt offering or holocaust (Lev 1,10–13). In fact, a sacrifice of this class formed the central part of the daily service in the former Temple. More specifically, the lamb sacrificed as part of the daily service was called the continual whole offering (in Hebrew: 'HaTamid'—התמיד): 'continual' because the smoke of this offering was continuously rising to God on the fire of the outer altar in the Temple, and 'whole' because the entire animal was offered up in this way.

In practice, the continual whole offering involved the sacrifice of one lamb in the morning and one in the evening, every day (Ex 29,38–42; Num 28,1–8), although in the Temple of Solomon (the first Temple) only one lamb was sacrificed each day— in the morning (2Kgs 16,15; Ezek 46,13–15). Added to the continual whole offering, the Law required that there should be an offering of cereal and a libation of wine (Num 15,1–16). The cereal was burnt with the members of the sacrifice on the outer altar, and the wine was poured out at the base of that altar, in the same place as the blood of the victim (Sir 50,15; Lev 4,34; 5,9).

Returning to the Apocalypse, a certain correspondence becomes evident between the continual whole offering (the Tamid) and the Lamb that is seen at the centre of the liturgical activity taking place in the Sanctuary of God. In fact, the 'Lamb that was slain' not only corresponds to a sacrifice of this type, but also seems to fulfil its role in a unique way:

a) The Lamb has ascended to heaven and is seen there in his entirety (Ap 5,6), so displaying one of the typical characteristics of the continual whole offering—its complete dedication and total reversion to God.

b) The 'Lamb that was slain' is alive and lives forever with God (Ap 21,23; 22,3), thus manifesting the other essential feature of the continual whole offering—its continual presence before God.

The Apocalypse is the only Book in the New Testament that directly represents the sacrifice of Jesus Christ as the continual whole offering. In the other books of the New Testament, there is only a very brief and indirect reference to this association; in the account of the Passion of Jesus, it is recorded that he died on the cross at the ninth hour, which is to say at three o'clock in the afternoon (Mt 27,46–50 and par.). In those days, this was exactly the time of the evening offering, in the daily service at the Temple (Acts 3,1).[34]

---

[34] It is confirmed also in the *Mishnah*, m. Pesahim 5:1, and in Josephus, *Antiquities* XIV, 65 (7:480–81).

Chapter 5

The Blood of the Victim

Despite the diversity of offerings and the multiplicity of situations for which they were prescribed, all sacrifices shared a common purpose—that of bringing the one for whom the sacrifice was offered into a closer relationship with God. The whole process is called expiation, or atonement,[35] and was accomplished specifically by the blood of the victim: "For the life of the flesh is in the blood and I have given it to you to offer on the altar to make atonement for your own lives; for blood makes atonement by means of the life in it" (Lev 17,11).

From the details given in the text of the Apocalypse, it is clear that the blood of the Lamb has a profound expiatory effect:

a) it acquires a people for God from every tribe and tongue, people and nation (Ap 5,9);

b) it liberates them from their sin (Ap 1,5);

c) it makes them "a kingdom and priests for our God and they shall reign on the earth" (Ap 5,10);

d) it enables them to purify themselves from their imperfections (Ap 7,14; 22,14);

e) it makes them partners in the defeat of the devil (Ap 12,11).

The association of this class of sacrifice (the whole offering or holocaust) with atonement is already implicit in the Old

---

[35] The origin and growth of the importance of 'expiation', or 'atonement', in the ancient cult is explained in detail by J. Pedersen, in *Israel: Its Life and Culture,* 2:358–75. According to this author, it is difficult to overestimate the significance of the concept of atonement in Jewish society during the second Temple period: "Whatever the view taken of sacrifice, it always contained germs of what developed into the idea of atonement" (Pedersen, op. cit., 359).

Testament (Lev 1,4; 16,24). In the Apocalypse, however, this association is rendered explicit in the sacrifice of the Lamb, which possesses the qualities of a single and most perfect sacrifice; one in which the power to make atonement (a property of the blood of a sin offering) is united with the continuity and integrity that characterized the continual whole offering. It is in the context of this unique and eternal sacrifice that the death and Resurrection of Jesus Christ are recalled and represented in the visions of the Apocalypse.

The fact that the Lamb is identified not only with the sacrificial offering, but also with the 'one like a son of man' who performs the office of the high priest, is of great importance in determining the specific character of the heavenly liturgy. The appearance of the Lamb standing before the Throne, displaying the signs of his sacrifice (Ap 5,6), recalls the great event that took place on the Day of Atonement, when the high priest entered the 'Holy of Holies' with the blood of the victims, and performed the expiatory rite for the Sanctuary: "For on that day atonement shall be made for you, to cleanse you, so that before the Lord you shall be clean from all your sins. It is a Sabbath of solemn rest for you, and you shall afflict yourselves; it is a statute forever. And the priest who is anointed and consecrated to serve in his father's place shall make atonement, wearing the holy linen garments; he shall make atonement for the holy Sanctuary, and he shall make atonement for the tent of meeting and for the altar, and he shall make atonement for the priests and for all the people of the assembly" (Lev 16,30–33).

The Lamb, therefore, not only makes atonement for the priests and the community by shedding his own blood, but his appearance before the Throne in heaven corresponds to the execution of the rite of expiation for the Sanctuary,[36] which the high priest performed on the Day of Atonement (Heb 9,18–22). It follows that the liturgy of the heavenly Sanctuary corresponds in some way

---

[36] The consequence of this act of expiation, for the heavenly Sanctuary, will be explained later (I. 9, iii).

to that of the Day of Atonement, as it was practised at the former Temple in Jerusalem.[37]

Before examining this correspondence in detail, it would be helpful to summarize the principal elements of the heavenly liturgy that have been identified so far:

1. The Sanctuary of God exists in two parts in the Apocalypse: a superior part in heaven, where the author sees the Throne of God, the lights of the lampstands and the altar of incense, and which corresponds to the 'Holy of Holies' in the former Temple; and an inferior part on the earth, which contains the seven lampstands and corresponds to the 'Holy Place' combined with the inner court of the former Temple.

2. In the inferior part, 'one like a son of man' is seen participating in the liturgy that is unfolding in this sacred setting, and can be identified as the high priest.

3. In the superior part, the high priest appears in front of the Throne as the victim of a ritual sacrifice—the 'Lamb that was slain'—in a way that recalls the rite of expiation that used to be performed on the Day of Atonement, in the ancient Temple. Furthermore, the victim has features that recall those of the continual whole offering, whose sacrifice formed the basis of the daily service in that institution.

These elements only give a superficial impression of the character of the liturgy that is being celebrated in the Sanctuary of God. With the purpose of describing it in greater detail, and then interpreting its significance, it is first necessary to outline the activity that took place on the Day of Atonement in the former Temple.

---

[37] This profile of the liturgical theme of the Apocalypse strongly recalls the main theme of the Letter to the Hebrews. In fact, such is the affinity between these two Scriptures that the Letter can be considered a useful introduction to the liturgical aspects of the Apocalypse.

Chapter 6

The Day of Atonement in the Ancient Temple

Information on the Day of Atonement in the former Temple derives from two main sources: the Old Testament and the Mishnah, both of which contain descriptions of the procedure in the post-exilic Temple (the second Temple).

In the Old Testament, the Day of Atonement is described as a day on which atonement was made for the Sanctuary, the altar and all the sins of the House of Israel;[38] it had to be held every year, as an eternal law. On this day, the Israelites had to humble themselves with fasting and refrain from doing any kind of work, as on a Sabbath of absolute rest.

There are three texts which regard the Day of Atonement: the first (Lev ch.16) describes in detail the special rite of expiation that used to be performed by the high priest in the Temple on that day. The second text (Lev 23,26–32) is a severe reminder to the members of the community to humble themselves and not to work on that day, and the third (Num 29,7–11) deals with the supplementary offerings that had to be made "apart from the sin offering for atonement, the continual whole offering with its cereal offering, and their drink offerings" (Num 29,11). In brief, none of the three texts of the Old Testament clearly explain the entire procedure for the Day of Atonement in the ancient Temple. However, in a form that complements the Old Testament sources,

---

[38] all the sins of the House of Israel: with one exception of little importance (Lev 5,20–26), no sacrifice was able to atone for those transgressions of the Law which had been done deliberately, 'with a high hand' (ביד רמה). The penalty for these transgressions was the removal of the transgressor from the community (Num 15,30–31). The specific rite of expiation for the Day of Atonement, however, was able to make atonement for all sins, including those performed deliberately (Lev 16,16.34; Spatafora, *From the God of the Temple*, 21–25).

33

the Mishnah does offer a comprehensive account of the liturgical activity that was performed on that day, in a tractate entitled 'Yoma', which simply means 'the Day'. Here follows a summary of the principal liturgical events described in this tractate:

a) As on every day in the Temple, the Day of Atonement started with the morning service, which included the sacrifice of a lamb as the continual whole offering (the Tamid). The only difference from the usual procedure was that, on this day, all the main ritual actions were performed by the high priest, and not by the ordinary priests[39](m.Yoma 3:1–5).

b) The morning service was followed by a special rite of expiation. For this rite, the high priest bathed himself and then put on the sacred white garments made of ordinary linen, the significance of which has already been discussed.[40] He removed these garments when the rite of expiation was finished (m.Yoma 3:6–7).

c) The special rite of expiation involved the offering of three animals as sin offerings: a bullock and a goat were sacrificed to the Lord, and another goat was led away into the desert, as a live offering for Azazel[41](m.Yoma 3:8–9; 4:1).

d) In the first place, the high priest sacrificed the bullock for his own sins, those of his own family and of his fellow priests. Then he sacrificed the goat for the sins of the community. Between these two sacrifices, the high priest entered the 'Holy of Holies' with a large amount of incense—much more than the amount he was given to offer in the Sanctuary during the daily service—in

---

[39] These actions will be mentioned later, in the description of the daily morning service (I. 7).

[40] See above at I. 3 ('The Priest').

[41] Azazel: according to the first Book of Enoch and other ancient sources, Azazel is the chief of the demons (rebel angels). The account in 1Enoch 10:1–8 describes how he was thrown down from heaven because he had deceived mankind, and was then imprisoned in the desert to wait for the final Judgement (2Pet 2,4; Jude 6). Related to this tradition was the belief that the desert was inhabited by demonic spirits (Tob 8,3; Mt 4,1; 12,43). The connection between the rite of expiation, Azazel and the prophecy of the Apocalypse is discussed later (I. 9, xv).

order to fill the chamber with smoke. To complete the rite of expiation for the Sanctuary, he returned twice to the 'Holy of Holies' to sprinkle it[42] with the blood of each sacrifice. After this he sprinkled the veil of the Sanctuary and the altar of incense. He sprinkled the outer altar as well, before pouring out the remainder of the blood at its base (m.Yoma 4:2 – 5:6).

e) The high priest then approached the third animal, the goat (the so-called 'scapegoat') chosen by lots to be sent as a live offering to Azazel. Placing his hands on the head of the goat, he pronounced a confession for all the transgressions of the Israelites and the animal was then led out into the desert, to return their guilt to Azazel (Lev 16,22). In practice, the goat was taken to the top of a cliff at a place a few miles outside Jerusalem, before being pushed alive and backwards into the ravine below (m.Yoma 6:1–6).

f) While the goat for Azazel was being led across the desert, the high priest burnt the fatty parts of the first two sacrifices on the outer altar. He then escorted the carcasses to a place outside the city where they were burnt (m.Yoma 6:7–8), for it was not permitted to burn them on the outer altar (Lev 16,27; Heb 13,11).

g) To indicate the conclusion of the rite of expiation, the high priest took the scroll of the Law and prepared to read to the members of the community who had gathered in the inner court. He

---

[42] to sprinkle it: according to the description of the rite in the Book of Leviticus (ch.16), the high priest sprinkled the mercy seat, otherwise called the propitiatory (כפורת). This was the name for the cover of the Ark, which was behind the veil in the Tent and contained the tablets of the testimony (Ex 25,10–22; 37,1–9). On each side of the mercy seat, there was a golden statue of a cherub, and between these cherubs, above the Ark, the Lord spoke with Moses (Ex 25,22; 30,6; Num 7,89). In later times, the Israelites took the Ark with them when they went to war, as a visible sign of the Presence of God (1Sam chs. 4–6). Finally, it was placed inside the 'Holy of Holies' in the Temple built by King Solomon, where it represented the place of God's Throne (1Kings 8,5–13). At the start of the exile, the Ark of the Covenant and its cover, or mercy seat, disappeared and have never been found. The 'Holy of Holies' in the postexilic Temple was left completely empty, and it was said that the reappearance of the Ark would herald the end of days (2Macc 2,4–8; Jer 3,16; cf. Ap 11,19).

recited the three texts that deal with the Day of Atonement and finished by pronouncing some benedictions. At precisely the same moment in which the high priest read from the scroll of the Law, the carcasses of the two sin offerings were burning outside the city (m.Yoma 7:1–2).

h) After the offering of the supplementary sacrifices for the Day of Atonement, the liturgy for the day finished with the evening service, which included the second continual whole offering of the day. At the end of the day, the high priest gave a banquet to celebrate his safe return from the 'Holy of Holies' (m.Yoma 7:3–4).

In summary, the parts of the liturgy for the entire Day of Atonement in second Temple times, with their corresponding sacrifices, were as follows:

the morning service: (Ex 29,38–42; Num 28,1–8)	• the continual whole offering (1 lamb)
the rite of expiation: (Lev ch.16)	• the two sin offerings to the Lord (1 bullock and 1 goat) • the live offering for Azazel (1 goat)
the supplementary sacrifices for the Day of Atonement:[43] (Num 29,7–11; Lev 16,3.24)	• a sin offering (1 goat) • a whole offering for the high priest (1 ram) • other whole offerings (1 ram, 7 lambs and 1 bullock)
the evening service: (Ex 29,38–42; Num 28,1–8)	• the continual whole offering (1 lamb)

---

[43] supplementary sacrifices for the Day of Atonement: a certain rabbi (R. Akiba) said that some of these sacrifices (the 2 rams and the 7 lambs) were offered with the continual whole offering of the morning service, while the others (the goat and the bullock) were offered with the continual whole offering of the evening service (m.Yoma 7:3).

Returning to the Apocalypse, it is evident that a great simplification has taken place: the blood of one Lamb has achieved, once and for all, more than the blood of all the bulls and goats, rams and lambs that were prescribed for the annual Day of Atonement (cf. Heb 10,1–18). The heavenly liturgy is based on only one sacrifice, that of the Lamb, which therefore corresponds to the first sacrifice of the annual Day of Atonement: this was the continual whole offering of the morning service, the first part of the liturgy for that day.

So before being able to clarify and define the main elements of the heavenly liturgy described in the Apocalypse, in order to compare them with the liturgical activity in the former Temple, it is essential to make a detailed examination of the daily morning service.

Chapter 7

The Daily Morning Service in the Ancient Temple

There is no complete account of the daily morning service in the Bible, although similar features can be recognized in the account of the expiation of the Temple during Hezekiah's reform (2Chr 29,18–30) and in a eulogy for Simon the high priest (Sir 50,1–21). The only complete description of this liturgical service is to be found in the Mishnah, in a tractate entitled 'Tamid', which means 'the continual'. Here follows a summary of the essential elements of the daily morning service, derived from this tractate:

1. Before dawn: the inspection of the Temple courts was followed by the preparation of the outer altar and of the lamb that was chosen to be sacrificed as the continual whole offering (m.Tamid 1; 2; 3:2–5).
2. At dawn: the lamb was sacrificed at the sound of the opening of the great gate into the Sanctuary (m.Tamid 3:7; 4:1). Its blood was then collected in a basin and tossed over the outer altar. The remainder of the blood was poured out at the base of the altar (m.Tamid 4:1).
3. Within the Sanctuary, the seven-branched lampstand was trimmed and refuelled, and the altar of incense was cleaned (m.Tamid 3:6,9).
4. At the same time, the corpse of the lamb was prepared for burning on the outer altar: it was first dismembered and its members were then taken to the base of the outer altar, to the lowest part of the access ramp (m.Tamid 4:2–3).
5. All the priests gathered to recite the Ten Commandments (Deut 5,6–22), followed by the 'Shema Israel' (Deut 6,4–9), other passages of the Law (Deut 11,13–21; Num 15,37–41) and some benedictions. Then lots were drawn to decide who would offer

the incense and, to the priest who was chosen, incense was given (m.Tamid 5:1–4).

6. A great sound was produced using an instrument called the 'magrefah';[44] heard in a wide area surrounding the city of Jerusalem, this sound announced that incense was about to be offered (m.Tamid 5:6).

7. Burning ashes were then taken from the outer altar to the altar of incense inside the Sanctuary and the priests entered to prostrate themselves. The incense offering followed immediately (m.Tamid 5:5; 6:1–3).

8. After this the priests gathered on the steps in front of the Sanctuary for the pronouncement of the priestly blessing (Num 6,24–26; m.Tamid 7:2).

9. The members of the sacrifice (the continual whole offering) were then taken up the ramp, thrown on to the fire of the outer altar and burnt (m.Tamid 7:3). The cereal offering was added to the continual whole offering on top of the altar (m.Tamid 3:1; 4:3). The consumption of these offerings in the fire represented the culmination of the liturgy: the 'presentation' of the offerings before God.

10. The trumpets were sounded (m.Tamid 7:3).

11. Finally the libation of wine was poured out at the base of the outer altar, and this was accompanied by the Levites, with musical instruments and singing of Psalms. At every break in the singing, the trumpets were sounded and the assembled people prostrated themselves (m.Tamid 7:3–4).

The daily evening service followed the same order, except that the offering of incense took place after the continual whole offering had been 'presented' on the outer altar (m.Yoma 3:5).

---

[44] the 'magrefah': is the name of an ancient musical instrument, about which almost nothing is known. Since the name means a 'shovel', or even a 'rake', it has been proposed that it must have looked like a shovel. In fact, the only thing that is known for sure is that this instrument produced a very loud sound: when it was sounded, two people talking in Jerusalem could not hear each other (m.Tamid 5:6), and the sound could even be heard in Jericho, about thirty kilometres away (m.Tamid 3:8).

Chapter 8

The Liturgy in the Sanctuary of God

After examining the liturgical procedure for the annual Day of Atonement and, in particular, for its first part (the morning service), it is worthwhile returning to the liturgy described by St. John in the Apocalypse. Reading the Apocalypse in the light of these ancient traditions, analogous liturgical elements can be identified and the sequence of the heavenly liturgy can be defined. An outline of this sequence is presented in the following list: the column on the right contains references to related passages in the text of the Apocalypse. The numbers in the column on the left refer to the paragraphs in the previous chapter, in which the corresponding parts of the daily morning service are described. Those elements without a number in the left-hand column correspond to liturgical activities that were performed specifically on the Day of Atonement. An explanation of this liturgical sequence will be offered in the next chapter,[45] with a detailed discussion of differences and similarities.

3	The 'one like a son of man' reproves and exhorts the seven churches.	Ap 1,10–20; chs. 2–3
–	The 'Lamb that was slain' appears before the Throne in the heavenly Sanctuary, takes the scroll and proceeds to break its seven seals.	ch. 5
5	The breaking of the first four seals.	6,1–8

---

[45] See I. 9 ('Discussion').

4	After the breaking of the fifth seal, the souls of the martyrs appear under the altar in heaven.[46]	6,9
6	After the breaking of the sixth seal, there are signs of the imminent manifestation of the Lord's anger.	6,12–17
8	The 144,000 are sealed on their foreheads.	7,1–8
7	After the breaking of the seventh seal, there is a silence in heaven and *much* incense was offered on the golden altar before the Throne, with the prayers of all the saints.	8,1.3–4
9	Fire from the golden altar is thrown on to the earth.	8,5
10	The seven trumpets are sounded.	chs. 8–11
11	The seven angels pour out the seven bowls on the earth; there is singing in heaven accompanied by harps and followed by prostrations.	chs.15–16; 14,2–3; 15,2–4; 19,6–8; 7,11; 11,16
–	The beast and the false prophet are thrown into the lake of fire, to be followed by Satan;	19,20; 20,10;
	the lake of fire is 'outside the city'.	22,15; cf. 21,8

---

[46] the altar in heaven: is the altar described subsequently in the text as the golden altar before the Throne (Ap 8,3), on which incense is offered. As already noted (I. 1), this corresponds to the altar of incense, covered with gold, which Moses commissioned and then placed inside the Tent (Ex 30,1–10; 37,25–28). Later, in the former Temple, this altar was situated inside the Sanctuary, in the 'Holy Place'.

– the resurrection for Judgement before the   20,12;
Throne: scrolls are opened, including the   cf. 21,27
scroll of Life[47] that belongs to the Lamb.

– The marriage and wedding-feast of the Lamb.   19,7–9;
                                                  chs.21–22

---

[47] the scroll of Life: is the same as the 'Book of Life' mentioned in other parts of the Bible (e.g., Ex 32,32–33; Ps 69,29; Dan 12,1; Mal 3,16–18). Even though the Greek word (βίβλος, βιβλίον) can mean either 'book' or 'scroll', it is better in this context to translate it by 'scroll' to facilitate its identification with the sealed scroll that was given to the Lamb (Ap ch.5) and is also called 'the scroll of Life of the Lamb' (Ap 21,27).

Chapter 9

Discussion

i. *The beginning of the liturgy*

One of the first things to be noticed is that all the elements of the daily morning service are represented in the heavenly liturgy, except for the preparation and slaughter of the lamb, and the tossing of its blood (see the summary given above: I. 7, 1 & 2). The analogous actions are not recounted in the Apocalypse. Nevertheless, the opening of the gate of the Sanctuary, the slaughter of the lamb and the outpouring of its blood are all recalled in such a way as to indicate that the corresponding events in the Apocalypse have already happened:

- *the gate of the Sanctuary has been opened*—because John sees an open door in heaven and passing through, he finds himself inside the heavenly Sanctuary (Ap 4,1–2);
- *the lamb has been slaughtered*—since the Lamb is seen inside the heavenly Sanctuary 'like one that had been slain' (Ap 5,6);
- *the blood of the lamb has been poured out*—since the blood of the Lamb has already acquired, for God, people from all over the world (Ap 5,9–10).

Given that the slaughter of the Lamb signifies the death of Jesus Christ on the cross, these allusions confirm that the Easter events form the historical background to the visions of the Apocalypse. Furthermore, the fact that the slaughter of the lamb forms the starting point of the daily morning service in the former Temple, indicates by analogy that the death of Jesus Christ on the cross signals the start of the heavenly liturgy described in the Apocalypse.

ii. *The servicing of the lampstands*

Although, in reality, the heavenly liturgy starts with the slaughter of the Lamb, its description in the Apocalypse begins instead with the vision of the trimming and refuelling of the seven lampstands by the one who is 'like a son of man' and represents the high priest (Ap 1,10–20). As already indicated,[48] this vision corresponds to the servicing of the seven-branched lampstand that was performed every morning, at the beginning of the daily morning service (see above, I. 7, 3) and immediately after the slaughtering of the lamb and the tossing of its blood. The fact that, on the Day of Atonement, this function was carried out by the high priest himself confirms that the introductory vision of the Apocalypse concerns a liturgy that is analogous to the one that was held on the Day of Atonement in the ancient Temple at Jerusalem.

Since the seven lampstands refer to the seven churches, this vision of the trimming and refuelling of the lampstands precisely corresponds to the reproof and encouragement transmitted to the churches in the messages that follow in the text (Ap chs.2–3). In this way, the 'one like a son of man' keeps the churches united to their angels in heaven, just as the trimming and refuelling of the lampstand were necessary to keep the lamps alight in the Sanctuary of the former Temple.

iii. *The Lamb taking the scroll*

Two events follow in the heavenly liturgy, which correspond to specific parts of the annual rite of expiation, performed in the Temple on the Day of Atonement: a) the appearance of the Lamb before the Throne; b) the Lamb taking possession of the scroll from the One sitting on the Throne.

a)   The significance of the Lamb's appearance before the Throne is clarified by identifying the Lamb with the 'one like a son of

---

[48] See I. 2 ('The Spirit of God').

man', who represents the high priest.[49] This event corresponds to the entrance of the high priest into the 'Holy of Holies' with the blood of the sacrifices, in order to perform the annual rite of expiation for the Sanctuary (Lev 16,32–33; see above, I. 6, d). It is implied therefore, that the appearance of the Lamb before the Throne with his own blood has an expiatory effect on the heavenly Sanctuary. In fact, this expiation is represented in the Apocalypse as the defeat of Satan together with his angels, and their expulsion from heaven so that "no longer was any place to be found for them in heaven" (Ap 12,7–11).

b)   Taking possession of the scroll corresponds specifically to the part of the ancient expiatory rite that indicated its conclusion, when the high priest took the scroll of the Law in order to read to the assembly (see I. 6, g). The fact that the Lamb takes the scroll at this point, long before the end of the heavenly liturgy, indicates that the act of expiation has been completely fulfilled and that there will not be any other sacrifices for the expiation of sins, the atonement of souls and the reconciliation of men with God.

This observation has important consequences for the interpretation of those features of the Apocalypse that appear to correspond to the three animal sin offerings prescribed by the Law, for the annual Day of Atonement in the former Temple. This apparent correspondence will be examined in detail at the end of this discussion.[50] At this stage it is important just to note that, in the heavenly liturgy, the possibility for the perfect atonement of souls does not depend upon any representation of the live sin offering to 'Azazel' (the scapegoat). Neither does it involve any form of sacrifice for the sins of the high priest,[51] because the high priest is the Lord himself. Only one sacrifice is necessary to make atonement, once and for all, and this has been freely and completely given

---

[49] As already demonstrated; see above at I. 3 ('The Priest').
[50] See below at I. 9, xv.
[51] The bullock in the annual rite of expiation (Lev 16,6.11).

through Jesus Christ, the Lamb of God: "It is done!" (Jn 19,30; cf. 1,29).

iv. *The breaking of the first four seals of the scroll*

After taking possession of the scroll, the Lamb proceeds to break its seals. The breaking of the first four seals and the missions assigned to the four horsemen correspond to the recital of the Ten Commandments (Deut 5,6–22), the 'Shema Israel' (Deut 6,4–9), and other passages of the Law (Num 15,37–41; Deut 11,13–21; see I. 7, 5). These passages serve to remind the community to observe and put into practice all the commandments (Num 15,17–41), whilst at the same time indicating the benefits of observing them and the tragic consequences of disobeying them (Deut 11,13–21).

Just as the recital of the Ten Commandments and the 'Shema' affirmed the sovereignty of God among his people, so also in the heavenly liturgy the mission of the man on the white horse (Ap 6,1–2) represents the victorious force of the Kingdom of God, transmitted to mankind by means of the Gospel. In a complementary way, the negative effects of the horsemen who follow (Ap 6,3–8) indicate the tragic consequences of rejecting the Kingdom of God, and recall the prophetic warnings frequently repeated in the Old Testament, concerning the curses that would afflict the people if they should rebel against God and disobey his commandments (Lev 26,14–46; Deut 28,15–69; Jer 29,17–19; Ezek 5,1–17).

v. *The breaking of the fifth seal*

After the breaking of the fifth seal, the souls of the martyrs appear under the altar in heaven, in such a way as to recall the placing of the members of the continual whole offering at the lowest part of the ramp leading up to the outer altar (see I. 7, 4). In contrast to the procedure in the ancient Temple, the Lamb in the Apocalypse was not dismembered before being offered as a sacrifice to God, but he ascended to heaven in one piece and remains there as a whole offering that is continually before God.

Instead, the dismembering of the sacrificial lamb, and the placing of its members at the base of the altar are represented, in the heavenly liturgy, in this vision of the souls of the martyrs under the altar in heaven (Ap 6,9–10). Just as the members of the sacrificed animal were cut from its body and then placed at the base of the altar, so some members of the Body of Christ have been taken from the Church on earth by martyrdom, and have been placed below the altar in heaven.

Since the Church constitutes a much larger offering than the body of a sacrificial animal, a longer time is needed to prepare for her 'presentation' to God on the altar. St. John's vision represents these preparations in progress, as the martyrs under the altar were told to wait "for a short time more, until also their fellow servants and their brothers had been consecrated,[52] those about to be killed just as themselves" (Ap 6,11).

From this analogy between the Church and the body of the sacrificial animal, it is implied that martyrdom is the means by which the Church is prepared for her 'presentation' before the Lord.[53]

In the context of the heavenly liturgy, the identification of the Church with the body of the Lamb, Jesus Christ, is reflected in the apostolic doctrine that defines the Church as the 'Body of Christ' (1Cor 12,27; Rom 12,5; Eph 4,11–16).

vi. *The breaking of the sixth seal*

After the breaking of the sixth seal, John had a vision of the signs in heaven and on earth that anticipate the imminent manifestation of the anger of God and of the Lamb (Ap 6,12–17). Among the liturgical activities that took place on the Day of Atonement it is difficult to find any action that might correspond in some way to this vision, and so help to explain it. Having said this, however, there is one event that seems to be analogous in its function as a sign: the sound that was produced by an instrument

---

[52] "…until also…had been consecrated…": this is our translation for the Greek words ἕως πληρωθῶσιν, which literally mean '…until also…had been filled…'. The explanation for this translation is given below in n. 236.

[53] Cf. *Catechism of the Catholic Church*, nos. 675–677.

called 'the magrefah', immediately before the offering of incense
(see I. 7, 6). Also this sound, which was audible as far away as
Jericho according to some witnesses (m.Tamid 3:8), acted as a sign.
At the sound of this instrument, the priests ran into the Sanctuary to
prostrate themselves, the Levites prepared to accompany the liturgy
with the singing of psalms, the head of the congregation separated
those who were ritually impure (m.Tamid 5:6) and the people in the
surrounding area stopped what they were doing and turned to pray.

Just as the sound of the 'magrefah' signalled that the most
solemn part of the morning service was about to begin, and everyone
ran to his post, so also the vision of the upheavals that follow the
breaking of the sixth seal signal the start of the most solemn part of
the heavenly liturgy, and in both situations the liturgy continues with
the offering of incense.

vii. *The sealing of the 144,000 men*

The correspondence between the vision of the 144,000,
sealed on their foreheads with the name of God and of the Lamb,
and the pronouncement of the priestly blessing in the daily morning
service (see I. 7, 8) becomes clearer by referring to the exact
wording of this blessing. The priests of the ancient Temple blessed
the people with the following formula: "The Lord bless you and
keep you; the Lord let his face shine upon you, and be gracious to
you; the Lord lift up his countenance upon you and give you peace.
So shall they put my name upon the people of Israel, and I will bless
them" (Num 6,24–27).

In the Apocalypse, the act of putting the name of God on the
Israelites is performed directly from heaven without any human
intermediary, and is represented by the impression of the seal of the
living God on the forehead of each of the 144,000 men chosen from
every tribe of the House of Israel (Ap 7,1–8). Later John sees them
with the name of the Lamb and of his Father inscribed on their
foreheads (Ap 14,1).

However, the blessing is not only given to the 144,000, but
to all those who take to heart the prophetic words of the Apocalypse
(Ap 1,3; 14,13; 16,15; 19,9; 20,6; 22,7.14). Furthermore, the

innumerable multitude of martyrs standing in front of the Throne in heaven, are also blessed and protected by God (Ap 7,9.15–17). Then, in the New Jerusalem, all the servants of God will see his face and will have his name on their forehead (Ap 22,3–4).

viii. *The offering of incense*

In the heavenly liturgy, there is a direct connection between the offering of incense and the prayers of the saints: "And the smoke of the incense went up with the prayers of the saints from the hand of the angel before God" (Ap 8,4). This connection between the offering of incense and the prayers of the saints displays a direct correspondence with the incense offering in the daily service of the former Temple (see I. 7, 7), since it was also held to be a time of prayer (Lk 1,10; Jdt 9,1; Ps 141,1–2).

As the Lamb lives forever in the Presence of God (Ap 22,3), there is clearly no relation between the offering of incense in the heavenly liturgy and that performed by the high priest as part of the specific rite of expiation on the Day of Atonement, when 'the cloud of the incense covered the mercy seat which is upon the testimony, so he would not die' (Lev 16,13). However, one small detail in the description of the offering of the incense in the Apocalypse recalls an aspect of the analogous part in the rite of expiation: the fact that the angel was given *much* incense to offer (Ap 8,3). The high priest was given *much more* incense to offer in the 'Holy of Holies', as part of the rite of expiation on the Day of Atonement, than the amount usually given to the priest to offer in the Sanctuary during the daily service (see I. 6, d).

The comparison between the heavenly liturgy and the daily service on the Day of Atonement reveals another difference with a particular significance: while, on the Day of Atonement, the high priest himself performed all the main tasks in the daily morning service (see I. 6, a), including the offering of incense in the Sanctuary, it is significant that in the Apocalypse it is not the 'one like a son of man' who offers incense, but another angel.[54] This implies that the one who is 'like a son of man' and corresponds to the high priest is occupied with some other task—a task which will be examined later in this discussion.[55]

ix. *Understanding the correct order*

In the daily service, the priestly blessing followed the offering of incense (see I. 7, 7 & 8), while in the heavenly liturgy the vision of the sealing of the 144,000 (Ap 7,1–8), which corresponds to the priestly blessing, is described before the account of the incense offering (Ap 8,1–4).

The cosmic upheavals prophesied with the breaking of the sixth seal (Ap 6,12–17) are delayed to allow the sealing of the 144,000, so that they will be able to survive on the great Day of the anger of God (Ap 6,17; 7,1–3). As a result, the upheavals will in fact take place after the breaking of the seventh seal, at the sound of the trumpets, and conclude with the outpouring of the seven bowls containing the last plagues (Ap 6,12–17; 11,18–19; 16,18–21).

The events that are announced by the seven trumpets and follow the breaking of the seventh seal, are therefore a recapitulation of what is described at the breaking of the sixth seal, with the result that the narrative sequence of this part of the text does not reflect the true sequence of events.

---

[54] another angel: in the heavenly liturgy the functions of the angels correspond to those of the priests in the liturgy of the ancient Temple—one angel performs the offering of incense (Ap 8,3), angels sound the trumpets (Ap 8,2.6), pour the libations (Ap 16,1) and prostrate themselves before the Throne (Ap 7,11–12). Just as the 'one like a son of man' represents the high priest, so also the angels represents his priestly colleagues in the heavenly liturgy. However, the role of the angels in the Apocalypse is certainly not limited to the liturgical ministry: they also transmit messages and warnings (e.g., Ap 2,1; 14,6–11), revelations and interpretations (Ap 17,1.7; 21,9); they control the elements and forces of nature (Ap 7,1; 9,11; 14,18–19; 16,5) and fight in the wars of God (Ap 12,7; 19,14; 20,1). In spite of all this, they are the fellow-servants of the witnesses of Jesus, of the prophets and of all those who take to heart the words of the Apocalypse (Ap 19,10; 22,9).

[55] See below I. 9, xiv.

In this context, the order of the daily morning service acts as a guide for interpreting the sequence of events described after the breaking of the sixth and seventh seals: according to this order the sealing of the 144,000 men (Ap 7,3) occurs after the offering of the incense in heaven (Ap 8,3).

The text itself provides confirmation of this interpretation of the order of events, based on the order of the daily morning service: "How much longer, Holy and True Master, until you judge and avenge our blood on the inhabitants of the earth?" (Ap 6,10). This prayer for the prompt administration of divine justice is the only petition, or prayer, of the saints reported at this point in the text of the Apocalypse, and can therefore be identified as one of the prayers that rise with the smoke of the incense offered by the angel in heaven (Ap 8,4). The response to this petition cannot therefore be expected to occur before the incense has been offered.

The preparations for the manifestation of God's anger, which start with the sealing of the 144,000, are a sign that the martyr's petition for the administration of divine justice has been heard, and that therefore the incense has already been offered. In this way, it is possible to confirm that the order of the heavenly liturgy follows that of the daily morning service.

x. *The kindling of the offerings*

Following immediately after the offering of incense, fire from the golden altar of incense is thrown to the earth (Ap 8,5). Since this action corresponds to that part of the daily service in which the offerings were thrown on to the fire of the outer altar and burnt (see I. 7, 9), it follows that the motive for throwing fire on to the earth is to kindle the offerings.

In the daily morning service, the offerings were thrown on to the fire, whereas in the heavenly liturgy the fire is thrown on to the offerings. The evident disparity between the two procedures reflects fundamental differences between the ancient Temple and the heavenly Sanctuary. In the former Temple, a fire was always kept alight on the outer altar (Lev 6,2.5.6) and fire from this altar was taken to the altar of incense inside the Sanctuary, when the moment arrived for the offering of the incense (see I. 7, 7).

Instead, the situation in heaven is the reverse: there is always a fire burning on the altar of incense[56] inside the heavenly Sanctuary and fire from this altar is thrown on to the earth when the moment arrives to kindle the offerings (Ap 8,5). Since the fire from heaven is the Holy Spirit[57](Ap 4,5) and the offerings who receive this fire are the faithful who offer themselves in spiritual worship, "as a living sacrifice, holy and pleasing to God" (Rom 12,1), the action of throwing heavenly fire on to the earth can be understood as a 'new Pentecost'.

The final effect of throwing fire on to the earth is revealed in the vision of the conquerors of the beast standing in front of God's Throne, on the glassy sea mixed with fire (Ap 15,2–3). By analogy with the corresponding part of the daily morning service in the former Temple, in which the offerings were presented to God on the outer altar and then consumed in the fire (see I. 7, 9), this vision of the conquerors represents the presentation of the offerings before God. Stretching out before the Throne like the floor of the heavenly Sanctuary (Ap 4,6; cf. Ex 24,10), the glassy sea mixed with fire corresponds to the hearth of the outer altar, on which the offerings were presented to God in the former Temple, at the culmination of the daily service. The vision of the glassy sea[58] therefore represents

---

[56] there is always a fire burning on the altar of incense: the fact that there is an angel in charge of the fire on the altar, suggests that the fire is always burning (Ap 14,18; cf. Is 6,6; Ezek 10,2). It is probably this angel who offers incense and then throws fire from the altar on to the earth (Ap 8,3–5).

[57] See above, I. 2 ('The Spirit of God').

[58] the glassy sea: this feature of the vision recalls another element of the inner court of the ancient Temple—the bronze 'sea' (ים in Hebrew) that stood between the outer altar and the Sanctuary (see plan on p. 13). The 'sea' contained water for the priests to purify themselves before entering the Sanctuary or serving at the altar (Ex 30,17–21; 1Kgs 7,23–26). In the same part of the Temple, there were also ten basins with water for washing the offerings (1Kgs 7,38–39; 2Chr 4,6). In the Apocalypse, all this water is represented by the glassy sea which is seen before the Throne (Ap 4,6), whose surface forms the floor of the heavenly Sanctuary (cf. Ex 24,10). Situated between the earth and the heavenly Sanctuary, the glassy sea appears to have the

the blazing offerings being presented before God, after being transferred to the heavenly Sanctuary at the culmination of the liturgy.

xi. *The sounding of the seven trumpets*

After fire from the heavenly altar has been thrown on to the earth, the seven trumpets are sounded, just as the two silver trumpets were sounded at the corresponding point in the daily service (see I. 7, 10). In the ancient Temple, the trumpets announced the culmination of the daily service (the presentation of the offerings on the altar) and heralded the pouring of the libation of wine at the base of the outer altar.

In exactly the same way, the trumpets described in the Apocalypse announce the culmination of the heavenly liturgy: "And the seventh angel blew, and there were loud voices in heaven saying: the kingdom of the world has become our Lord's and his Christ's, and he shall reign forever....And the Sanctuary of God in heaven was opened, and the Ark of his Covenant was seen in his Sanctuary..." (Ap 11,15.19).

At the same time, the trumpets herald the pouring of the seven bowls filled with the last plagues: "and the Sanctuary of the Tent of testimony in heaven was opened[59] and out of the Sanctuary came the seven angels with the seven plagues....And I heard a loud voice from the Sanctuary saying to the seven angels: Go and pour out the seven bowls of the passion of God on the earth" (Ap 15,5–16,1). It is therefore evident that there is a correspondence between

---

same function as the water in the ancient Temple: that of purifying those who enter the heavenly Sanctuary (Ap 7,13–15). The vision of the glassy sea mixed with fire (Ap 15,2) represents the blazing offerings after passing through this sea.

[59] It should be noted that the opening of the Sanctuary is reported twice in the text (Ap 11,19 & 15,5). It is essential to recognize that these two references describe the same event, and therefore establish a link between the end of the trumpet series and the beginning of the bowl series (see Bauckham, *Climax of Prophecy*, 9). Between the intervening section (Ap 12,1 – 15,4) and the previous chapter (Ap ch.11), there are verbal-thematic links indicating an overlapping of these passages. An analysis of these 'overlapping sections' and other features of the literary structure of the Apocalypse are presented in the Appendix at the end of this study.

the pouring of the libation of wine in the daily service and the outpouring of the bowls in the heavenly liturgy described in the Apocalypse.

xii. *The pouring of the seven libation bowls*

Confirmation of the correspondence between the seven bowls filled with the seven last plagues[60] and the libation of wine that was poured out at the end of the daily morning service (see I. 7, 11) can be found in the text of Apocalypse, in the verses that identify these plagues with the wine of the passionate anger of God.[61] This wine represents the judgements of God that fall on the unredeemed world at the end of time (Ap 16,6–11), and clearly correspond to the libation of wine that was poured out at the base of the altar, at the conclusion of the daily service in the former Temple.

The fact that the libation of wine used to be poured out at the base of the outer altar, while in the Apocalypse the bowls containing

---

[60] the seven bowls filled with the seven last plagues: in this context the word 'bowl' is translated from the same Greek term (φιάλη) that is used for the bowls that contained the incense, or prayers of the saints (Ap 5,8). The fact that the same vessels are used for the plagues indicates that it is by means of these plagues that the prayers of the saints (Ap 6,10) are answered.

[61] the verses that identify these plagues with the wine of the passionate anger of God: in the text, the content of the bowls is described in two ways: as plagues (Ap 15,1.6.8; 21,9) and as 'the passion (θυμός) of God' (Ap 15,1.7; 16,1). In the same context 'the passion of God' is described as wine poured from a cup (ποτήριον: Ap 16,19). In a related context 'the wine of the passion of God' is mixed in the cup of his anger (ὀργή), to give to the followers of the beast (Ap 14,10). In the following passage, the origin of the wine is traced to the eschatological harvest, in particular to the vintage and to the treading of the grapes 'in the great winepress of the passion of God' (Ap 14,17–20). The full description of this wine is not given until the conclusion: the one sitting on a white horse is identified as the one who treads the winepress that produces the wine of the passion of the anger of God (Ap 19,15). The wine, then, represents the passionate anger of God. Its description illustrates a method, frequently employed by the author of the Apocalypse, of constructing an image piece by piece using different but related expressions in various contexts (see Thompson, *Apocalypse and Empire*, 43–45, ch. entitled 'Accumulation of Images'). The image of the wine and the cup for the administration of divine justice originates with the prophets of the OT (Jer 25,14–28; Is 51,17–23; Ps 75,9; 60,5; Ob 16; Hab 2,16).

the wine of God's passionate anger are poured out over almost all the natural world, indicates that in the heavenly liturgy almost all the natural world is considered to be the base of the altar.[62]

In this part of the heavenly liturgy, the great multitude of martyrs sings a new song in heaven, a song of salvation (Ap 7,9–17; 14,2–3; 15,2–4) that finishes with the Hallelujah (Ap 19,1–8). This activity of the martyrs is analogous to the singing of hymns and psalms by the Levites, in the corresponding part of the daily service (2Chr 29,27–30; Sir 50,18).

xiii. *The presentation of the offerings*

There is a remarkable similarity between the effects of the sounding of the trumpets (Ap ch.8–11) and the effects of pouring out the seven bowls described in the Apocalypse (Ap ch.16). The natural elements are affected in a similar way, first by the trumpet plagues and then by the bowl plagues.[63] The main difference consists in the degree of damage that they cause: the trumpet plagues cause damage to only a third part, whereas the plagues strike the elements in their entirety.

This close resemblance between the effects caused by the trumpets and those caused by the bowls in the heavenly liturgy reflects the liturgical use of the trumpets (see I. 7, 10) and of the

---

[62] the base of the altar: the seven bowls are poured on to the earth, the sea, the rivers and springs of water, then on to the sun, the throne of the beast, the River Euphrates, and finally over the air (Ap ch.16). So almost all of the created world represents the base of the altar, whose hearth—as indicated in I. 9, x above—constitutes the 'floor' of the heavenly Sanctuary. On this 'floor' the golden altar of incense is seen (Ap 8,3), and at the feet of this altar, the first martyrs (Ap 6,9). The cosmic symbolism of the altar described in the Apocalypse is prefigured by the outer altar described by the prophet Ezekiel (Ezek 43,13–17).

[63] The similarity of the effects of the trumpet and bowl plagues was first noted by Victorinus of Pettau, in the 3rd century AD, and gave rise to various theories of 'recapitulation', by which is meant the deliberate repetition of whole sections of text. The conclusions of this study oppose the idea that the bowl series is simply a repetition of the trumpet series, and it interprets the similarity between the two as the superimposition of the effects of the bowl plagues on those of the trumpet plagues. In other words, the two series are consecutive, and by no means identical.

bowls of libation (see I. 7, 11) in the daily service of the ancient Temple. The sounding of the trumpets led to the pouring of the libation, which was a sign to start the singing of the psalms. At every pause in the singing, the trumpets sounded and the people prostrated themselves (m.Tamid 7:3). The effects of both the trumpets and the libation were superimposed and resulted in a great act of adoration and celebration involving the assembled people of Israel.

So also in the heavenly liturgy the sounding of the trumpets leads to the pouring of the bowls, whose effects are superimposed on those of the trumpets and result in a great act of adoration and celebration involving the people of God. At the basis of both these liturgical actions, helping to explain the similarity of their effects, is the same liturgical event that is announced by the trumpets and completed with the bowls. This event is the culmination of all the liturgical activity: the presentation of the offerings before God.

xiv. *The conclusion of the liturgy*

The last parts of the heavenly liturgy are clearly similar to the situation at the conclusion of the liturgical activity on the Day of Atonement, in the ancient Temple.

The scroll of Life is opened at the final Judgement, just as the high priest opened the scroll of the Law and read to the assembly at the end of the annual rite of expiation on the Day of Atonement (see I. 6, g). However, there is an important difference: while the high priest read from the scroll immediately after receiving it, in the Apocalypse there is a long interval between the Lamb taking possession of the scroll (Ap 5,7) and the time when he reads it out at the final Judgement (Ap 3,5; 20,12).

As explained at the beginning of this discussion (in section iii above), the act of taking the scroll soon after the start of the heavenly liturgy indicates the conclusion of the act that corresponds to the expiatory rite, with the result that no other sacrifice is either necessary or valid for making atonement. The sacrifice of the Lamb is unique and eternal, and there will be no other sacrifice for the reconciliation of mankind with God. The long interval between the Lamb taking the scroll and eventually reading it out at the final

Judgement has been established, then, as a time of conversion (Ap 6,1–2) and repentance (2Pet 3,9; Ap 9,20).

The fact that, at the breaking of the fifth seal of the scroll, the martyrs under the altar were told to wait a *short time* more until God judges and avenges their blood (Ap 6,11) implies that the breaking of the first five seals of the scroll occupies almost all of this long interval, up to a *short time* before the manifestation of God's judgements.[64] After the breaking of the seventh and last seal, the Lamb is able to open the scroll, but there is still a short period of time before he reads it out at the final Judgement—the period during which the trumpets are sounded and the bowls are poured out. Although the text of the Apocalypse does not specify precisely what the Lamb does with the scroll during this brief period, this can be inferred from the following passage: "The one who overcomes will be dressed like this in white clothes, and I will never scrub his name from the scroll of Life, and I will proclaim his name before my Father and before his angels" (Ap 3,5).

After the breaking of the seventh seal, therefore, the Lamb can open the scroll and begin to perform judgement by cancelling names that are written in it.[65] It is a period of intense scrutiny, which accurately recalls a Jewish tradition concerning the New Year and

---

[64] the breaking of the first five seals of the scroll occupies almost all of this long interval, up to a short time before the manifestation of God's judgements: in concrete terms, this means that the breaking of the seals represents the greater part of the Christian era, from the Ascension of Christ up until the start of the eschatological period. The sounding of the trumpets signals the start of the eschatological period, and the outpouring of the bowls bring this period to an end.

[65] cancelling names that are written in it: the scroll can not be opened and modified before its seven seals have been broken. This implies that the scroll of Life originally contains the names of every person, and for this reason it is called 'the scroll of Life from the foundation of the world' (Ap 13,8; 17,8). Judgement therefore consists in the Lamb removing names from the scroll during the period between the opening of the last seal and the final Judgement, at which time he will proclaim in front of God and his angels those names which he has not removed (Ap 3,5; 20,12–15). Only those whose name remains inscribed will be able to enter the Holy City after the Judgement (Ap 21,27), and those whose name has been erased will be sent to eternal perdition (Ap 20,5).

the Day of Atonement.[66] According to this tradition, the New Year is considered as an annual day of judgement, on which all creatures pass before the penetrating eyes of the Lord in order to be examined; this day is announced by the sound of trumpets (Num 29,1–6) and initiates a period of penitence, which lasts 10 days and finishes with the Day of Atonement.

It is said that three books are opened in heaven: one for those who are completely wicked, one for those who are thoroughly pious, and one for everybody else. Judgement for the few who are either completely wicked or thoroughly pious is already clear, but for the great majority of people it is suspended until the end of the Day of Atonement, after the period of 10 days, by which time the decision will be sealed as to whether a man will live or die. The final decision takes account of all the prayers, mortifications and rituals performed during the penitential period and on the Day of Atonement.

All the characteristics of this Jewish tradition are present in the Apocalypse, not merely in the context of a new year, but in the eschatological context of 'a new heaven and a new earth', which will be realized at the end of the heavenly celebration of the Day of Atonement. The breaking of the last seal of the scroll and the silence in heaven initiate a period of intense examination, prayer and penitence for the faithful, announced by the sound of trumpets (Ap 8,1–6). All human beings pass before the eyes of the Lamb, as Lord and Judge; he examines the attitudes and the conduct of each person with the purpose of recording his final decision in the scroll of Life, as to whether a man will live eternally or die. It is a testing time (Ap 3,10) and "if anyone was not found written in the scroll of Life, he was thrown into the lake of fire" (Ap 20,15).

During this period, therefore, the Lord scrutinizes hearts and minds (Ap 2,23) and does not perform the incense offering as would

---

[66] This tradition is recorded in the *Mishnah,* m.Rosh Hashanah 1:2, and in the *Babylonian Talmud*, Rosh Hashanah 16a and 16b. The origin of this tradition goes back to the annual New Year festivities that were held in the ancient kingdom of Babylonia (see Schauss, *Jewish Festivals*, 156–58).

normally be expected of the high priest in the corresponding part of the daily service on the Day of Atonement.[67]

xv. *Analysing the role of the agents of iniquity*

The reading of the scroll of the Law by the high priest at the end of the annual rite of expiation, coincided with the burning of the carcasses of the two sin offerings outside the city. At the same time, the live sin offering was being led away across the desert to Azazel (see I. 6, f & g). It is not a coincidence that, in the Apocalypse, at the same time that scrolls are being opened for the Judgement (Ap 20,11–12), the beast, the false prophet[68] and Satan are burning in the lake of fire (Ap 20,10), which is also 'outside the city' (Ap 22,14–15; cf. 21,8).

It is understood, then, that there is some kind of correspondence between the beast, the false prophet and Satan on one hand, and the three animals that were offered in the annual rite of expiation on the other. From this observation *two different interpretations* arise, which convey opposing attitudes towards the sacrifice of the Lamb. It has already been stressed[69] that after this sacrifice no other atoning sacrifice for souls is either necessary or valid.

In the first interpretation a clear rejection of the atoning sacrifice of the Lamb is implied. At the end of the specific rite of expiation on the Day of Atonement, the carcasses of the two sin offerings sacrificed to the Lord were burning outside the city, at the same time as the high priest was reading from the scroll of the Law (see I. 6, g). Arising from this observation, there seems to be an analogy between the beast and false prophet on one hand and the

---

[67] This answers the question raised earlier, at I. 9, viii.

[68] the false prophet: is the name given in the text (Ap 19,20) to the 'beast that ascends from the land', i.e., the man who institutes the cult of the 'beast that ascends from the sea', so that this beast may be admired and worshipped by all those whose name is not inscribed in the scroll of Life of the Lamb (Ap ch. 13). In the subsequent discussion the 'beast that ascends from the land' is called the false prophet, to avoid confusion with the 'beast that ascends from the sea'.

[69] See above at I. 9, iii.

two sin offerings to the Lord on the other (a bullock and a goat), leaving Satan to be identified with the scapegoat—the live sin offering to Azazel.

Since the means for the atonement of souls has been fully provided by the sacrifice of the Lamb, the line of interpretation arising from this deceptive resemblance of the beast and false prophet to the two sin offerings represents a total rejection of the expiatory sacrifice of the Lamb. This interpretation, then, can be regarded as characteristic of those who, in reality, reject the sacrifice of Jesus Christ as a means of atonement for their sins. In other words, it signifies the extreme antichristian position that has been present in the world since the coming of Jesus Christ and is finally embodied in the beast,[70] the false prophet and Satan.

Keeping in mind the error of this position with respect to the Faith in Jesus Christ, it is worthwhile examining the interpretation that arises from it, because it indicates how the beast and his false prophet manage to deceive those who are attracted, or even forced, to worship the beast (Ap 13,8) and Satan (Ap 13,4).

The two sin offerings to the Lord were considered to be especially holy (Lev 6,18.22), so much so that those who took their carcasses outside the city to burn them, had to wash thoroughly to deconsecrate themselves before re-entering the city[71] (Lev 16,28).

---

[70] embodied in the beast: in this study the 'beast' refers to the 'beast which ascends from the sea' (Ap 13,1–2), and is described as a monster formed from elements of all four of the animals seen by the prophet Daniel (Dan 7,2–8). Just as these four animals represented four successive kingdoms in the ancient world (Babylonia, Media, Persia and Greece), so the beast represents a power in the contemporary world which reflects elements of all these ancient kingdoms. Since the beast rules from below the waters of the Abyss (see n. 79), its seven heads and ten horns can not be identified with certainty before the beast is revealed in all its fullness during the eschatological period (Ap 11,7; 13,5; 2Thess 2,3–12). This full manifestation of the beast is related specifically with its seventh head, which represents a leader (Ap 17,9) who survives a fatal wounding (Ap 13,3) to become an international ruler with astonishing power (Ap 13,4–8). In this capacity he is described as the eighth head of the beast (Ap 17,11), who reigns for 42 months and is aided by the false prophet (see n. 68 above). In the following discussion, this ruler is intended whenever the 'beast' is mentioned.

[71] de Vaux, *Ancient Israel*, IV 14.2, 460–61.

The blood of these animals was used for the expiation of the holiest places as well as for the sins of the priests and the whole community.

In an analogous role, the beast and the false prophet are two figures that promote the belief that they are performing a divine and salvific role for mankind, in the context of a restored Temple at Jerusalem. This role expresses the complete and utter rejection of the atoning sacrifice of the Lamb, whose blood expiates the sins of all those who turn to God.

Furthermore, this comparison prompts the identification of Satan with the third animal: the live sin offering to Azazel, or scapegoat.[72] The interpretation that derives from this comparison unmasks the blasphemous logic of Satan, already present in our society. Just as the scapegoat received the sin of the House of Israel, and transferred it back to its origin, Azazel, so also Satan is involved in an imitation of the same procedure. Since the evil spirit (Satan) is incapable of removing sin from people, this procedure consists in liberating them, not from their guilt, but from their feeling of guilt, by transferring to God the blame for all the disorder in creation. This process involves the denial that their guilt, or sin, arises from their rebellion against God and is responsible for all the disorder in creation (Gen ch.3). Their denial excludes the need for repentance and God's forgiveness through Jesus Christ. As a result, people become hardened in their wickedness, losing their ability to discern the spirits and recognize the deceptions of the evil one. Furthermore, by falsely projecting himself as the scapegoat that innocently took upon itself the guilt of others, Satan is able to exonerate himself from blame for the rebellion against God and all the disorder in creation. Finally, he proceeds to transfer the blame for this disorder on to God himself, making men think that God, the all-powerful Creator, is a blind 'creative force' that works through trial and error.

---

[72] scapegoat: it is interesting, but without any apparent connection, that in paintings of the Renaissance the evil spirit is commonly represented as a figure with the head and feet of a goat. It is said that this representation derives from descriptions of the servants of the god Bacchus, otherwise known as Dionysius, in pagan mythology.

This diabolical logic urges men to consider themselves superior to God (cf. 2Thess 2,4) and to entrust themselves blindly to their own strength, believing that their future lies in their own hands. In this way, they imagine that their scientific knowledge will enable them to eliminate the prevailing disorders,[73] and create a 'new order'. This form of 'salvation' requires a sophisticated knowledge of nature ('science'), applied, or even enforced, for the so-called improvement of the quality of life on earth, but which in truth is only leading to its destruction.

Moreover, considering themselves as gods, men feel confident to judge the Holy Scriptures and all that is attributed to divine revelation or inspiration, rejecting whatever they consider obsolete, irrelevant, disconcerting or restricting their apparent 'freedom' of conscience and action.[74] In fact, these are the consequences of rejecting the wisdom that blames Satan for the rebelliousness and sin that have lead to man's separation from God (Gen ch.3).

The second interpretation explains the true relation between the beast, false prophet, and Satan on one hand and the three animal sin offerings on the other, and so reflects the Christian position. Since atonement is completely and perfectly realized through the sacrifice of the Lamb, the true role of the beast and the false prophet in the history of salvation is totally detached from the process of making atonement for mankind; *the beasts do not by any means participate in the reconciliation of men with God.*

The true role of the beast and the false prophet in the heavenly liturgy is indicated by the fact that they are *thrown alive* into the lake of fire (Ap 19,20). This confirms the absence of any profound relation with the two sin offerings to the Lord, because

---

[73] prevailing disorders: e.g., aquired and inherited diseases, congenital abnormalities, mental disorders, psycho-social problems, discrimination, crime, anti-social behaviour, overpopulation, accidents, famine, ecological disturbances, environmental pollution, civil and national warfare, and terrorism.

[74] the apparent 'freedom' of conscience and action: is the problem considered in depth and summarized in section 32 of the encyclical letter *The Splendour of Truth* by Pope John Paul II.

these had to be *killed* and their corpses burnt outside the city (Lev 16,27). Furthermore, the fact that the beast and false prophet come to be *thrown alive* into the lake of fire suggests a genuine correspondence with the live offering to Azazel, the scapegoat that was *thrown alive* from the top of a cliff (see I. 6, e).

Before studying this correspondence more closely, it is necessary to make a detailed examination of the function of the scapegoat in the annual rite of expiation.

After the sacrifice of the two sin offerings to the Lord, the goat destined for Azazel was brought before the Lord. The high priest placed his hands on the head of the goat and, in front of the assembly, pronounced a confession for all the sins of the House of Israel, intentional and non-intentional, thus transferring them on to the goat. Then a priest or a Levite led the goat into the desert, loaded with all the sins of Israel. He took it to the top of a cliff several miles out of Jerusalem and there he pushed it alive and backwards into the ravine below. The one who had accompanied the goat returned impure and had to wash himself before he was able to re-enter the city.

The point where the scapegoat was thrown over the cliff corresponds to the place where, according to the account in the first Book of Enoch, Azazel had been bound and thrown as a punishment for his crimes. It is related that Azazel was one of the leaders of angels who seduced the daughters of men (cf. Gen 6,1–4) and taught men how to make weapons and ornaments (1Enoch 8:1–2). It is written that the archangel Raphael was commanded to: "Bind Azazel hand and foot, and cast him into the darkness: and make an opening in the desert, which is in Dudael, and cast him therein. And place upon him rough and jagged rocks, and cover him with darkness, and let him abide there for ever, and cover his face that he may not see light. And on the day of the great judgement he shall be cast into the fire....And the whole earth has been corrupted through the works that were taught by Azazel: to him ascribe all sin" (1Enoch 10:4–6,8).[75]

In the above context, the purpose of throwing the live sin offering off the cliff, at this place, was to return the sins that it was carrying to their origin, Azazel, who was confined to the invisible region below (Lev 16,10.22).

In summary, the live sin offering was a means whereby the unexpiated sin of the community could be gathered up and returned to its source, Azazel, to await the final Judgement and eternal destruction.

Returning to the Apocalypse, there is a striking resemblance between Azazel and Satan: Satan[76] deceives the whole world (Ap 12,9); was thrown out of heaven by the archangel Michael and his angels (Ap 12,7.9); was bound and imprisoned by an angel in the Abyss (Ap 20,1–3), and will remain there until being released for a short time, just before the final Judgement (Ap 20,7–9). He will then be thrown into the lake of fire (Ap 20,10).

Furthermore, the description of the false prophet seems to allude to the scapegoat that was sent to Azazel: he is described as a beast of the earth, which has two horns like a lamb and speaks like a dragon (Ap 13,11). Since lambs do not have horns, the two horns could be those of a goat[77] that resembles a lamb, because like a lamb it represents a kind of sin offering. He speaks like a dragon because he received his authority from the beast (Ap 13,12), who in turn had received it from the dragon (Ap 13,2), namely Satan (Ap 12,9).

---

[75] Quoted from Charles, *Apocrypha and Pseudepigrapha of the Old Testament in English*, 2:193–94.

[76] Satan: in the Apocalypse, this evil spirit is also called the devil, the dragon, the ancient serpent and the one deceiving the whole world (Ap 12,9). In this part of the study, the spirit behind these names is referred to as 'Satan'.

[77] the two horns could be those of a goat: the text at this point leaves the impression that the author does not wish to be too specific in describing this beast as a goat, even though it may be true. It is probable he wished this figure to have a double significance, both as the scapegoat and as Behemoth, the legendary monster who is often represented as an ox in the ancient Jewish tradition (see n. 84).

In fact the description of the false prophet as a live animal with two horns, which has a function analogous to that of a sin offering, is somewhat reminiscent of the scapegoat sent to Azazel, in the ancient rite of expiation. The difference, however, is in the fact that the false prophet receives authority from the beast to serve Satan, and not God.

In the annual rite of expiation, the high priest confessed the unexpiated sins of the community before God and so transferred them into the goat, making a separation between the sinner and his sins. The goat then carried the sins to their source, Azazel.

In the Apocalypse, however, the high priest does not intervene on behalf of God in the analogous process, to separate the sinner from his sins. Instead, the false prophet has the task of taking away not only the sins that remain unexpiated, but also the sinners themselves, all those whose name has been erased from the scroll of Life (Ap 13,8; 17,8). The way in which the false prophet removes them is described in the text: he attracts, deceives or compels these people to identify themselves with the beast, by worshipping him through an image, or by receiving his mark (Ap 13,12–17). The act of worshipping the beast or its image, or of receiving his mark, has the tragic consequence of identifying the person with irredeemable sin,[78] and from that time onwards he is liable to destruction in the lake of fire (Ap 14,9–11).

As the scapegoat removed unexpiated sin from the community in the ancient rite, so also at the conclusion of the heavenly liturgy, the false prophet causes the removal of sin, not by expiating it, but the reverse—by making it incapable of expiation and so provoking the eternal destruction of both the sinner and his sin.

---

[78] Confirmation that these people identify themselves with irredeemable sin is their blasphemy against God, when they are afflicted by the final plagues (Ap 16,9–11. 21). In the act of blaspheming God, they also demonstrate their identification with the beast (Ap 13,5–6). According to the NT, blasphemy against God and against his Spirit is an eternal sin because it can not be forgiven (Mk 3,29; Mt 12,32; 1Jn 5,16–17; Heb 6,4–6; 10,26–31). The entire process recalls, and further develops, St. Paul's explanation in 2Thess 2,9–10.

The scapegoat in the ancient rite carried away the sins, to return them to Azazel, the source of evil. In an analogous way, also the false prophet returns the sin, now irrevocably identified with the sinner, to Satan. In fact, this process of returning the sin to Satan occurs every time the false prophet causes people to identify themselves with the beast, since the beast receives his power, his throne and great authority directly from Satan (Ap 13,2–4).

Furthermore, the beast is formed in the image of Satan, with seven heads and ten horns; the beast is scarlet (Ap 17,3) while the dragon is fiery red (Ap 12,3); the beast is a man whose number is 666 (Ap 13,18) and Satan is a fallen angel (Ap 12,9); the beast ascends from the Abyss (Ap 11,7; 17,8), the place where Satan is bound (Ap 20,2–3). Recalling that the Abyss is formed from peoples, crowds, nations and tongues[79](Ap 17,15), the beast can be identified with that part of the Abyss where Satan is bound, or, stated more simply, the beast is nothing other than Satan bound up in a human form.[80]

---

[79] the Abyss is formed from peoples, crowds, nations and tongues: this can be deduced by comparing several passages in the Apocalypse: the prostitute who sits on many *waters* (Ap 17,1) is also seen to be sitting on the beast with seven heads and ten horns (Ap 17,3), which is submerged in the *Abyss* (Ap 17,8), before arising from the *sea* (Ap 13,1) to kill the two witnesses (Ap 11,7). In these passages, the terms '*waters*', '*Abyss*' and '*sea*' are synonyms, whose meaning is given in the text, when it is explained that the waters on which the prostitute sits are peoples, crowds, nations and tongues (Ap 17,15). All these terms, therefore, refer to human society throughout the world, *above which* the prostitute presently sits, *over which* the beast will come to rule (Ap 13,7) and *from which* people have been redeemed by the blood of Christ (Ap 5,9; 7,9). Similarly, for St. Augustine the Abyss symbolizes "the countless number of godless men whose bitter hatred of God's Church comes from the abysmal depths of their hearts" (Augustine, *City of God*, bk. 20, ch. 7, Fathers of the Church series, 24:267).

[80] Satan bound up in a human form: it is explained in the text that Satan is bound up so that he may not tempt the nations any more (Ap 20,3) until the end of the period of a thousand years; in other words, his spiritual power is very limited during this period, even though it is not altogether abolished (see n. 87). The significance of his imprisonment is explained in depth by St. Augustine in *City of God*, bk. 20, chs. 7–8.

The incarnation of Satan in the beast[81] parodies not only the Incarnation of God in Jesus Christ, but also many aspects of this divine mystery:

1. One of the heads of the beast is 'as though it had been slain to death' (Ap 13,3), a feature which imitates the Passion of Jesus Christ, who appears in heaven as a Lamb that had been slain (Ap 5,6).

2. The head of the beast lives because his mortal wound had been cured (Ap 13,3), a fact that appears to mimic the Resurrection of Jesus Christ, who was dead and returned to Life (Ap 1,18; 2,8).

3. The beast ascends from the Abyss to reign over every tribe, tongue, people and nation (Ap 11,7; 13,1–2.7), in a way that emulates the Ascension of Jesus Christ to the Throne of God in heaven, from where 'he will govern the nations with an iron rod' (Ap 12,5).

4. By means of a false prophet (Ap 13,12), Satan and the beast come to be worshipped by the inhabitants of the earth, whereas it is through a true prophet, John, that Jesus Christ communicates his Revelation to his servants, so that God will be glorified (Ap 1,1–2; 19,10; 22,6.8–9).

5. Finally the beast is thrown alive into the lake of fire along with his false prophet, and there they will be tormented day and night forever (Ap 20,10). Their eternal condemnation is contrasted with the eternal Life of God's servants in the Holy City, where they will reign forever and ever (Ap 22,3–5).

---

[81] The incarnation of Satan in the beast: is summarized in the description of the beast as 'the one who was and is not and is about to come up out of the Abyss' (Ap 17,8.11). This name imitates the Name of God ('the One who was and is and is to come', Ap 1,8; 4,8) and denotes a challenge to God's Sovereignty by the beast and the evil spirit he embodies. This imposture recalls the conduct of the person described by St. Paul as 'the man of lawlessness, the son of perdition', "who opposes and exalts himself above every God or object of worship, finally taking his seat in God's Sanctuary, proclaiming himself to be God" (2Thess 2,4).

When the beast is thrown into the lake of fire, Satan is liberated[82] and goes out to deceive all the nations from the four corners of the earth; soon afterwards, he too is thrown into the lake of fire (Ap 20,7–10).

In summary, perhaps the most memorable event in the annual rite of expiation in the former Temple—the scapegoat or live offering to Azazel—is represented in the Apocalypse by the figure of the false prophet. However, this final part of the liturgy is clearly detached from the expiation, or atonement, achieved through the sacrifice of the Lamb. Coercing men to identify themselves with the beast, who is none other than the incarnation of Satan, the false prophet really does cause the removal of unexpiated sin, not like Christ the Lamb, through the reconciliation of the sinner with God, but instead through the tragic and eternal condemnation of the impenitent sinner (Ap 14,9–11; cf. 2Thess 2,11–12). This role not only reveals an affinity with the function of the sin offering to Azazel, but also leads to a clarification of the relationship between the beast and Satan, as described in the Apocalypse.

xvi. *The messianic banquet*

At the end of the Day of Atonement, the high priest gave a banquet to celebrate his safe return from the 'Holy of Holies' (see I. 6, h), the most sacred part of the former Temple, where there was a danger he might die (Lev 16,2.13). For a different reason, there will also be a banquet at the end of the heavenly liturgy, to celebrate the glorious return of Christ the Lamb: "blessed are they that are invited to the wedding-feast of the Lamb" (Ap 19,9).

---

[82] Satan is liberated: according to this interpretation, the liberation of Satan for a short time at the end of the millennial reign of Christ (Ap 20,3.7) immediately follows the defeat of the beast by the one who is sitting on the white horse, that is to say, by Jesus Christ at his second coming (Ap 19,11–21). Since the second coming is followed immediately by the fulfilment of God's eternal kingdom (Ap 11,15–18), there can be no interval between the end of the millennial reign and God's eternal kingdom. The problem of the interval is considered by St. Augustine in *City of God*, bk. 20, chs. 8 & 13.

At the start of the great feasts in the ancient Temple in Jerusalem, the curtain that covered the entrance of the Sanctuary was opened to allow the pilgrims, who were in the inner court, to see inside.[83] In the Apocalypse, the celebration of the marriage of the Lamb starts with an analogous action: "and the Sanctuary of God in heaven was opened..." (Ap 11,19; 15,5).

Various visions in the Apocalypse reflect the festive spirit of celebration in heaven over the fulfilment of God's mystery (e.g., Ap 7,9–17; 11,15–18; 19,1–9) and the marriage of the Lamb. However, there is only one vision that deals specifically with the theme of the banquet. This vision seems entirely detached from the celebration of the saints and martyrs in heaven and recalls a very ancient rabbinical tradition.

According to this tradition,[84] there will be a contest at the end of time between the two great monsters created on the fifth and sixth days of creation, and kept apart since then: Leviathan, who lives in the depths of the sea, and Behemoth, who lives in the desert to the east of the garden of Eden. It is said that these two monsters will clash and destroy each other, and a huge banquet will be prepared from their flesh, to be shared by all the righteous people who survive the 'birth pains of the Messiah'.

In the Apocalypse, the elements of this tradition are present, although the details are very different. The context of the battle is eschatological, but the combatants are not limited to the two creatures analogous to Leviathan and Behemoth, namely the 'beast from the sea' (Ap 13,1) and the 'beast from the land', or false

---

[83] For the existence of this curtain, see Ex 26,36; 40,28; 1Macc 4,51; and Josephus, *Antiquities*, III, 127–129 (Loeb Classical Library series, 4:376–77). Allusions to the opening of this curtain at the start of the pilgrim festivals can be found in the *Babylonian Talmud*, Yoma 54b, and in Josephus, *Antiquities*, III, 128. For a summary of the procedure at the pilgrim festivals, see *Encyclopedia Judaica*, s.vv. 'Sacrifice' (col. 610) and 'Temple' (col. 978).

[84] The literary sources of this tradition are the following: 1Enoch 60:7–11,24; 4Ezra 6:49–53; 2Baruch 29:4; *The Babylonian Talmud*, Baba Batra 74b and 75a; Leviticus Rabba 13:3 (*Midrash Rabbah*, 4:167) and Esther Rabbah 2:4 (ibid., 9:36). A summary can be found in Ginzberg, *Legends of the Jews*, 1:26–31; Klausner, *Messianic Idea in Israel*, 298–99; and Brod, *Days of Moshiach*, 156–58.

prophet (Ap 13,11). The other combatants include all the rulers of the earth with their armies, assembled for the battle of the great Day of God the Almighty, in the place called Harmagedon (Ap 16,14–16). The conquerors are the righteous, with Christ the Lamb at their head (Ap 17,4; 19,11–21), but they do not eat the flesh of the two beasts after defeating them, since these two beasts are thrown alive into the lake of fire; neither do they eat flesh of any other kind. The banquet of God, in fact, is not intended for the righteous, but rather for the birds of heaven, and it consists of the flesh of all the defeated armies: "Come, gather for the great feast of God, to eat the flesh of rulers and the flesh of military officers and the flesh of strong men, and the flesh of horses and of their riders, and the flesh of all people, both gentlemen and servants, both small and great..." (Ap 19,18–21; cf. Ezek 39,4.17–20).

Chapter 10

Summary and Conclusions

In defining the elements of the heavenly liturgy described in the Apocalypse and then comparing them with descriptions of the liturgical activity at the former Temple of the Jews in Jerusalem, it has been shown that these elements represent the liturgy for the Day of Atonement, in which Jesus Christ reveals himself fulfilling the roles of both high priest and atoning sacrifice. The most obvious differences and similarities that arise from this comparison have been presented and examined. The majority of the differences can be explained by the inexhaustible efficacy of the sacrifice of Jesus Christ, in atoning for sin and thus reconciling men with God.

The Passion and Resurrection of Jesus Christ occupy a central place in the visions of the Apocalypse. They are not only eternally recalled in the figure of the 'Lamb that was slain', but they are also the starting point of the liturgy that unfolds around the Lamb, within the Sanctuary of God.

It is evident from the foregoing comparison that the order and individual elements of this heavenly liturgy correspond closely to those of the daily morning service, as practised in the former Temple. However, added to this basic sequence of liturgical actions, there are also elements analogous to the liturgy that was specific for the Day of Atonement.

These observations can be explained by the fact that the liturgy in the Apocalypse represents, in a condensed and simplified way, the liturgy that was performed on the Day of Atonement at the Temple in Jerusalem. As the fulfilment of every kind of sacrifice, the Lamb substitutes all the sacrifices that were offered on the Day of Atonement, and therefore corresponds to the first sacrifice on that day: the lamb chosen as the continual whole offering in the morning service. As a result, the heavenly liturgy described in the Apocalypse corresponds closely to the morning service, as it was performed on the Day of Atonement, and includes other liturgical elements that recall the specific rite of expiation for that day.

As previously observed, the introductory vision of the seven golden lampstands and the subsequent messages to the churches (Ap 1,10–20; chs.2–3) represent the trimming and refuelling of the seven-branched lampstand at the start of the morning service in the ancient Temple. The appearance of the Lamb before the Throne of God in heaven (Ap 5,6) corresponds to the entrance of the high priest into the most sacred part of the Temple on the annual Day of Atonement, in order to achieve expiation with the blood of the victims. The missions of the first four horses and their horsemen (Ap 6,1–8) represent the part of the morning service reserved for the reading of the Ten Commandments and other parts of the Law. The souls of the martyrs who appear under the altar in heaven (Ap 6,9) correspond to the members of the sacrifice, after being transferred to the base of the outer altar in the former Temple. The sealing of the 144,000 men that is described in the Apocalypse (Ap 7,1–8) corresponds to the pronouncement of the priestly blessing. The offering of a great quantity of incense with the prayers of the saints on the golden altar in heaven (Ap 8,3–4) recalls the same action in the morning service of the former Temple, which was also considered as a time of prayer for all the community. The angel who throws fire on to the earth from the altar in heaven (Ap 8,5), evokes the act of throwing the offerings on to the fire that was always kept alight on the outer altar. The sounding of the seven trumpets (Ap chs.8–11) and the outpouring of the bowls (Ap chs.15–16) together with the singing of the celestial choirs described in the Apocalypse (Ap 7,9–17; 14,2–3; 15,3–4; 19,1–8) are analogous to the use of the trumpets and bowls at the culmination of the morning service, a time when the Levitical musicians used to sing psalms and praise to God.

At the conclusion of the heavenly liturgy, the scroll of Life, which had been given to the Lamb a long time previously (Ap 5,7–14), is opened and read out at the final Judgement (Ap 20,11–12), just as the high priest used to read from the scroll of the Law at the end of the special rite of expiation on the Day of Atonement. In the Apocalypse all the agents of iniquity, including Satan himself, are thrown alive into the lake of fire, to bring an end to sin forever, whilst in the annual rite of expiation the scapegoat was thrown alive from a cliff, only temporarily removing sins from the community.

Defined in this way, the heavenly liturgy includes a large number of the liturgical elements mentioned in the text of the Apocalypse, but not all. For example, the filling of the heavenly Sanctuary with the smoke of the glory and power of God (Ap 15,8) is not included, and neither are the allusions in the text to the Jewish Feasts of Tabernacles (Ap 7,1–17) and Pentecost (Ap 14,1–5). These elements will be treated in the third section of this study, together with a more detailed examination of the concluding part of the heavenly liturgy, whose meaning has not been thoroughly investigated in this section.

In conclusion, the Passion and Resurrection of Jesus Christ constitute the starting point of a liturgy that is currently being celebrated in heaven; this liturgy continues up until the end of time and represents a synthesis of the liturgy that was performed on the Day of Atonement at the ancient Temple of the Jews in Jerusalem. Being the principal activity in the heavenly Sanctuary, the liturgy not only provides a framework that embraces the entire sequence of visions in the Apocalypse, but also determines the course of events on earth.

The heavenly liturgy, therefore, imposes its order on every part of the Revelation and on all the events prophesied in the Apocalypse, uniting them in a single and coherent Vision dominated by the theme of Atonement—the Love of Christ reconciling mankind with God. The Apocalypse, in fact, is nothing else but the revelation of the course of this liturgy of reconciliation taking place in heaven, and of its consequences for the lives of the peoples, believers and non-believers, on earth.

Chapter 11

Implications

The findings of this part of the study resonate in various aspects of Christian life and devotion, but there are three implications, in particular, that need to be stated clearly. The first concerns the re-establishment of the ancient sacrificial cult of the Jews, the second is about the interpretation of the Book of Apocalypse in general, and the third refers to the interpretation of one part of the Apocalypse in particular, the part that describes the 'Millennium'.

i. *For the re-establishment of the ancient cult*

Representing a synthesis of the liturgy that was performed on the most solemn and important day in the ancient calendar of the Jews, the liturgy revealed in the Apocalypse presents itself as the fulfilment of the ceremonial Law, or rather that part of the Law that dealt with the ancient sacrificial cult (cf. Mt 5,17–19). It is in this context that Jesus Christ, as in no other book of the New Testament, reveals himself fulfilling every type of sacrifice in the form of the continual whole offering. More than any other type of sacrifice, the continual whole offering formed the basis of the ancient sacrificial cult of the Jews, and it was a tragedy for them when this sacrifice was suspended, as happened temporarily following the profanation of the Temple by emissaries of Antiochus Epiphanes in 167 BC (1Macc ch.1), and then definitively when Roman armies destroyed the Temple in 70 AD.

In the form of the continual whole offering, then, Jesus Christ reveals himself in a way that most clearly demonstrates that the sacrificial cult of the Jews has been completely fulfilled and is now obsolete. It follows that every intention or attempt to reconstruct the Temple and re-establish the cult[85] is opposed to the truth of God revealed in Jesus Christ.

ii. *For the interpretation of the Apocalypse*

The clarification of the heavenly liturgy carries two significant implications for the interpretation of the Book of Apocalypse. The first concerns the fact that, on the analogy of the liturgy of the former Temple, the liturgy revealed in the Apocalypse follows a very precise chronological order. Since the events described in the visions of the Apocalypse are determined by this order, it follows that these events also succeed one another in a definite temporal order.

The second implication derives from the fact that the culmination of the liturgy in the former Temple coincided with its conclusion, and was indicated by the blowing of trumpets and the outpouring of the libation. In an analogous way, the culmination of the heavenly liturgy can be identified with its conclusion, which takes place at the end of time and is also signalled by the sounding of trumpets and the outpouring of libation bowls. The fact that the greater part of the text of the Apocalypse is concerned with this conclusive part of the heavenly liturgy, from chapter 8 onwards, indicates that the greater part of the Apocalypse is a prophecy of what will happen at the end of time—it is an eschatological prophecy and ought to be interpreted as such.[86]

---

[85] every intention or attempt to reconstruct the Temple and re-establish the cult: this is one of the 'achievements' of the reign of 'the beast from the sea' and his partner 'the beast from the land', and will be considered in III. 3 ('The Pseudo-messianic Reign').

[86] it is an eschatological prophecy and ought to be interpreted as such: these findings agree not only with the interpretation of the Apocalypse that prevailed in the Early Church, but also with the views of the faithful throughout the centuries (the 'sensus fidei'), on the basis of which the word 'Apocalypse' has become virtually synonymous with the 'end of the world'. More significantly, these findings offer a rational basis for rejecting the 'preterist' interpretation of the Apocalypse, according to which the greater part of this Book refers primarily to the persecutions suffered by the Early Church, under the Roman imperial authorities (see n. 2). Basing itself on the restrictive assumption that St. John was only addressing the situation that

iii. *For the interpretation of the 'Millennium' (Ap 20,2–6)*

The heavenly liturgy, which began with the Passion of Jesus Christ and lasts until the final Judgement at the end of time, corresponds to the annual Day of Atonement in the former Temple, and therefore represents one day in heaven. On the basis of the ancient biblical formula stating "that one day with the Lord is like a thousand years and a thousand years is like one day" (2Pet 3,8), it is possible to understand more fully the context and the significance of the passage in the Apocalypse that describes the reign of Christ with his saints as a period of a thousand years, often called the 'Millennium' (Ap 20,2–6).

In reality, this period does not represent the length of time determined by a thousand revolutions of the earth around the sun, following the second coming of Christ (Ap 19,11–21); instead it represents the unspecified period of time on earth that coincides with the day in heaven, which is analogous to the Day of Atonement in the former Temple. The Millennium, then, should be identified with the present age of salvation,[87] which follows the Passion and

---

prevailed at the time he was writing (the end of the 1st century AD), the 'preterist' interpretation fails to explain many features of the sacred text, especially its orientation toward, and attention to, the eschatological period of history. Unfortunately this interpretation has found its way into the commentaries of the Bibles most widely used by Catholics (e.g., the Jerusalem Bible, the New American Bible, La Biblia Latinoaméricana) and continues to be promoted actively by the ecclesiastical Authorities (e.g., Conferenza Episcopale Italiana, *Incontro Alla Bibbia*, 54).

[87] The Millennium, then, should be identified with the present age of salvation: since we are living in the Millennium, it is implied that Satan is locked and chained in the Abyss (Ap 20,3). This is difficult to reconcile with the presence of his 'sign' in heaven (Ap 12,3). How can the evil spirit be represented in heaven, and have influence there, while he is locked and chained in the Abyss? This question articulates the mystery of iniquity. "Why do you wonder? I will tell you the mystery of the woman, and of the beast with seven heads and ten horns that is supporting her" (Ap 17,7) says the angel to St. John, referring to Babylon, the great prostitute, whose sins "have piled up to heaven" (Ap 18,5). The fact that her sins have reached up to heaven indicates that it is through the sins of the prostitute that Satan is able to exercise his influence in heaven and on earth, despite being locked and chained in the Abyss (for further discussion of this subject, see III. 4: 'The Mystery of Iniquity').

Resurrection of Jesus Christ and lasts up to his second coming, at the time of the final Judgement.

This conclusion about the Millennium agrees with the interpretation of St. Augustine of Hippo,[88] which forms the basis of the teaching of the Catholic Church concerning the reign of Christ, but it contradicts the opinions of those who are called 'millenarians'.[89] These people, in fact, deny the reality of the millennial reign of Christ in the present age, and are expecting that it will start after the second coming of Christ.

However, referring to the original expression of the formula about the period of a thousand years, it is evident that even the opinions of the millenarians have been anticipated: "For a thousand years in your sight [O Lord] are like a yesterday which has passed, like a watch in the night" (Ps 90,4). For those who are not able to recognize the Millennium in the present age, it will be revealed at the end of time as 'a yesterday already passed' and eternity will follow.

There is one day in particular, the Sabbath, which expresses the character of both the Day of Atonement and the Millennium, in such a way as to confirm the link between them. Concerning the Day of Atonement it is written: "It shall be a Sabbath of solemn rest[90] for

---

[88] Augustine, *City of God*, bk. 20, chs. 6–9.

[89] those who are called 'millenarians': they interpret the millennial reign of Christ with his saints as the destiny of the Church in an interval between the second coming of Christ and the final Judgement. Although this 'literalistic' interpretation of Ap 20,4–6 has a very long history, it has never been adopted by the Catholic Church: firstly because it was associated with the unrestricted enjoyment of sensual pleasures, and secondly because it implicitly denies that already, in the present age, the millennial reign of Christ subsists in the Church; see *Catechism of the Catholic Church*, nos. 663–672, 680. For this reason the millenarians tend to be Protestants. A variant of this interpretation, called 'dispensationalism', identifies the millennial reign of Christ, not with the destiny of the Church, but with the restoration of Israel centred on Jerusalem, in fulfilment of ancient prophecies interpreted in a fundamentalist way (see n. 272). According to this view the Church will no longer exist during this period, because at the second coming of Christ she will 'seized up into the air to meet the Lord' (Ladd, *Commentary on the Revelation*, 12, 260–61).

[90] a Sabbath of solemn rest: is the translation of שבת שבתון, which literally means 'a Sabbath of Sabbaths'.

you and you shall afflict your souls: from the evening of the ninth day of the month until the following evening, you will celebrate your Sabbath" (Lev 23,32).

In the biblical tradition, the concept of the Millennium originates from the account of creation in seven days (Gen 1,1 – 2,4), and in this way became identified with the seventh and last day, called the 'Sabbath'. In the account of creation every day was thought to represent a thousand years, according to the words of the Psalm (Ps 90,4), and the seventh and last period of a thousand years, which corresponds to the day on which God rested from his work, was anticipated to be a period of rest, peace and blessing on earth, under the leadership of the Messiah, the Sovereign anointed by God.[91]

It is therefore, above all, the theme of 'rest' that links both the Day of Atonement and the Millennium with the Sabbath,[92] and for this reason the theme of sabbatical, and millennial, rest[93] is clearly reflected in the text of the Apocalypse (cf. Heb 3,7 – 4,11), in the following contexts:

a) the martyrs under the altar in heaven were told to *rest* a short time more until the judgements of God take place at the end of time (Ap 6,11);

b) those who die in the Lord (the saints) are able to *rest* from their labours; nevertheless their good works follow them (Ap 14,13).

The fact that the saints work for salvation on earth and take their rest in heaven guides the authentic interpretation of the millennial reign of Christ with his saints. The Millennium does not consist in

---

[91] Cf. 1Enoch chs. 91–104; 2Enoch chs. 30–33.

[92] Sabbath: the word 'Sabbath' derives, in fact, from the Hebrew verb לשבות, which means 'to refrain from work' or 'rest' (Gen 2,2–3).

[93] The relationship between the Sabbath rest and the millennial reign of Christ indicates exactly how Jesus Christ fulfilled the OT Law concerning the Sabbath (Ex 20,8–11; Deut 5,12–15; cf. Mt 5,17). Just as the Sabbath formed the basis of an eternal Covenant between God and Israel (Ex 31,12–17; 35,1–3), so also the Sabbath rest continues to be at the base of the new and eternal Covenant established in Jesus Christ.

the enjoyment of sensual pleasures, nor in the absence of wickedness in the world, but in the participation of the faithful in the vocation and mission of the Christian community.

PART II

THE ROLE OF PROPHET
AND PROPHECY

Chapter 1

Defining the Problem

Following the introductory vision of the Lord's angel in the midst of seven lampstands, the author describes his ascent 'in spirit' to the Throne of God within the heavenly Sanctuary, in order to be shown what will happen in the future. There he sees Christ, represented as a Lamb, taking a sealed scroll from God and proceeding to break its seals. After the breaking of each seal, the author sees and describes a vision of the consequences in heaven and on earth. When the seventh seal is broken, he reports a silence in heaven for the hearing of prayers, and fire from the altar before the Throne is cast down to the earth. Then the author describes a series of seven trumpet-blasts and their consequences, as revealed to him in heaven.

However, before the sound of the seventh trumpet, the author again finds himself on earth, in another vision of the Lord's angel. This change in the author's situation creates an interruption in his narration of the heavenly liturgy—an interruption that begins with his preparation for a renewal of prophetic activity.[94] Then,

---

[94] With the advent of Jesus Christ, the role of prophecy changed: it no longer focused on the prediction of future events, but on the act of salvation already realized by Christ's coming (1Pet 1,10–12; 2Pet 1,19; Ap 19,10). Jesus himself said: "the Law and the Prophets were until John; since then the kingdom of God is being announced and everyone is straining themselves to enter" (Lk 16,16; cf. Mt 11,13). It is therefore no longer legitimate to consult the prophets of the Old Testament for information regarding the future, even though many of the events that they prophesied have not yet been fulfilled, especially those concerning the fulfilment of the promises of God. Instead, the role of the Law and the Prophets consists in their witness to the Messiah, who has already come to fulfil the promises of God and so determine what must happen in the future: "I still have much to tell you, but you cannot bear it now. When the Spirit of truth comes, he will guide you to the whole truth; for he will not speak on his own authority, but whatever he hears he will

immediately after he had been told that he should "prophesy again about many peoples, nations, tongues and kings" (Ap 10,11), he received a command that forms the subject of this part of the study, because it strongly recalls the theme of the Temple: "And a cane similar to a rod was given to me while saying: get up and measure the Sanctuary of God and the altar and those who are worshipping there. And reject the court that is outside the Sanctuary and do not measure it, because it was given to the nations, and they will trample the Holy City for forty-two months" (Ap 11,1–2).

Most commentators agree that this passage introduces one of the most obscure parts of the whole of the Apocalypse. There is therefore little agreement about its significance, and at least five different modes of interpretation have been proposed.[95] These differ according to the way they identify the main elements of the command: whether the reference to the Temple is literal or metaphorical, and whether the command refers to the past, the present or the future.

Ever since Wellhausen suggested that this passage originated from a zealot oracle composed in the final weeks of the siege of Jerusalem in AD 70, there has been a persistent tendency to

---

speak, and he will declare to you the things that are to come. He will glorify me, because he will take from what is mine and declare it to you" (Jn 16,12–14). In contrast to the Old Testament, the New Testament does not contain many prophecies of future events, and the greater part of those that are recorded concern the eschatological period of history leading up to the coming of the Lord in glory (Mt ch. 24; Mk ch. 13; Lk 17,22–37; 21,5–36; 1Thess 4,15–18; 2Thess ch. 2; 1Cor 15,20–28; 2Tim 3,1–9; 2Pet 3,1–13; Ap chs. 8–22). Of all the prophecies in the New Testament, the Apocalypse is unique because Jesus gave it to the churches with the specific purpose of informing his servants about what will happen in the future (Ap 1,1; 22,6). As such, the Apocalypse precisely fulfils the function of the Spirit of truth, to 'declare the things that are to come' (Jn 16,13). Revealing how Jesus Christ fulfils the Law and the Prophets up to, and beyond, his coming in glory, the Apocalypse replaces the prophets of the Old Testament as the principal source of information about the future.

[95] See Prigent, *Apocalypse of St. John*, 337; Mounce, *Book of Revelation*, 218; Wikenhauser, *L'Apocalisse di Giovanni*, 270. For an explanation of the difficulties, see Prigent, *Apocalypse of St. John*, 337, and for the five different modes of interpretation: Beale, *Book of Revelation*, 557–59.

treat it as an insertion and not as an integral part of the text. As a result, few commentators seriously investigate the meaning of the entire command within its present context, and most of them comment only on some small element or aspect of it. Among the authors who examine the command more thoroughly, several seem to be aware that the author, St. John, is given an active role to fulfil, but they attach little or no importance to this. Those scholars who reflect on this activity interpret it as an example of a symbolical prophetic action, similar to the kind of actions frequently performed by the ancient prophets[96] (e.g., 1Kgs 22,11; Is 8,1–4; 20,1–6; Jer 13,3–11; 19,1–15; 27,1 – 28,16; Ezek 12,1–7; 24,1–14; Acts 21,10–11).

However, there are overwhelming objections to this explanation of the task given to the author of the Apocalypse. There is no further information about how, when, or even if the required action was ever performed. Furthermore, many years before St. John wrote the Apocalypse, the Temple had been destroyed by Roman forces in a way that frustrates any comparison with the details of the command that was given to him. Since there is no possibility of identifying a specific action taken by the author in obedience to this command, then it is unrealistic and inappropriate to consider this as a symbolical prophetic action. Indeed, this line of investigation has not resolved any of the problems associated with the interpretation of the command itself or of the text that follows it.

In view of the remarkable lack of agreement or progress in the interpretation of this command in its present context, a thorough examination is required before turning to the contents of the prophecy that the author was given in order to be able to 'prophesy again'.[97]

---

[96] E.g., Aune, *Revelation 6–16*, 603; Bauckham, *Climax of Prophecy*, 266; Mounce, *Book of Revelation*, 219.

[97] In view of the need to study this passage thoroughly, it is important to mention the only major textual problem. In Ap 11,2 the critical text (Nestle-Aland, *Novum Testamentum Graece*) gives the following reading: "and reject the court that is outside the Sanctuary..." and is supported by the most reliable manuscripts (P[47], A, P, 040, 2053 etc.). The alternative reading is this: "and reject the court that is inside

In fact, the immediate context of the command given to St. John acts as a guide for its interpretation. The command (Ap 11,1–2) is situated between two references to the act of prophesying: in the first the author describes his preparation to "prophesy again about many peoples, nations, tongues and kings" (Ap 10,8–11), and in the second he recounts with remarkable detail the prophetic mission of the two witnesses (Ap 11,3–13). From this entirely prophetic context, it is difficult to escape the conclusion that the command to measure 'the Sanctuary of God, the altar and those worshipping there' concerns the author's vocation to 'prophesy again' (Ap 10,11). In effect, the command presents itself as the order to 'prophesy again', expressed, however, in a metaphorical way.[98]

As a description of one thing in terms which are suggestive of another, metaphor is just one of many non-literal forms of language: it is used to say something new that can not be said in any other way.[99] The present context concerns a metaphorical expression which, in terms that are suggestive of an activity in the Temple, says something new about the author's commission to 'prophesy again'. Since the metaphorical expression is pronounced by a divine and spiritual spokesman, it is implied that the new insights that it conveys are related to the spiritual significance of the prophetic activity to which it refers. In other words, the use of this metaphorical expression is intended to communicate the spiritual significance and essential purpose of the prophecy that the author is required to prophesy from this moment.

---

the Sanctuary...", and is found in ℵ, 2329, the Syriac version, the Vulgate, and in the Commentary of Victorinus of Pettau. However, since there was no court inside the Sanctuary the alternative reading is not coherent and probably derives from a scribal error.

[98] In fact, this can be seen as the opposite of a symbolical prophetic action. In the case of a symbolical prophetic action, the prophet was asked to perform a symbolical action by means of which he could communicate a certain prophecy, whereas here St. John is required to communicate a prophecy by means of which he can perform a symbolical action. Far from being 'a prophetic action', we are here dealing with something that could be termed 'an action-prophecy', which—like an 'action-plan'—is indispensable for planning and realizing a desired purpose.

[99] *Dictionary of Biblical Interpretation*, s.v. 'metaphor'.

Understood in this way, the metaphorical expression acts as a key to the interpretation of the prophecy, confirming—for the part of the text which follows—the hypothesis proposed in the introduction to this study, that the theme of the Temple is so important that it should be considered as the 'organizing principle'. To interpret the command of measuring in a literal way would not only be a fundamentalist error, but would also overlook and ignore this interpretative key.

Since the command to measure the Temple is another way of expressing the order to prophesy, one expects to find the prophecy, which the author has been given to prophesy, in the text which immediately follows. In order to understand this prophecy, and the command that precedes it, it is necessary to return to the author's preparation to 'prophesy again'.

Chapter 2

The Preparation of the Prophet

After seeing how Christ took the scroll from God and broke its seven seals, the author of the Apocalypse found himself again on earth, in front of a mighty angel holding a little open scroll in his hand, and declaring that the mysterious plan of God is about to be fulfilled. The author goes on to describe his preparation to prophesy again in the following way: "And the voice which I heard from heaven was again speaking to me and saying: Go, take the open scroll that is in the hand of the angel standing on the sea and on the land. And I went towards the angel, telling him to give me the little scroll. And he says to me: take and eat it; it will make your stomach bitter, but in your mouth it will be as sweet as honey. And I took the little scroll from the hand of the angel and ate it, and in my mouth it was as sweet as honey, and when I swallowed it my stomach was made bitter. And they say to me: you must prophesy again about many races and nations and tongues and rulers" (Ap 10,8–11).

The fact that the author takes the little scroll from the hand of the angel after Christ had taken the sealed scroll from the Throne, strongly recalls the transmission of the Revelation of Jesus Christ, outlined in the opening verse of the Book: "The Revelation of Jesus Christ which God gave to him to show his servants what must soon take place, and which he made known by sending his angel to his servant John" (Ap 1,1). The reflection of the first words of the text at this point permits the identification of the little scroll with 'the Revelation of Jesus Christ…which he made known…to his servant John' by means of his angel.

Since the 'Revelation of Jesus Christ' is the main subject of the entire Apocalypse, its identification with the little scroll indicates the start of the most important part[100]—the part in which is revealed 'what must soon take place' (Ap 1,1). In fact, here, at the centre of the Book, there is a new beginning, one to which the first half has been converging, and from which the second half unfolds.

Apart from its particularly significant situation at the centre of the Book, the account of the author's preparation to prophesy again is set in the interval between the sixth and seventh trumpet-sounds, following a solemn declaration that: "there shall be no more time, but in the days of the sound of the seventh angel, by the time he is going to blow, also will have been fulfilled the mystery of God, as he announced to his servants the prophets" (Ap 10,6–7). The setting of the account at this point, immediately before the sound of the seventh and last trumpet (Ap 11,15–19), indicates that the preparation of the author to prophesy again is linked in a special way to the period immediately preceding the eschatological fulfilment of the divine project for mankind. It is implied that by eating the little scroll, the author was prepared to prophesy about the final, or eschatological, period of history.

The way the author recounts his vocation to prophesy this eschatological prophecy is very similar to the way the prophet Ezekiel described his vocation (Ezek 2,8 – 3,3), when he was beside the River Chebar, after having received a vision of the Throne of God. Just as Ezekiel was given a scroll to eat, which was sweet in his mouth but left him 'bitter in the heat of his spirit'[101](Ezek 3,14), so also the author of the Apocalypse was told to eat the little scroll that proved to be sweet in his mouth and bitter in his stomach. The prophet Ezekiel was given a scroll on which was written "weeping and wailing and woe" (Ezek 2,10), and in a similar way John

---

[100] The importance of the following part of the text is also indicated by the fact that it occupies the central part of the book (Ap 11,1 – 15,4). In ancient documents, the central part was often reserved for the most important information (e.g., the account of the greatest event in the Jewish calendar, the Day of Atonement, is situated in the central part of the Pentateuch, Lev ch.16).

[101] 'bitter in the heat of his spirit': is based on a literal translation of מר בחמת רוחי in Ezek 3,14.

received his prophetic vocation in the context of the three Woes that afflict the people living on the earth, in the wake of the sounding of the last three trumpets (Ap 8,13).

However, in contrast to the vocation of Ezekiel to prophesy about matters which concerned only the House of Israel, the author of the Apocalypse is required to prophesy about things which concern "many peoples and nations and tongues and rulers" (Ap 10,11).

Chapter 3

The Measuring Rod

After being called by God, a prophet was usually told what to do and what to prophesy (cf. Ezek 3,4–11). After St. John was called to prophesy again, it can be assumed that he would have been given a new prophecy. The author, however, reports that he was given 'a cane (κάλαμος) similar to a rod (ῥάβδος)', and was commanded to measure certain things (Ap 11,1).

Since canes were used as instruments for measuring, it is reasonable that St. John was given a cane in order to carry out the command to measure. Nevertheless, it has already been emphasized that this command is a metaphorical expression representing the order to 'prophesy again', and so the cane given to John should rather be interpreted as a metaphor.

The metaphorical significance of a cane used for measuring is indicated by the use of the word 'canon', which derives from the Hebrew word for a cane (קנה). Until the second century AD, 'canon' (κανών) was the term used in the Church to refer to 'the rule of faith' that the faithful should follow in order to be of one mind (Phil 3,16; Textus Receptus).[102]

In its metaphorical context, therefore, the measuring cane given to St. John represents a rule of faith for believers, which enables them to be of one mind (cf. Acts 4,32; Phil 1,27). Since this cane was given to John in order to carry out his obligation to 'prophesy again', it can also be identified with the prophecy that was given to him for this purpose. In summary, the cane represents the

---

[102] After the 2ⁿᵈ century AD, the use and the significance of the word 'canon' in the Church changed slightly: 'canon' came to mean the collection of books chosen by the Church, in which the rule of faith is clearly expressed, i.e., the Canon of the Old and New Testaments (see *New International Dictionary of New Testament Theology*, 3:399–402).

prophecy that St. John must now prophesy, and this prophecy acts as a rule of faith for those who believe.

Despite indicating the significance of the 'cane' (κάλαμος), these findings do not explain why it should be similar to a 'rod' (ῥάβδος), in view of the fact that John was given 'a cane similar to a rod' (Ap 11,1). In order to determine why it should be 'similar to a rod', it is important to recognize those aspects of the prophetic vocation of St. John that correspond to the experience of Moses on Mt. Sinai.

In the first place, there is a correspondence between the events that precede the author's meeting with the angel carrying the little scroll, and the events that preceded the meeting between Moses and the Lord's angel on Mt. Sinai: the plagues which follow the sounding of the trumpets (Ap chs.8–9) are described with explicit allusion to the plagues which Moses announced[103] in order to liberate the people of Israel from Egypt.

In the second place, the cloud, the column of fire and the 'voices' of the seven thunders described by St. John in his meeting with the powerful angel (Ap 10,1–4), all recall the signs and portents that accompanied the revelation of God on Mt. Sinai (Ex 19,16–21). The little open scroll corresponds to the 'Word of God' given to Moses in the form of the Law (the Torah or Pentateuch), and therefore presents itself as a new Torah.[104]

---

[103] the plagues which Moses announced: even though there are allusions to the plagues of Egypt in the descriptions of the plagues that follow the trumpet-blasts in the Apocalypse (Ap chs. 8–9), they are neither systematic nor methodical. In fact, the plagues of the trumpets appear to be different in almost every way, except in kind, and so the same 'kind' of expression is the most appropriate to describe them. The 1st trumpet plague (Ap 8,7) recalls the plague of the hail (Ex 9,23–25; Wis 16,16–19); the 2nd plague (Ap 8,8–9) recalls the plague of blood (Ex 7,20–21); the 4th plague (Ap 8,12) recalls the plague of darkness (Ex 10,21–23); the 5th plague (Ap 9,1–11) recalls the plague of the locusts (Ex 10,12–15) and the intervention of the destroying angel (Ex 12,23); the 6th plague (Ap 9,13–19) and the refusal of people to repent (Ap 9,20–21) recall various passages of reflection and commentary on the plagues of Egypt (Wis chs. 11–12).

[104] as a new Torah: there are indications in other parts of the text that confirm this statement. Like the Torah, the Apocalypse was also written in obedience to a

Furthermore, just as the revelation on Mt. Sinai involved Moses in the construction and consecration of a Dwelling for God (Ex 25,8), so also John is entrusted with an analogous task: that of measuring 'the Sanctuary of God, the altar and those who are worshipping there' (Ap 11,1–2).[105]

---

command of the Lord (Ap 1,11.19; 21,5; cf. Ex 34,27–28; Deut 31,19.21.24–27); it was revealed by his angel (Ap 1,1–2; cf. Acts 7,38); it promises divine blessing to those who keep and observe its words (Ap 1,3; 22,7; cf. Lev 26,3–13; Deut 12,26–27; 28,1–14; 30,16) and it contains a solemn warning to whoever may wish to change the text (Ap 22,18–19; cf. Deut 4,2). The importance of the Exodus theme in the Apocalypse (see Bauckham, *Theology of the Book of Revelation*, 70–73) also links it with the Torah and further supports the identification of the Apocalypse as a new Torah. In fact, in the Christian tradition, the acknowledgement of Jesus as Messiah and the representation of the Christian life as a *new* exodus leading to the formation of a *new* Israel by means of a *new* Covenant, all contributed to the expectation of a *new* Torah. Some modern authors (especially Davies, *Torah in the Messianic Age*; id., *Paul and Rabbinic Judaism*, xxvii–xxxviii, 72–73, 147–76, 223–25, 262–66) have argued that this expectation was fulfilled in the person of Jesus, or in the giving of his Spirit, but neither of these proposals agrees with the written character of that which has come to be known as the 'Torah' (or Pentateuch). The Jewish tradition also expects that the coming of the Messiah will bring about a change in the Torah, which has been termed a new Torah by some authorities (see Klausner, *Messianic Idea in Israel*, 445–50; Scholem, *Kabbalah and its Symbolism*, 66–86; id., *Messianic Idea in Judaism*, 19–24, 53–58, 65–77). In the shared biblical tradition, the concept of a new Torah revealed to a second Moses (based on Deut 18,14–22) is found in the prophecy of Ezekiel (chs. 40–48) and especially concerns the ceremonial Law. Although this differs substantially from the Torah of Moses, points of contact can be identified showing that Ezekiel's intention was to present his prophecy of the new Temple as a new Torah (see Block, *Book of Ezekiel 25–48*, 498–501 and subsequent commentary), in the same way as the author of the Apocalypse.

[105] It becomes clear, therefore, that the author, St. John, is being presented as a 'second Moses'—'the prophet like Moses' whom God promised to Moses with the following words: "I will raise up for them [the people of Israel] a prophet like you from among their own people and I will put my words in his mouth, and he shall tell them everything that I command him" (Deut 18,18). At the time of Jesus, the messianic expectation of the Jews was concentrated on three main figures (see Jn 1,19–25): the Messiah himself, the 'Elijah' who was to precede him (Mal 3,23–24), and 'the prophet' (that is to say, 'the prophet like Moses'). In the New Testament texts, the difference between 'the prophet' and the Messiah is not completely clear (sometimes it seems to refer to the same person, e.g., Jn 6,14–15; at other times to two different people, e.g., Jn 7,40–43, Mt 17,1–8, Lk 9,19–20). In the Christian

As the renewal of the author's prophetic activity evokes the prophetic ministry of Moses in this way, there is an obvious analogy between 'the cane similar to a rod', which was given to John, and 'the rod of God' with which Moses performed his miracles (Ex 4,17.20).[106] As the miracles performed by the two witnesses vividly recall those made by Moses (Ap 11,6), it is implied that the prophetic activity of the two witnesses is realized by means of the 'cane similar to a rod', which represents the prophecy given to John in order that he could prophesy again. This link between the author's prophetic vocation and the prophetic mission of the two witnesses

---

tradition, Elijah is identified with John the Baptist (Mt 11,9–14; 17,12–13; Lk 1,17) and the Messiah with Jesus (Mt 16,13–17, etc.). 'The prophet' was frequently identified with Jesus by his hearers and disciples (as in Jn 5,46–47; 6,14; 7,40; Acts 3,22–26; 7,37), but within a short time of his Ascension this title for Jesus was replaced by other more elevated titles (see the *Jerusalem Bible*, note on Mt 16,14). It was therefore expected of the risen Jesus, as Lord, to raise up 'the prophet like Moses' from among the Jews, and to put his word in the prophet's mouth (as in Deut 18,18). Indeed, this part of the Apocalypse reveals Jesus Christ, as Lord, raising up a 'prophet like Moses' in the person of John, the author of the Apocalypse, and putting his words in John's mouth. As a result "every soul that does not listen to that prophet will be utterly cut off from the people" (Acts 3,23). In the Christian tradition, therefore, Jesus is the Messiah, John the Baptist is Elijah and John of the Apocalypse is 'the prophet like Moses'. These conclusions discredit the assertion, attributed to God in *The Koran* (7:157; 33:40; 61:6), that this prophet is Mohammed, the founder of Islam.

[106] There is also an internal allusion to the rod of iron with which the Messiah (Ap 12,5; 19,15) and his faithful followers (Ap 2,27) shepherd the nations. But the violent way in which they use the rod to shepherd the nations, 'like pots of clay are smashed' (Ap 2,27; cf. Ps 2,9), corresponds to the judgmental function of the double-edged broad sword that comes out of the mouth of the risen Christ (Ap 1,16; 2,16; 19,15.21). In fact, both the rod and the sword are mentioned in parallel in Ap 19,15: just as Christ will strike the nations with the sword that comes out of his mouth, so also, in a similar way, he will 'shepherd' the nations with the rod of iron. Understanding the sword as a symbol for the Word of God (Heb 4,12; Eph 6,17; Mt 10,34), it is proposed that the rod of iron also represents the Word of God, but presented in a special form—the form that is given to St. John under the figure of a 'cane similar to a rod' (Ap 11,1). Therefore, the measuring rod, which is identified with the prophecy given to St. John in order to prophesy again, not only corresponds to the rod of God given to Moses to perform miracles, but also to the rod of God given to the Messiah and to his followers, in order to shepherd the nations.

(Ap 11,3–13) indicates that these two witnesses are the announcers of the prophecy given to St. John in order to prophesy again 'about many peoples, nations, tongues and rulers'.

In conclusion, the cane that represents the prophecy given to John as a rule of faith, for the direction of the people of God, also acts like a rod for performing miracles, similar to the rod of Moses.

Chapter 4

The Task of Measuring

The identification of the measuring rod with the prophecy that was given to St. John, in order that he could 'prophesy again', determines what is meant by the act of measuring. 'Measuring' signifies witnessing the prophecy given to John in order that he could 'prophesy again'. The author did this by writing the prophecy in a book (Ap 1,2), while the two witnesses do this by announcing it publicly (Ap 11,3–13).

The author set about performing the task of measuring by writing the prophecy of the Apocalypse and sending it to the seven churches. This task will continue all the time that the prophetic words of his book (Ap 22,18) are witnessed in and by the Church, and will finish only when there is no longer a need to witness them—with the realization of the prophecy itself. Given that the prophecy concerns events in the eschatological period of history, it is clear that the task entrusted to St. John will continue up until the end of history, well beyond his mortal life-span.

Even though St. John is no longer present physically, the witnessing of his prophecy continues to fulfil the task entrusted to him. In this way, John continues to have an effective and lasting presence in the Church—a spiritual presence which precisely recalls the enigmatic passage in the fourth Gospel about the future of the beloved disciple: "Peter turned and saw the disciple whom Jesus loved following them—the disciple who had leaned against his breast at supper and said, "Lord, who is going to betray you?" When Peter saw him, he said to Jesus, "Lord, what about this one?" Jesus said to him, "If I want him to remain until I come, what is it to do with you? You follow me!" So the rumour spread among the members of the community that this disciple would not die. Yet Jesus did not say that he would not die, but, "If I want him to remain until I come, what is it to do with you?" It is this disciple who is testifying these things in writing, and we know that his testimony is true" (Jn 21,20–24).

The active and lasting presence of the author in the Church not only fulfils Jesus' prophecy about the beloved disciple, but also identifies John, the author of the Apocalypse, with the same beloved disciple. Beyond all questions of literary style, it also confirms the identification of the author of the Apocalypse with the author of the fourth Gospel.[107]

---

[107] the identification of the author of the Apocalypse with the author of the fourth Gospel: the first serious argument against the Church's tradition of identifying John the Apostle as the author of the Apocalypse was devised by St. Dionysius, Bishop of Alexandria in the 3rd century AD, in order to confute a group of millenarians in his diocese. Without daring to reject the Apocalypse, but confessing his poor understanding of it, Dionysius based his argument on a comparison of the style and the words used in the Apocalypse with those of the Gospel and the Letters of John (his discussion is preserved in Eusebius, *Ecclesiastical History*, VII, 25, 2:197–209). Certain that they could not have been written by the same hand, and appalled by the literary style of the Apocalypse, Dionysius concluded that it was not written by the Apostle John, but by another author with the same name, unknown to the Church of his day. Shared by many scholars up to this day, this opinion of Dionysius continues to challenge the testimony of the Early Church concerning the authorship of the Apocalypse—a testimony recorded in writing by at least two saints who lived in the same region as John, within living memory of his lifetime (Justin martyr, who lived in Ephesus from 132–135 AD, and St. Irenaeus of Lyons who was born in Smyrna around 140 AD and educated there). The importance of the question of authorship becomes clear when due consideration is given to the importance of the Apocalypse in the Church. The prophecy of this Book can be received as a 'rule of faith' because we know that the testimony of the author, understood to be the Apostle, is true (Jn 21,24). In fact, the apostolic authorship of the Apocalypse was one of the main reasons for including it in the Canon of the New Testament. The fact that the author of the Apocalypse presents himself as a prophet, and not as an apostle, should not be an obstacle in identifying him with the beloved disciple and author of the fourth Gospel. Among the Jews in those days, a man was forbidden to participate in public life until he had reached the age of 30 years. So, on account of his young age, John would not have been permitted to fulfil the role of an apostle, preaching the Gospel in public like the other apostles (in the Acts of the Apostles, it is recorded that John accompanied the Apostles at times, but there is no report of any preaching by him). It is therefore probable that he remained as a disciple (תלמיד) and that, in the light of the Incarnation, he dedicated himself to study the scriptures and traditions of his people, including the apocalyptic writings

It is suggested above that the sign of the completion of the task of measuring is the realization of the prophecy that the author received and recorded in writing immediately after being commanded to measure 'the Sanctuary of God, the altar and those worshipping there'. However, the first event described in the prophecy is actually the mission of the two witnesses, which involves the public witnessing of the prophecy. The mission of the two witnesses, therefore, initiates the realization of the prophecy and so brings to completion the task of measuring entrusted to St. John.

It was previously noted that the command to measure the Sanctuary (Ap 11,1–2) is situated between two references to the act of prophesying: in the first the author describes his preparation to 'prophesy again' (Ap 10,8–11), and in the second he recounts the prophetic mission of the two witnesses (Ap 11,3–13). It is now clear that both references are related to the metaphorical task of measuring: the first concerns the beginning and the second describes the end of the task entrusted to St. John, of measuring 'the Sanctuary of God, the altar and those who worship there'.

---

and perhaps even the beliefs of the Essenes. Leading St. John along this path of study and contemplation, the risen Lord was preparing him to receive his prophecy (the Apocalypse), and so become his prophet—'the prophet' that was expected in those days (see above, n. 105).

Chapter 5

The Place to be Measured

The metaphorical significance of the 'cane similar to a rod' requires a metaphorical interpretation of the place that St. John has to measure: "the Sanctuary, the altar and those who worship there. And reject the court that is outside the Sanctuary and do not measure it…" (Ap 11,1–2).

The details of the command given to St. John are strongly reminiscent of the plan of the ancient Temple, which can therefore serve as a guide in the interpretation of the command. Taken as a whole 'the Sanctuary of God, the altar and those who worship there' correspond to the most central part of the former Temple, namely to the inner court and all that it contained. The court that is 'outside the Sanctuary'[108] corresponds to the rest of the Temple—a large court which surrounded the inner court and was called the outer court.

However, since the measuring rod is understood as a prophecy that functions as a rule of faith, and the act of measuring

---

[108] The court that is 'outside the Sanctuary': the wording of this expression has caused some commentators to interpret the court as analogous to the inner court, not the outer court, since that was the court immediately outside the Sanctuary edifice. As a consequence, the altar would represent the incense altar within the Sanctuary, and 'those worshipping there' would correspond to the priests, as only the priests were allowed to enter the Sanctuary (see Bauckham, *Climax of Prophecy*, 268–69). However, there is another explanation that confirms the correspondence between the court that is mentioned and the outer court. In the first part of this study (see I. 1), it was noticed that, due to the lack of a veil, the Sanctuary of God in the Apocalypse is composed of two parts: an upper part which corresponds to the Sanctuary of the ancient Temple, and a lower part that corresponds to the inner court. So the court that is 'outside the Sanctuary' corresponds to the court that was outside the inner court, i.e., the outer court of the ancient Temple. The altar, therefore, corresponds to the altar of holocausts, and 'those worshipping there' correspond to representatives of the entire House of Israel. The use of the term 'Sanctuary' to refer to the most sacred zone recalls the use of the same term (מקדש) by the prophet Ezekiel.

describes the witnessing of this prophecy, so the Temple certainly does not refer to a building made of inert materials. It must refer to a Dwelling for God made up of people who can respond to the prophecy by accepting or rejecting its words. As in other parts of the New Testament, the Temple in this command refers to the people of God—those who constitute the Church in the broadest and most universal sense of the term.[109]

The form of worship that Jesus preached was no longer centred on the Temple at Jerusalem; the purpose of that Temple was fulfilled by his sacrifice, and with his Resurrection the construction of a new Temple[110] was begun: "So then you are no longer strangers and aliens, but you are fellow citizens with the saints and members of the household of God, built upon the foundation of the apostles and prophets, with Christ Jesus himself as the cornerstone. On him the whole building is being put together to become a holy Sanctuary in the Lord; on him you also are being built together into a dwelling-place for God in the Spirit" (Eph 2,19–22).

The construction of the new Temple of God on earth with 'living stones' (1Pet 2,4–10) forms the New Testament background for the 'Revelation of Jesus Christ' that was given to St. John. In the Apocalypse, therefore, reference is made to the construction of the new Temple in such a way as to confirm that the building materials are the faithful and that the risen Lord is the builder: "The one who

---

[109] the Church in the broadest and most universal sense of the term: "Hence the universal Church is seen to be 'a people brought into unity from the unity of the Father, the Son and the Holy Spirit'" (Lumen Gentium 4, *Conciliar and Post Conciliar Documents*, 1:352). "All men are called to belong to the new People of God. This people, therefore, whilst remaining one and only one, is to be spread throughout the whole world and to all ages in order that the design of God's will may be fulfilled: he made human nature one in the beginning and has decreed that all his children who were scattered should be finally gathered together as one" (Lumen Gentium 13, op. cit., 1:364). In the widest and most universal sense of the term, the Church may also include people who have grown up under the guidance of other religions (i.e., Judaism or Islam).

[110] For detailed treatment of this subject, see especially Congar, *Mystery of the Temple*; McKelvey, *The New Temple*.

conquers—I will make him a pillar in the Sanctuary of my God, and never will he go out again" (Ap 3,12).

So the construction of the messianic Temple represents the reconciliation of people with God, in every age and place, through the love of Jesus Christ (Heb 12,22–24). Since the forgiveness and reconciliation of the people of Israel were always associated with the annual Day of Atonement in the ancient Temple, it is no coincidence that in the Apocalypse the construction of the new Temple of God takes place at the same time as the liturgy in the heavenly Sanctuary, which is analogous to that of the Day of Atonement.[111]

In this context, the command given to John to measure certain elements in the new Temple of God (Ap 11,1–2) reveals that the author and the prophecy given to him are directly involved in the process of construction.[112] In every building process the materials have to be measured so that they fit together properly, according to the builder's designs. The task of measuring indicates that it is a precise and carefully planned project.

There are indications in the Apocalypse that the construction of the messianic Temple, in which St. John is participating with the measuring rod, concerns the fulfilment of a vision revealed to the prophet Ezekiel during the Babylonian exile (Ezek chs.40–48). In Ezekiel's vision, an angel with a measuring rod leads the prophet around every part of the future Temple, giving him the measurements of each part. The record of this vision forms the plan of a new Temple (Ezek 43,10–12), which was never realized by the

---

[111] This is the conclusion of the first part of this study.

[112] Most of the commentators assert that the purpose St. John's measuring task is simply to indicate the part of the Church that will be protected and preserved. Understood in the context of the construction of the new Temple, however, this task has a much greater significance: it contributes in an essential way to the edification and completion of the Church. It could even be said that the Church will not be able to reach her state of completion and perfection without the participation of the prophet John and his prophecy. Confirmation that the role of the author exceeds that of simply indicating the preservation of a part of the Church is the fact that he was asked to 'reject the outer court and not measure it'. It would be superfluous to add the instruction 'not to measure it', if 'measuring' only signified 'outlining the part to be protected and preserved'.

Jews following their return from exile, since it presented problems of interpretation[113] and its execution was therefore left to the Messiah, whenever he may come.

In the Apocalypse, the prophet himself has the measuring rod in his hand[114] and was asked to perform what Ezekiel was asked only to record in writing. It is implied that the new prophecy revealed to St. John, and identified with the measuring rod, helps to fulfil the plan given to Ezekiel by the angel. In other words, the author of the Apocalypse is the authentic interpreter of the vision described by Ezekiel, and brings this vision to fulfilment by means of his prophecy.[115]

---

[113] The problem was based on the fact that there were discrepancies between the Torah of Ezekiel and the Torah of Moses. Despite having a great respect for the Torah of Moses, it is evident that Ezekiel was proposing his writings (chs. 40–48) as a new Torah (on this theme and for a summary of the discrepancies, see Block, *Book of Ezekiel 25–48*, 498–501; also Hamerton-Kelly, "The Temple and the Origins" in *Vetus Testamentum*, 20, 1–15).

[114] the prophet himself has the measuring rod in his hand: this is true for the part of St. John's vision that concerns the construction of the new Temple. However, in his vision of the Holy City, the New Jerusalem that descends from heaven after the final Judgement, the situation of the prophet is similar to that of Ezekiel: the angel has a measuring rod and takes measurements which the prophet then reports in writing (Ap 21,15–17). The conclusion is that the author of the Apocalypse represents the fulfilment of the final vision of Ezekiel (chs. 40–48) in two stages: before the final Judgement—the construction of the new Temple; after the Judgement—the materialization of the New Jerusalem, in which there will not be a temple (Ap 21,22).

[115] Owing to the discrepancies between the Torah of Ezekiel concerning the Temple and that of Moses (see above, n. 113), it is possible to identify features of the new Temple described in the Apocalypse that indicate a specific intention to fulfil the plan of Ezekiel: (a) the simplicity of the inner court of the Temple described by Ezekiel (Ezek 40,47; see Eichrodt, *Ezekiel*, 545–46, 549) is reflected in the three elements that John has to measure, namely 'the Sanctuary of God, the altar and those worshipping there' (Ap 11,1–2). (b) Just as the Temple is separated from the Holy City in the plan of Ezekiel (Ezek 45,1–6; 48,8–20), so also in the command given to John a separation between the Temple and the Holy City is implied (Ap 11,1–2; see below at II. 8). (c) Ezekiel's plan for the Temple requires the complete exclusion of the nations (Ezek 44,5–9) and, in the command given to John, this is accomplished by rejecting the outer court (Ap 11,1–2). (d) In contrast to the Mosaic regulations that prescribe two continual holocausts each day (Ex 29,42, Num 28,3),

To summarize, in the metaphorical command given to the author of the Apocalypse, the measuring rod is the prophecy revealed to him so that he may 'prophesy again', the act of measuring signifies the witnessing of this prophecy and the place where this prophetic activity takes effect is actually amongst the people of God. This activity begins with the writing of the Apocalypse and continues until the eschatological period of history, at which time it will be brought to completion by the mission of the two witnesses of the Lord. In some way, the prophet and his prophecy are involved in a process of edifying and perfecting the Church. To know more about their role, it is necessary to return to the command given to John and examine it in more detail.

---

the Torah of Ezekiel prescribes only one per day, as an eternal law (Ezek 46,13–15). As already observed in the first part of this study, only one continual holocaust—the Lamb—is described for the Day represented in the Apocalypse, and he remains before God for all eternity (Ap 21,22). (e) Differing from the regulation in the former Temple, which required the priests to wear ceremonial garments of fine linen for daily use (Ex 39,27–29), the Torah of Ezekiel specifies that they should be made of ordinary linen (Ezek 44,17–18). In the Apocalypse, the angels who perform the priestly functions of pouring libation bowls, as part of the heavenly liturgy, wear garments of ordinary linen (Ap 15,6).

Chapter 6

The Command to Measure

The command given to St. John, following his preparation to 'prophesy again', divides naturally into two distinct but related parts:

1. "Get up and measure the Sanctuary of God and the altar and those worshipping in it" (Ap 11,1b).
2. "And reject the court which is outside the Sanctuary and do not measure it, because it was given to the nations" (Ap 11,2a).

In the first and main part of this command, the author is asked to use the measuring rod to measure 'the Sanctuary, the altar and those worshipping there', all of which correspond to the innermost parts of the former Temple, also considered the most sacred parts because of their proximity to the Presence of God. In its metaphorical context, the inner parts of the Temple represent the part of the Church that is closest to God, understood in practice to refer to those members who remain faithful to the Word of God and to the Christian vocation. As noted previously, the rod is a prophecy given to St. John, which acts as a rule of faith and is recorded in the part of the text that follows, and the act of measuring corresponds to the act of witnessing this prophecy.

In brief, the witnessing of the prophecy that follows in the text directs and guides the faithful. From the eschatological context of the prophecy, it is implied that this direction applies especially to the Church at the end of history, just as she prepares for the fulfilment of the mystery of God and the coming of her Lord. So the prophecy that St. John is obliged to prophesy, at this point in the Apocalypse, directs the faithful in the attainment of their perfection, which is the perfection of the Church at the end of time.

As a whole, therefore, the three elements that St. John has to measure, namely 'the Sanctuary of God, the altar and those worshipping there', correspond to the most sacred part of the former Temple in Jerusalem and represent the Church at the end of time. The significance of each of the three elements is not evident from the context of this command, since it refers to the prophecy that follows in the text, and relates to information contained in it. The reference to the three elements that constitute the Church in its final form serves to emphasize their importance in the prophecy that follows, and suggests that their identification in this prophecy is an essential step in its interpretation.

The second part of the command is complementary to the first part. While the first part indicates the constructive aspect of the prophecy, the second part reveals its negative or 'de-constructive' aspect. The author is required to reject the outer court of the new Temple,[116] which represents the part of the Church that is furthest from the Presence of God, understood in reality as those members who have distanced themselves from the Faith. One thinks of baptised Christians who no longer adhere to the principles of their Faith—nominal Christians whose love for the world is greater than their love for God and his Word. In fact, the command to 'reject' translates a Greek word (ἐκβάλλειν) that literally means 'throw out' and is frequently used in the New Testament to refer to the rejection and exclusion of people from the faithful community (Mt 5,13; Lk 13,28; 14,34–35; Jn 6,37; 12,31; 15,6).

In its metaphorical context, the command to 'throw out' the outer court does not imply some violent or forceful action by the author, but rather suggests that there is something in his prophecy that is displeasing to this part of the Church. Therefore these nominal Christians refuse to accept or take notice of John's prophecy and, as a result, they come to be 'thrown out'. The fact that the author is specifically asked not to measure the outer court

---

[116] to reject the outer court of the new Temple: without an outer court, the plan of the new Temple recalls that of the Tent of Meeting that Moses built (see p.14).

indicates that the next part of his prophecy is not by any means directed at this part of the Church. It is evident that there is no middle ground between the part of the Church that receives the prophecy as a rule of faith, and the part that does not accept it as such and is excluded because of its refusal.

The cause of the rejection of the outer court is reported to be "because it has been given to the nations" (Ap 11,2a). The meaning of this expression can be deduced from the pejorative sense of the word 'nations' (ἔθνη), which derives from the Old Testament use of the original Hebrew word (גויים). In this context, the word refers to the idolatrous and impure people who do not worship the true God[117] and are elsewhere called pagans or gentiles. The giving of the outer court of the Temple to the 'nations' therefore refers to the apostasy of those who are Christians[118] by name but not in deed, since they imitate the 'nations' and surrender themselves to the values of the world. On account of their apostasy, their love for the world becomes greater than their love of God and of his Word, and so they refuse to accept the prophecy given to St. John and are correspondingly excluded from the true community of Faith.

In its entirety, therefore, the witnessing of the prophecy given to the author not only informs and directs the faithful about the way to proceed during the eschatological period of history, but also makes a distinction between the believers and the non-believers in the Christian community. In fact the witnessing of the prophecy written by St. John creates a profound division within the people of God,[119] between those who choose to remain faithful to the Word of God (the inner court composed of the 'Sanctuary of God, the altar

---

[117] See *New International Dictionary of New Testament Theology*, 2:790–95.

[118] the apostasy of…Christians: as an eschatological sign, this distancing from the Faith is also mentioned in other prophecies of the New Testament (2Thess 2,3; Mt 24,10) and therefore forms a fixed element in the eschatological expectation of the Christian tradition.

[119] a profound division within the people of God: this effect of the prophecy recalls the internal division of contemporary Jewish society that was caused by the preaching, Passion and Resurrection of Jesus (Lk 2,34–35; Mt 10,34–36).

and those worshipping there') and those who surrender themselves to the values of the world (the outer court that has been given to the 'nations').

This interpretation of the effects of witnessing the prophecy given to St. John confirms its role as a 'canon' for the faithful, symbolized by the measuring rod. As a canon, the prophecy not only acts as a rule for the faithful to follow in order to be of one mind (cf. Phil 3,16; Textus Receptus), but also determines and defines who the faithful really are. In acting like a 'canon' within the Canon of the New Testament, the role of this prophecy is similar to that of the Pentateuch (the Torah) for the Jews, since this is also considered to be a 'canon' within the Canon of the Hebrew Scriptures (the OT).[120]

In so far as it is a measure of unity and agreement among faithful Christians, the prophecy also has ecumenical implications. All those people, from whatever religio-socio-cultural background, who agree to be guided by the Word of God expressed in this prophecy, come to be included in the messianic Temple in its final form, that is to say the perfected Church at the end of time. All those who refuse to accept it, whatever their social status, qualifications or experience, will find themselves totally excluded.

---

[120] This is another reason for considering the prophecy of the Apocalypse as a new Torah (see above, n. 104).

Chapter 7

The Outcome of the Command

The final part of the command given to St. John concerns the outcome of the task entrusted to him. The 'nations', together with the unfaithful Christians who are added to their numbers, "will trample the Holy City for forty-two months" (Ap 11,2b).

The wording of this part of the command distinguishes, though in a very subtle way, between what happens to the outer court of the Temple and what happens to the Holy City: the outer court is simply given to the 'nations' for an unspecified period of time, whilst the Holy City will be trampled by them for a specific period of time. The wording of the command avoids any explicit reference to the trampling of the outer court,[121] since those members of the Church who are identified with the outer court will not be trampled in the same way as the Holy City.

In fact, the wording of this part of the command attests to the difference between this Temple and the one that used to stand at the heart of the Holy City in ancient times. The Temple that is referred to in this command is no longer a material edifice at the centre of the Holy City, but as already explained it represents the faithful community, the Church, which has now spread throughout world.

Taking this modification into account, the Holy City in the command is no other than the historical Jerusalem. The biblical tradition does not recognize any other city as being the Holy City. It is therefore significant that despite the transformation of the ancient

---

[121] There is, however, an *implicit* reference, or allusion, to the trampling of the outer court. For further discussion on this, see n. 134 below.

Temple into a messianic Temple dispersed throughout the world, Jerusalem continues to be called the 'Holy City'.[122]

The meaning of the verb 'to trample' is also indicated in biblical literature, where it is used frequently with reference to the submission and profanation of the ancient Temple by pagan nations (Is 63,18; Dan 7,23; 8,13; 1Macc 3,45.51; 4,60; 2Macc 8,2). In the context of St. John's command, it is clear that the action of 'trampling' continues to have the same significance: that of submission and profanation[123] by non-believing peoples—not primarily with reference to the Temple, but to the Holy City (cf. Zech 12,3 in the Septuagint version).

The outcome of the task entrusted to the author is therefore expected to be a limited period of time during which non-believing peoples will have a strong physical presence in the Holy City, and will conduct themselves without respect for the holy character of this

---

[122] Holy City: "The phrase 'holy city' is a clear reference to Jerusalem" (Aune, *Revelation 6–16*, 608). In fact, up to this day 'Holy City' is the name given to Jerusalem, the city where the Lord of the two witnesses was crucified (Ap 11,8). However, when the two witnesses are killed just before the start of the 42-month period, the historical city of Jerusalem will no longer be called 'Holy City', but assumes the title of 'great city' from Babylon (Ap 11,8). She will no longer be 'spiritually' associated with the name of 'Zion', because she will be 'spiritually' called Sodom and Egypt. When the period of 42 months is finished, the name of 'Holy City' will be granted to the New Jerusalem that descends from heaven (Ap 21,2). It should be noted that the New Jerusalem will never be profaned, since "by no means shall anything impure enter her" (Ap 21,27). Since the command given to St. John anticipates the profanation of the Holy City (Ap 11,1–2), it would be a mistake to identify the Holy City in this command with the New Jerusalem, as some commentators do (Bauckham, *Climax of Prophecy*, 272 n. 50; Beale, *Book of Revelation*, 568; Ford, *Commentary on Revelation*, 170).

[123] To combat the opinion that the trampling the outer court and the Holy City signifies their persecution and physical destruction (Beale, *Book of Revelation*, 558 & 569; Bauckham, *Climax of Prophecy*, 272–73; Walker, *Holy City*, 246–59), it is necessary to insist on the difference between persecution and destruction on one hand, and the true biblical significance of trampling, namely that of submission and profanation, on the other. They are by no means equivalent. Confusion may have arisen because the two alternatives are closely related in historical experience, i.e., persecution and destruction are the consequences of resisting submission to, and profanation by, ungodly forces.

place. The text of the command specifies that the period in which Jerusalem will be profaned in this way will last for 42 months, that is to say, for three and a half years. This period of time not only recalls a long tradition of eschatological teaching based on the prophecy in the Book of Daniel,[124] but is also related to the period of 1260 days mentioned in the following verse (Ap 11,3).

In order to interpret either of these periods of time, it is necessary to broaden this study beyond the command given to the author and examine the use of these temporal expressions in the text that follows—the text that has already been identified as the prophecy that was given to the author in order that he could 'prophesy again'.

---

[124] One thinks especially of the eschatological discourse reported in the Gospels of Matthew and Mark. Differing from Luke, these Evangelists present a final period of great tribulation, which will be shortened for the sake of the elect (Mk 13,19–20; Mt 24,21–22). After the preaching of the Gospel in all the world (Mk 13,10; cf. Mt 24,14), this period will begin with the erection of 'the abomination of desolation'— mentioned by the prophet Daniel—in the holy place (Mt 24,15), where it should not be (Mk 13,14). At the end of this period, there will be signs in the heavens concluding with the universal vision of the Son of Man coming on the clouds in power and glory (Mk 13,24–27; cf. Mt 24,29–31). In all its details, this shortened period corresponds to the period of 42 months described in the Apocalypse, and also to the final period of persecution prophesied in the Book of Daniel.

Chapter 8

The Two Periods of Time

Even though the task of measuring the new Temple takes effect from the moment that St. John receives the new prophecy, there are certain indications in the text of the Apocalypse suggesting that it has a specific reference to a definite period of time in history. As already emphasized, the fact that the prophecy follows the announcement of the imminent realization of the mysterious plan of God (Ap 10,6–7) indicates that it refers to events leading up to this fulfilment at the end of time.

It is in this eschatological context, then, that the two periods of time mentioned at the end of the command given to St. John should be interpreted: "And reject the court which is outside the Sanctuary and do not measure it, because it was given to the nations, and they will trample the Holy City for forty-two months. And I will give to my two witnesses and they will prophesy for one thousand two hundred and sixty days dressed in sackcloth" (Ap 11,2–3).

The periods of 42 months and 1,260 days are repeated later in the text of the Apocalypse, and therefore have an important function in connecting certain events described in different parts of the prophecy. The period of 42 months connects the following events:
a)   the trampling of the Holy City by the 'nations' (Ap 11,2);
b)   the reign of a tyrannical ruler (the 'beast') over every tribe, tongue, people and nation, during which he is allowed to make war against the saints and conquer them (Ap 13,5–7).

The period of 1,260 days connects:
a)   the prophetic ministry of the two witnesses (Ap 11,3–13);
b)   the flight and protection of the woman, mother of the male child, in a place prepared by God in the desert (Ap 12,6).

111

Like the rest of the command given to St. John, the periods of 42 months and 1,260 days refer to events whose significance is explained later in the text, in the body of the prophecy. In this case, however, the link is even more significant. These two periods of time do not refer to single or isolated events, but to activities that characterize the entire message of the prophecy, and therefore impose a temporal structure on all that is described in it.

The period of 1,260 days describes a period of prophesying and witnessing, in which the woman flees to the desert to be protected in a place prepared by God, and the period of 42 months describes a period of persecution and tribulation, in which the Holy City will be trampled by the nations.

It is clear that each of these two periods has a completely different character: during the period of prophesying (1,260 days) the two witnesses have the divine power to overcome whoever might wish to harm them (Ap 11,5), whilst during the period of persecution the 'beast' (the term which refers to the ruling tyrant) is allowed to make war against the saints and to conquer them (Ap 13,7). The character of these two periods is so different that they cannot possibly take place at the same time—they are in fact mutually exclusive. If these two periods were identical, as the majority of commentators on the Apocalypse assert,[125] the two witnesses and the 'beast' would destroy each other simultaneously and that would be the end of the story. Instead, the text confirms that the two witnesses are not defeated by anyone, until the end of the period of 1,260 days, at which time the beast that ascends from the Abyss, or sea,[126] will make war against them, will conquer them and will kill them, thus indicating the start of his 42 month reign (Ap 11,7; 13,5). The two

---

[125] Among those who assert the identity of these two periods are: Ford, *Commentary on Revelation*, 177; Mounce, *Book of Revelation*, 221; Bauckham, *Climax of Prophecy*, 267; Beale, *Book of Revelation*, 565–67; Prigent, *Apocalypse of St. John*, 345; Aune, *Revelation 6–16*, 609–11.

[126] from the Abyss or sea: as explained previously (n. 79), these terms are synonymous in the Apocalypse.

periods, therefore, are consecutive: first the period 1,260 days, then that of 42 months.[127]

Since the period of 42 months equals three years and a half, and the period of 1,260 days is almost the same, it follows that these two consecutive periods represent the two halves of a total period of seven years. Understood in this way, the prophecy given to John so that he could 'prophesy again' manifests a temporal structure that recalls the final week of years (seven years) described in the

---

[127] The commentators who claim that these two periods refer to the same single period of time proceed to describe it as a symbolical period that represents the entire duration of the eschatological tribulation. However, no one has yet been able to explain why these two periods are described differently (see Beale, *Book of Revelation*, 565–68). One of the most sophisticated explanations to date is based on numerical symbolism (Bauckham, *Climax of Prophecy*, 400–404). Despite its sophistication, however, this explanation fails to clarify the presumed symbolical significance of the different periods of time, and its author is forced to conclude: "The two numbers 42 and 1260 thus prove so numerologically suggestive it is difficult to be sure what symbolical significance John may particularly have seen in them" (ibid., 402). The symbolical interpretation of these two periods is thrown into even greater confusion by the finding that (1) the two periods are consecutive, and that (2) between the first and second periods the beast ascends from the Abyss. If both periods are to be understood symbolically, how can one identify in history two consecutive periods of equal duration, in the midst of which the beast ascends from the Abyss? Alternatively, if only one of the periods is symbolic and the other is not, how can one decide which of the two ought to be interpreted symbolically, since both represent times of more or less the same duration? Furthermore, the events associated with both periods are described in such detail that only by stretching the credibility of the text, and the credulity of the reader, can they be considered in a symbolical or metaphorical way. Interpreting either the period 1,260 days, or that of 42 months, so as to exclude a literal fulfilment would require many of these details to be overlooked or ignored. Finally, there have been many attempts to identify a historical figure corresponding to 'the beast that ascends from the Abyss', but none have been convincing or conclusive. The most widely supported proposal identifies 'the beast' with Domitian, a Roman Emperor at the end of the 1st century AD. On evidence external to the Book of Apocalypse, this proposal has been challenged successfully by Thompson, in *Apocalypse and Empire* (see n. 2 above). On internal evidence, there can be little doubt that the prophecy of this event remains open to a future fulfilment (there has never been a Roman Emperor who destroyed his Imperial City in the way described in ch. 17, nor any leader who has conducted a persecution as widespread and systematic as the one foreseen in ch. 13).

prophecy of the 'seventy weeks', which is recorded in the Book of Daniel (Dan 9,24–27).

This prophecy concerns a period of seventy weeks of years before the time of the end,[128] in which the final week (seven years) is characterized by an alliance between a tyrant and many people. The second half of this week of years (three years and a half) is described in the prophecy, and in other parts of the Book of Daniel, in the following ways:

a) 'a time, times and half-a-time', when the saints of the most High will be oppressed and persecuted by the tyrant, who is identified with the little horn of the fourth beast which Daniel saw (Dan 7,23–25; 12,7);

b) 'half-a-week' (Dan 9,27) or '1,290 days' (Dan 12,11) which begin with:

  ❖ the abolition of the continual offering and oblation (which formed the basis for the morning and evening services in the former Temple);

  ❖ the erection of the 'abomination of desolation' (which refers to a sacrilegious idol erected in a part of the Temple[129]);

---

[128] the time of the end (עֵת קֵץ): signifies the final period of tribulation (Dan 8,17; 11,35.40) described in various ways in the last chapters of the Book of Daniel, always from the point of view of an author writing during the Babylonian exile (Dan 12,4.9). However, while the details of the description of this period correspond to the activity of the Syrian king, Antiochus Epiphanes, against the Jewish religion, the anticipated end was nothing less than the eschatological fulfilment that is still awaited (Dan 7,14.26–27; 9,24; 12,1–3.13).

[129] a sacrilegious idol erected in a part of the Temple: the debate on what was meant by the expression 'abomination of desolation' (שִׁקּוּץ שֹׁמֵם) is reviewed briefly by Collins in his *Commentary on the Book of Daniel*, 357–58, and includes two important points of view: (a) the relatively late tradition that identifies 'the abomination' as an image or idol of one of the pagan gods, erected by Antiochus Epiphanes (this was the opinion of St. Jerome in his commentary on Dan 11,31, and also the view expressed by the rabbinical tradition in the Babylonian Talmud, Ta'anith 28c). (b) The opinion of modern scholars, based on the Books of Maccabees and the writings of Josephus, that 'the abomination' refers to a pagan altar constructed above the altar of holocausts in the ancient Temple. There followed sacrifices that the Jews considered abominable. As it is difficult to imagine

c) a period of 2,300 evenings and mornings (1,150 days) in which the Temple and a part of the heavenly army will be trampled, the continual offering will be taken away and the iniquity that causes desolation will flourish (Dan 8,9–14.23–26);

d) 'a period of distress', such as there has never been since the nations came into existence (Dan 12,1).

In nearly all its details, the second half of this week of years and its principal events are reflected in the period of 42 months described in the Apocalypse.

In the prophecy of Daniel, the tyrant identified with the little horn of the fourth beast, and the 'abomination' erected by him, are recalled in the prophecy of the Apocalypse by the ruler representing the eighth head of the beast that comes up from the sea and by the sophisticated image through which he is worshipped[130] (Ap ch.13; 17,8.11). Just as, in the prophecy of Daniel, the tyrant oppressed and persecuted the saints of the Most High for 'a time, times and half-a-time', so also in the Apocalypse the beast and his false prophet are permitted to make war against the saints during the period of 42 months (Ap 13,7.9–10.15–17; 7,14).[131] The expression 'time, times and half a time' reappears in the Apocalypse, where it refers to the time in which the woman, mother of the male child, flees to the desert (Ap 12,14). Since this expression corresponds to the 42-month period of persecution described in the Apocalypse, it can be inferred

---

a pagan sacrificial rite without an image or idol of the pagan god, the view adopted in this study is a combination of the two opinions cited above.

[130] the sophisticated image through which he [the beast] is worshipped: by those whose name is not inscribed in the scroll of Life, which belongs to the Lamb (Ap 13,8; 17,8).

[131] "The Church will enter the glory of the kingdom only through this final Passover, when she will follow her Lord in his death and Resurrection. The kingdom will be fulfilled, then, not by a historic triumph of the Church through a progressive ascendancy, but only by God's victory over the final unleashing of evil, which will cause his Bride to come down from heaven. God's triumph over the revolt of evil will take the form of the Last Judgement after the final cosmic upheaval of this passing world" (*Catechism of the Catholic Church*, no. 677).

that this woman will continue to be nourished and protected at her place in the desert, during the period of 42 months.[132]

However, concerning the Temple and the Holy City, there are subtle differences between the prophecy of Daniel and that of the Apocalypse, which reflect the transformation that the Temple underwent at that time. In the prophecy of Daniel, reference is made to the abolition of the continual offering and the oblation during the period of persecution and oppression. Instead, in the prophecy of the Apocalypse, there is no reference to the suspension of the daily offerings at the start of the 42-month period, since the eternal fulfilment of these offerings is represented by the sacrifice of Jesus Christ, with which the liturgy of the heavenly Sanctuary begins.[133] Neither is there an explicit reference to the trampling of the Temple,[134] since the Temple in the command given to the author

---

[132] will continue to be nourished and protected at her place in the desert...: the woman, mother of the male child, flees to the desert and stays there for 1,260 days (Ap 12,6). However, later in the text it is stated that she stays in the desert for 'a time, times and half-a-time' (Ap 12,14)—the same expression of time that is mentioned in the prophecy of Daniel and corresponds to the period of 42 months. The information on the flight of the woman in Ap 12,14 is not therefore a repetition of that in Ap 12,6. In Ap 12,6 the information is reported with reference to the period of 1,260 days, while in Ap 12,14 it is reaffirmed, but this time with reference to the succeeding period of 42 months ('a time, times and a half-a-time'). So, the woman remains at her place in the desert for the entire final week of years (1,260 days + 42 months).

[133] This is the conclusion of the first part of this study.

[134] Neither is there an explicit reference to the trampling of the Temple: (see also II. 7 above). However, there is undoubtedly an implicit reference, or allusion, to the trampling of the outer court, which seems to recall and reinterpret one of the most obscure passages of Daniel's prophecy (Dan 8,9–14). This passage amplifies the description of events in the short period of the tyrant's (the 'little horn') domination, and speaks of the 'giving over' (Dan 8,12–13) of the Sanctuary and of 'an army', in order to be 'trampled' (Dan 8,10.13). Although it may be clear that the Sanctuary refers to the Temple in Jerusalem, it is certainly not evident what is meant by the reference to 'an army' (Dan 8,12; see Collins, *Commentary*, 334–35). However, before the trampling of the Sanctuary and the suspension of the daily sacrifice (Dan 8,12), it is recounted that a part of the army and of the stars of heaven are cast down to the earth and trampled, as a result of the activity of the tyrant (Dan 8,10). This description of the fall of some of the angels seems to be offered as a kind of spiritual

refers to the Church, now dispersed throughout the world. In the prophecy of the Apocalypse, it is only the Holy City that is trampled by the nations during the period of 42 months.

In the Book of Daniel, the period of persecution and desolation ends at a divinely determined time with the condemnation of the tyrant (Dan 7,10–11.26) and his removal by means of divine intervention (Dan 8,25; 9,27; 11,45) in circumstances of war and cataclysm (Dan 9,26–27). Linked to the end of his evil reign is the judgement at the end of time (Dan 12,2–3), the fulfilment of the eschatological ideal (Dan 9,24) and the establishment of the eternal reign of God on earth (Dan 7,27). So also in the Apocalypse of St. John, the period of 42 months ends with the condemnation of the beast and his false prophet, and their elimination by means of divine intervention in the war of the great Day of Almighty God (Ap 19,19–21). Immediately after this divine intervention, the final Judgement is held and the plan of God for mankind is fulfilled (Ap 10,6–7; 11,14–19; 20,11–15; chs.21–22).

The evident similarity between the period of 42 months on one hand, and the last half-a-week of years on the other, confirms a close correspondence between the two consecutive periods mentioned in the Apocalypse and the prophecy of the final week of years (seven years) described in the Book of Daniel. Since the period of 42 months is equivalent to three years and a half, and the period of 1,260 days has almost the same duration (only 18 days less), it follows that the prophecy in the Apocalypse also concerns a final

---

explanation for the apostasy of some of the faithful (Dan 9,27; 11,30–32), which then led directly to the suspension of the daily sacrifice and the trampling of the Temple. The account of the fall of the angels is taken up vividly in the visions of the Apocalypse (Ap ch.12): as a result of the war in heaven, a third part of the stars is thrown down to the earth at the start of the period of 1,260 days, in which the woman flees to the desert and the two witnesses announce the prophecy given to St. John. As already noted (at II. 6), the witnessing of this prophecy results in the exclusion of apostate Christians (the outer court), who together with the 'nations' (the idolatrous people from among the nations) trample the Holy City for 42 months. All the elements of Daniel's prophecy are present, but reinterpreted in such a way that the inner parts of the Temple (the contents of the inner court understood as the true community of faith) will not be trampled, or profaned, by the 'nations'.

week of years (seven years), which begins with the prophetic ministry of the two witnesses (Ap 11,3–13) and finishes with the eternal condemnation of the beast at the second coming of the Lord (Ap 19,19–21). The prophecy for this period of time forms the main subject of the third part of this study.

Chapter 9

Conclusions and the Importance of the Little Scroll

After swallowing the little scroll, the author of the Apocalypse was prepared to prophesy about many peoples, nations, tongues and kings (Ap 10,11). For this purpose, St. John was given a measuring rod and was commanded to measure the elements that constitute the inner court of the Temple that is in the process of construction. The command is expressed in a way that communicates the purpose and the spiritual significance of this renewal of his prophetic activity. The measuring rod is identified with the prophecy that follows in the text, the act of measuring signifies the witnessing of this prophecy and the Temple that is in the process of construction represents the Church, made up of people of every place and time who have been reconciled to God through Jesus Christ.

The prophecy forms the central message of the Apocalypse and refers specifically to events in the final seven years of history, before the second coming of the Lord. The first of these events is the prophetic ministry of the two witnesses, who interpret and publicly announce the prophecy given to St. John.

The witnessing of this prophecy has a double effect, as implied in the command given to the author: on the one hand it encourages and guides those who receive it with faith (the inner court), and instructs them how to proceed to the completion of God's Dwelling, which is to say the perfection of the Church at the end of time. On the other hand, the witnessing of the prophecy provokes the exclusion of those who refuse to accept it (the outer court), and is followed by the distressing period of 42 months that ends with the second coming of the Lord. The fact that this prophecy has such a determining role in the fulfilment of the entire plan of God for mankind raises questions about its origin, or, more precisely, about the little scroll in which it was transmitted to the author of the Apocalypse.

The first words of the Apocalypse refer to the transmission of the Revelation from God to Jesus Christ, and from Jesus Christ to St. John by means of his angel (Ap 1,1–2), and this corresponds, as already noted, to the events described in the first half of the text, which converge on the sending of the little scroll to John: Christ receives from God a sealed scroll and after breaking its seals, sends his angel to St. John with the little open scroll, asking him to eat it. Although it is not openly expressed in the text, it is implied that there is a connection between the sealed scroll that Christ had taken from God and the little scroll swallowed by St. John.

However, it must not be concluded that the sealed scroll, which was taken and then opened by Christ in heaven, is the same as that which was swallowed by St. John. From the information provided in the text, the sealed scroll entrusted to Christ is 'the scroll of Life from the foundation of the world',[135] which is opened at the final Judgement (Ap 20,12) and contains the names of all those who will be able to enter the Holy City after the Judgement has taken place (Ap 21,27). Those whose names are not written in this scroll will be liable to eternal condemnation (Ap 20,15). If this scroll were the same as the one that was swallowed by St. John, it could not then serve as a vital record at the final Judgement. For this reason the two scrolls cannot be identical.[136]

---

[135] Assuming that the Lamb takes possession of only one scroll, the text confirms that the scroll that now belongs to him is in fact 'the scroll of Life' (Ap 21,27). In another context, this scroll is called 'the scroll of Life from the foundation of the world' (Ap 17,8; cf. 13,8). Given that the biblical tradition regards the scroll of Life as a register of names (Ex 32,32–33; Ps 69,29; Lk 10,20; Phil 4,3), the description of the scroll as a register of names 'from the foundation of the world' indicates that the register includes the names of everyone that has lived on the earth, since the foundation of the world. Removing the names of people from this register is a metaphor for adverse Judgement (see Aune, *Revelation 1–5*, 223–25).

[136] Against Bauckham (*Climax of Prophecy*, 243–57), who, after dissolving the distinction between the terms used for the two scrolls (βιβλίον, βιβλαρίδιον), tries to demonstrate their identity on the basis of the correspondence between the account

Elsewhere in the text, it is stated that, before the final Judgement, the risen Christ has authority to erase names from the scroll of Life (Ap 3,5), but he obviously cannot do this before breaking all the seals in order to open it. Since this is also the moment in which the little open scroll is transmitted to St. John, it can be inferred that the sending of the little open scroll to St. John is connected in a particular way with the opening of the scroll of Life and the removal of names from it.

Unfortunately there is nothing in the Christian tradition or Scriptures that can help interpret this connection, and for this reason the significance of the little scroll has never been explained in a satisfactory way. The background that is necessary for the interpretation of this part of the Apocalypse can, however, be found in the Jewish tradition regarding the New Year. As already explained,[137] the annual feast of New Year initiates a period of judgement, which is announced by the sounding of trumpets and involves the opening of three scrolls. During this period, every living person passes before the eyes of the Lord in order to be examined, but judgement for most of them is suspended for a period of 10 days, up until the conclusion of the Day of Atonement. The judgement for every person—whether one will live or die in the new year—depends on his conduct during this 10-day period of penitence, between the New Year's Day and the Day of Atonement. Comparing this Jewish tradition with the experience of St. John, following the breaking of the last seal of the scroll of Life, can help to guide and complete the interpretation of this part of the Apocalypse.

Christ the Lamb breaks the seventh and last seal of 'the scroll of Life from the foundation of the world' and there follows a silence in heaven while the prayers of the saints are heard. The scroll of Life contains the names of all those who have ever lived, 'from

---

of the two scrolls in the Apocalypse (chs. 5 & 10) and that of the prophetic vocation of the prophet Ezekiel (Ezek 2,8 – 3,3). His argument, however, does not take any account of the fact that the sealed scroll is none other than the scroll of Life.

[137] For the previous presentation of the Jewish New Year tradition, see I. 9, xiv; for references to this tradition in ancient sources, see n. 66.

the foundation of the world'.[138] After breaking the final seal, Christ is able to open this scroll and perform judgement by erasing names from it (Ap 3,5). Trumpets are sounded (Ap chs.8–11) and it is a time of repentance (Ap 9,20–21), as in the Jewish New Year tradition. Every living creature passes before the eyes of the Lord and Judge, who examines the conduct of all the living with a view to reaching a final decision. It is a testing time (Ap 3,10), and "if anyone was not found written in the scroll of Life, he will be thrown into the lake of fire" (Ap 20,15).

This is the precise context in which the little open scroll is transmitted to John, who was then told to eat it as a preparation for writing the eschatological prophecy that will be publicly announced, in its time, by the two witnesses. The little scroll, then, concerns events in the period between the opening of the scroll of Life in heaven (Ap 8,1) and the pronouncement of its contents at the final Judgement (Ap 20,12). This is the time—analogous to the period of 10 days in the Jewish tradition—when Christ is able to remove names from the scroll (Ap 3,5).

With this in mind, it is possible to understand the connection between the two scrolls. The little scroll assimilated by St. John describes, in the form of prophecy, the conditions under which Christ will judge the conduct of every living person and register the result of his judgement by erasing names from the scroll of Life in heaven. So the little scroll concerns the way in which the final judgement will be decided, whereas the scroll of Life in heaven conveys the results of that judgement. The first reveals the *outer* form of the final Judgement, and the second discloses its *inner* content. The fact that the complementarity of the two scrolls can thus be expressed in terms of the relationship of outside to inside, suggests that the little scroll represents the writing on the back of the Lamb's scroll in heaven (Ap 5,1), whilst on the inside of that same scroll are recorded the names of all who have lived since the foundation of the world.[139]

---

[138] See n. 135 above.
[139] See n. 135.

In summary, the little scroll that is eaten by St. John represents the outer part of Christ's scroll of Life. The prophecy which issues from this experience concerns the final period of history (a final week of years), understood as a time when the decision will be taken as to who will live eternally, and who will die. As noted previously, the same prophecy not only defines who are the people of God but it also instructs and informs these people how to pass through the time of judgement.

The fact that the prophecy has its origin in the scroll of Life, and is also linked intimately with the execution of the final Judgement, confirms and underlines the divine importance of this prophecy. The next part of this study is dedicated to the interpretation of the prophecy, with the aim of determining, in particular, how the new Temple of God will attain completion.

PART III

THE FULFILMENT OF THE MYSTERY OF GOD

Chapter 1

The Two Witnesses

After being told that he must 'prophesy again' (Ap 10,11), St. John was commanded to measure 'the Sanctuary of God, the altar and those worshipping there' (Ap 11,1–2). Understood as a metaphorical expression representing the command to witness the prophecy given to him at this point, it is implied that this prophecy starts immediately, with the following words: "And I will give to my two witnesses and they will prophesy for 1,260 days dressed in sackcloth. These are the two olive trees and the two lampstands standing before the Lord of the earth" (Ap 11,3–4).

Even though St. John does not begin this prophecy like the ancient prophets, with the expression 'thus says the Lord', he nevertheless starts in the same way, with the Lord speaking in the first person. It is therefore clear that he is communicating the Word of the Lord.

The first part of this prophecy (Ap 11,3–13) concerns the mission of two people called by the Lord to be his witnesses, and then empowered by him to prophesy during the period of 1,260 days. As noted in the previous part of this study, however, the mission of these two witnesses involves the public announcement of the prophecy given to St. John so that he could 'prophesy again'.[140] Being at the same time a part of the prophecy and a description of how it will be announced, the account of the two witnesses can be understood as the introductory part of the prophecy itself.

This double aspect of the first part of the prophecy has important practical implications, for it means that the appearance of the two witnesses, and the actualisation of the mission assigned to them, also signals the realization of the prophecy given to St. John.

---

[140] See II. 3 ('The Measuring Rod').

In other words, the realization of this prophecy starts with its announcement by the two witnesses. Furthermore, since the realization of the prophecy removes any further need to witness it, the actualisation of the mission of the two witnesses also completes the task of witnessing—the task entrusted to St. John and described metaphorically as the measuring of the 'Sanctuary of God, the altar and those worshipping there'.[141] Finally, the fact that the mission of the two witnesses forms a part of the prophecy given to St. John means that their mission shares the same aims and has the same consequences as that of the prophecy itself. Repudiation of their divine mission therefore implies rejection and denial of St. John's prophecy, and leads to exclusion from that part of the Church which is represented by the inner parts of the Temple that St. John is commanded to measure.[142] It is in this sense that the two witnesses truly represent the Church, or, in other words, represent the true Church.

However, the precise way in which these two witnesses or prophets represent the Church should be clarified by reference to the description of them as "the two olive trees and the two lampstands that stand before the Lord of the earth" (Ap 11,4). The origin of this description is the prophet Zechariah's vision of two olive trees standing on either side of a lampstand that represents the House of Israel, with seven flames that signify the Presence of the Lord (Zech 4,1–6a.10b–14). Nevertheless, there are certain important differences between Zechariah's vision and the description of the two witnesses. Before comparing them in order to determine the significance of these differences, it is necessary to examine the description of the two witnesses more closely.

Each of the two witnesses is described symbolically as a unit consisting of a lampstand and an olive tree standing before the

---

[141] It should be noted that only a literal fulfilment of the mission of the two witnesses will unambiguously signal the realization of its prophecy and so bring to completion the task of measuring entrusted to St. John. Furthermore, according to biblical norms (Deut 18,21–22), prophecies of events that do not take place as announced should be considered false prophecies.

[142] See II. 6 ('The Command to Measure').

Lord.[143] In contrast to the seven lampstands in the opening vision (Ap 1,9–20), the two lampstands in this description are not identified with a specific church community. According to the plain meaning of the text, these two lampstands are identified with the two individuals who are given divine authority to carry out the mission described in this part of the prophecy (Ap 11,3–13).[144]

Furthermore, whereas the lights of the lampstands in the opening vision are supplied by the Lord, as the angels of the churches,[145] the description of the two witnesses as 'the two lampstands and two olive trees' contains no mention of any lights associated with the two lampstands. The implication is that the lights of these two lampstands are nourished and kept alight by oil from the two olive trees, in a way that invites comparison with the original vision of Zechariah (Zech 4,1–6a.10b–14).

---

[143] The fact that there are two witnesses is determined not only by the number of olive trees in Zechariah's vision, but also by the law which requires at least two witnesses for a testimony to be considered valid (Deut 19,5; Jn 8,17).

[144] Most commentaries manage to avoid giving a literal interpretation of this passage by explaining that the two witnesses are symbolical, allegorical or 'collective' figures representing the Church. According to the plain meaning of the text, the two witnesses do indeed represent the Church, though not as symbolical or 'collective' figures, but as living beings who have been called and empowered by the Lord for a specific mission. The text is so clear about this, that these two witnesses should be considered as two individuals unless proved otherwise. The most serious argument used to support the figurative or 'corporate' interpretation of the two witnesses clings to the identification of the lampstands with the churches in the opening vision (Ap 1,9–20; see Beale, *Book of Revelation*, 574, n. 1; Bauckham, *Climax of Prophecy*, 274). One commentator goes so far as to say it would be "a defiance of common sense to use the same distinctive symbol for two different ideas, within the compass of one book" (Kiddle, *The Revelation of St. John*, 181, quoted by Beale, *Book of Revelation*, 577). However, the symbol of the lampstand bearing the light of the Lord does not specifically represent the idea of a church community as such, but rather its role in bearing witness to the Lord. Since this symbol primarily represents the idea of 'witness', it can therefore be applied without contradiction to represent a nation (Zech 4,1–6a.10b–14), a church (Ap 1,9–20), an individual (Ap 11,4; Jn 5,35; Ps 132,17; Sir 48,1) or even the Old Testament prophetic message (1Pet 1,19).

[145] See II. 2 ('The Spirit of God').

However, the identity of the two olive trees in Zechariah's vision is not altogether clear.[146] When this prophet asks the interpreting angel what the *two olive trees* represent, his question is not answered (Zech 4,11). The prophet then asks again, but this time he presents his question in a different way: now he wants to know the meaning of the *two olive branches* that supply oil to the lampstand by a pipe (Zech 4,12). The angel replies to this question by saying that the two branches are "the two anointed leaders (literally 'sons of oil') who stand near the Lord of all the earth" (Zech 4,14). Their role in this vision is to provide oil to keep the flames alight. Taking the oil to symbolize the 'spirit', the lampstand the community of Israel, and its flames the Presence of God, then these two leaders 'offer their spirit'—they dedicate their lives—to maintaining the Presence of God among the people of Israel.[147]

---

[146] In fact, the whole passage is problematic: Zech 4,6b–10a is an insertion that completely interrupts the prophet's account of his vision (Zech 4,1–6a.10b–14) and judging by the style and content of verse 12, most commentators agree that this verse was also added at a later stage, for reasons which are not clear (cf. especially Petersen, *Haggai and Zechariah 1–6*, 234–37; also Mitchell, Smith and Bewer, *Haggai, Zechariah, Malachi and Jonah*, 164–65). A possible explanation is raised by examining the vision without, and then with, the addition of verse 12. Without verse 12, the lampstand in Zechariah's vision is easily recognized as a representation of the Lord himself (see Smith, *Micah-Malachi*, 202–206): its lights are his eyes (v.10b, cf. v.2) and standing beside him are the two 'sons of oil' (v.14, cf. v.3). This visual representation of the Lord was probably quite acceptable when it was written, before the Temple was rebuilt, but afterwards there was a real danger that the lampstand in the Temple would become the object of idolatrous worship, on the basis of Zechariah's vision (Zech 4,1–6a.10b–14, without v.12). The interpolation of verse 12 not only removes this danger by altering the symbolism of the vision, but does so in a way which suggests that verse 12 was added for this purpose, after the Temple had been built. Verse 12 describes how oil from a branch on each of the two olive trees is collected and distributed to the lampstand by a tube, thereby linking the olive trees to the lampstand at the same, human level. The lampstand now comes to symbolize the community of Israel, and only the flames of its lamps continue to represent the divine Presence.

[147] It is generally agreed that the two olive branches refer to two anointed leaders (or 'Messiahs') of the postexilic Jewish community, namely Joshua the high priest and Zerubbabel the governor (Mitchell, Smith and Bewer, *Haggai, Zechariah, Malachi and Jonah*, 165). However, the fact that Zerubbabel was never anointed, and that the

Although the significance of the *two olive trees* is not explained by the angel in Zechariah's vision, it can be deduced in the following way: on the one hand the two olive trees represent that which supports and nourishes the two olive branches, or 'anointed leaders', whose role is to maintain the Presence of God among the people of Israel. On the other hand, the two olive trees represent the living heritage of the first two figures who performed that role. They therefore recall the two great spiritual leaders who 'offered their spirit' to establish and maintain the Presence of God among the people of Israel: Moses, the recipient of the Law, was the first to 'offer his spirit' for this purpose (see Num 11,17.24–30), and the second was Elijah, one of the greatest of the prophets (see 2Kgs 2,9–12). As described in Zechariah's vision, therefore, the two olive trees represent the two traditions, called the Law and the Prophets, which were founded by Moses and Elijah and continue the work initiated by them.

At this point, the connection between the two witnesses and the two olive trees can be confirmed from the fact that the spiritual powers manifested by the two witnesses explicitly recall the powers of Moses and Elijah (Ap 11,5–6). By evoking the spirit and power of Moses and Elijah, the two witnesses can be identified as living expressions of the two traditions derived from these two ancient prophets—the Law and the Prophets. So the two witnesses are not a material reappearance of Moses and Elijah in person, but two witnesses of the Lord who, in the fulfilment of their mission at a certain time, demonstrate the spirit and power of Moses and Elijah. This point is further emphasized by the fact that they work together

---

restored community did not become a Sovereign State, but remained under foreign domination, gave rise to the suspicion that Zechariah's vision was not fulfilled by contemporary events. The fact that the basic elements of the vision—the lampstand and the two olive branches (without the trees)—have reappeared as the insignia of the modern State of Israel is a sign that the vision retains its validity, to this day, as a symbol of the ideal Jewish community.

as a pair, and not as two individuals with separate powers, one acting like Moses and the other like Elijah.[148]

The full significance of the description of the two witnesses as two olive trees and two lampstands emerges from the analogy with Zechariah's vision: the two olive trees (the Law and the Prophets) provide the oil (the Spirit of Prophecy) which keeps alight the flames (the light of the Lord) on the lampstands (the two witnesses). In brief, the two witnesses embody the witness of the Law and the Prophets to the Lord of all the earth.[149]

As mentioned previously, however, there are important differences between this description of the two witnesses and the original vision of Zechariah. First and foremost, the role of the two olive trees, including all its branches, has changed. They no longer symbolize leaders who maintain the witness of their community, but instead they represent the tradition of the Law and the Prophets fuelling the witness of two particular individuals—the two witnesses.

As the two olive trees and the two lampstands standing before the Lord of the earth, these two witnesses appear to fulfil the vision of Zechariah concerning the Presence of God among the Israelites. However, in Zechariah's vision there were seven flames and not just two. It is thus implied that for the complete fulfilment of

---

[148] This is a point strongly emphasised by Giblin, who epitomizes the two witnesses by saying: "typologically, these two theological twins are more alike than Tweedledum and Tweedledee" (Giblin, *The Book of Revelation: The Open Book of Prophecy*, 112–14).

[149] the witness of the Law and the Prophets to the Lord of all the earth: the importance of this witness is reflected in many other parts of the New Testament (e.g., Jn 1,45; 5,39.46; Rom 3,21–22). It appears also in the synoptic accounts of the Transfiguration (Mk 9,2–8; Mt 17,1–13; Lk 9,28–36) where Moses and Elijah represent the Law and the Prophets. Of all the writings in the NT, however, it is the Book of the Apocalypse itself which reflects most strongly the witness of the Law and the Prophets to the risen Lord Jesus Christ (Beale, *Book of Revelation*, 76–99). The identification of the two witnesses with the witness of the Law and the Prophets is therefore entirely consistent with the fact that they are the announcers of the prophecy of this Book. It suggests furthermore, that they come to embody this witness by assimilating its contents.

Zechariah's vision, the witnessing of the two witnesses must be added to that of the universal Church, as represented by the seven stars and the seven lampstands in the opening vision (Ap 1,9–20).[150]

These findings indicate that the witnessing of the two witnesses is unique in relation to that of the Church. Rather than simply representing, or reproducing, the mission of the Church, the witness of these two is, in fact, complementary to it. The unique significance of their mission, however, can only be appreciated in relation to the setting and content of their prophetic mission.

The setting of their mission is reflected by its context in the Apocalypse. As noted in the last section, the author's preparation to 'prophesy again', which culminates in the account of their prophetic mission, takes place in the interval between the sixth and seventh trumpet-sounds. In fact the account of the mission of the two witnesses is followed by the description of the seventh and last trumpet-sound and an acclamation of praise for the fulfilment of God's plan for mankind (Ap 11,15–19), which includes the final Judgement. Therefore, the final Judgement and the fulfilment of the divine plan form the goal towards which the mission of the two witnesses is orientated, a fact which is readily confirmed by their emphasis on repentance, manifested by dressing in sackcloth.[151]

---

[150] Since the number 'seven' is understood to represent 'totality' or 'completion', the seven lampstands represent all the churches in every part of the world—the universal Church (see n. 24 above). In addition to the seven lampstands representing the universal Church, the two lampstands signifying the two witnesses makes a total of nine lampstands. Here is a curious correspondence with the number of lights on the modern Hanukkah lamp, consisting of eight main lights and one central light (or 'shammash') from which the others are lit. However, although the custom of lighting a new light on each day of the feast of Hanukkah goes back to the first century AD, the modern form of the lamp, with nine lights, was not adopted until the late mediaeval period (Schauss, *Jewish Festivals*, 208–36; *Encyclopaedia Judaica*, s.v. 'Hanukkah lamps').

[151] To those educated in the biblical tradition, wearing sackcloth is a sign of sorrow and repentance (Is 22,12; Jer 4,8; Jon 3,6–8; Mt 11,21). As noted by Prigent (*Apocalypse of St. John*, 271), the wearing of sackcloth by the two witnesses means that their mission is, above all, a call to repentance. In many ways, their mission reproduces the 'sign of Jonah' which was the only sign that Jesus promised to give

Furthermore, the prophecy which they witness derives from the scroll of Life, and warns of the conditions under which Judgement will take place.[152]

In a similar way, the content of their prophecy can also be inferred from the text. After the description of the seventh trumpet-sound, the announcement of the fulfilment of God's plan and the final Judgement, the text continues as follows: "And the Sanctuary of God in heaven was opened, and the Ark of his Covenant was seen inside his Sanctuary, and there were lightnings and noises and thunders, an earthquake and a great hail" (Ap 11,19). Next there is a complete change of subject and a long passage (Ap 12,1 – 15,4) describing a series of visions concerning events that take place during the two consecutive time-periods: one of 1,260 days followed by the other of 42 months. The opening of the Sanctuary in heaven is then resumed with the following account: "And after this, I looked and the Sanctuary of the Tent of testimony in heaven was opened, and out of the Sanctuary came the seven angels with the seven plagues..." (Ap 15,5).

The resumption of the account of the opening of the Sanctuary at this point confirms that the intervening passage (Ap 12,1 – 15,4) breaks the flow of the text by returning to the time-periods mentioned previously, which represent a final 'week of years'.[153] Since these time-periods determine the temporal structure of the prophecy given to St. John and then prophesied by the two witnesses, it is clear that the intervening passage represents the core of that prophecy.

In broad outline, this part of the text contains two subjects which strongly recall the ministries of Moses and Elijah: the exodus of the mother of the male child to the wilderness during the period of 1,260 days, and the conflict with a false and idolatrous religion during the period of 42 months. Since the leaders of this false

---

the scribes and Pharisees, when they asked for one (Mt 12,38–42; 16,1–4; Lk 11,29–32).

[152] See II, 9 ('Conclusions and the Importance of the Little Scroll').

[153] See II, 8 ('The Two Periods of Time').

religion are presented as a false messiah and his false prophet,[154] it is understood that one of the main concerns of the prophecy, which the two witnesses prophesy, is the imminent realization of this false messianic expectation. Ignoring the New Testament fulfilment of the coming of the Messiah, the two pseudo-messianic leaders are liable to be identified with the two olive branches in Zechariah's vision, which represent two anointed leaders, or Messiahs, of the community of Israel.

It is in the context of the imminent appearance of these two false messianic leaders that the mission of the two witnesses has a specific significance and purpose: they not only witness to the true fulfilment of Zechariah's vision by the risen Lord Jesus Christ, but also give warning about its false fulfilment by those two leaders who, at the appointed time, will seek to identify themselves with the two olive branches or 'sons of oil'.[155]

The appointed place and time for this false messianic reign is also made known by means of the two witnesses. At the end of their public mission lasting 1,260 days (Ap 11,3), they are killed in

---

[154] In the text itself, these two leaders are actually described as the 'beast from the sea' or Abyss (Ap 11,7; 13,1) and the 'beast from the land' (Ap 13,11). Later in the text, the 'beast from the land' is directly identified as the false prophet (Ap 16,13; 19,20; 20,10), and the 'beast from the sea' can be recognized as a false messiah by the fact that he is promoted by the false prophet (Ap 13,11–17), worshipped and admired like God (Ap 13,8.15) and finally presented as the ultimate antagonist of the risen Christ (Ap 17,4; 19,19–20). Furthermore, in conjunction with Satan, the two beasts are portrayed as false counterparts of God, his Messiah and their prophet, John, the author of the Apocalypse.

[155] To clarify these circumstances, an understanding of the hopes and expectations of Orthodox Judaism is required. Not believing in the messianic roles of Jesus of Nazareth or John the Baptist, the Orthodox Jewish establishment continues to await the realization of its messianic expectations, in the form of a messianic leader like Moses and a messianic prophet like Elijah (Klausner, *Messianic Idea in Israel*, 13–25; 451–57; Brod, *Days of Moshiach*, 109–10; 175–78; 126–27). It is in this context that the mission of the two witnesses, in the spirit and power of Moses and Elijah, can best be understood. Evoking the messianic expectation of Orthodox Judaism, they witness to its true fulfilment by the risen Lord Jesus Christ, just before it is falsely realized by the false messiah and his prophet.

Jerusalem[156](Ap 11,8) on the orders of the false messiah himself (Ap 11,7), at the start of his brief and blasphemous reign of 42 months (Ap 11,2; 13,5–8).

The fact that the death and resurrection of the two witnesses occupies the greater part of the account of their mission (Ap 11,7–13) suggests that these events constitute the most important part of their witness to the true fulfilment of Zechariah's vision, by the risen Lord.

After the two witnesses have been killed, their corpses are left exposed for three-and-a-half days in a public place in Jerusalem.[157] According to the text of the Apocalypse, the bodies of these two prophets will then be raised from the dead, giving a vivid testimony to the Christian faith in the Resurrection of Jesus. The exposure of the corpses of the two witnesses can be interpreted, therefore, as an attempt to challenge and discredit this faith (cf. Mt 28,11–15): the false messiah gives orders for the corpses of the two witnesses to be left on the street, under guard and exposed to view,

---

[156] There has been much debate about the identity of "the great city which is spiritually called Sodom and Egypt, where indeed their Lord was crucified" (Ap 11,8). The main objection to recognizing Jerusalem in this description is that the title 'great city' refers to the city which is called Babylon elsewhere in the text and can readily be identified as Rome. The objection can be overcome by arguing that the 'great city' refers to any city that has a close association with the beast (cf. Ap 17,3). The transfer of the title to Jerusalem, at this point in the prophecy, corresponds to the arrival of the beast in order to kill the two witnesses and start his 42–month reign. During this period, the Holy City of Jerusalem is subjected to profanation by the 'nations' (Ap 11,2) and is 'spiritually' called Sodom and Egypt. Both Sodom and Egypt were places which the people of God had to leave in a hurry, in obedience to divine instructions. It is implied, therefore, that during this period Jerusalem is no longer 'spiritually' called Zion, since the exodus of God's people from the city leads to a separation of Zion from the historical city of Jerusalem (cf. Mk 13,14–23; Mt 24,15–28).

[157] The death of the two witnesses is celebrated by people throughout the world (Ap 11,9–10). Against a literal interpretation of the two witnesses as two individuals, it is argued that it would be impossible for so many people at once to know about the death of just two individuals (Ford, *Commentary on Revelation*, 181; Beale, *Book of Revelation*, 574, n. 3). Nowadays, however, such a controversial event would be broadcast immediately around the world by the international media.

for a short while longer than Jesus lay in the tomb. Instead of discrediting the Faith, however, this challenge has the opposite effect: after the three-and-a-half days, the resurrection of the two witnesses precipitates the conversion of many unbelievers in the city (Ap 11,11–13), and is described in a way that evokes the resurrection of the people of Israel, as prophesied in Ezekiel's vision of the valley strewn with dry bones (Ezek 37,1–14).

The time, place and character of the death and resurrection of the two witnesses, all confirm that the most important part of their mission is directed especially towards the Jewish nation, therefore realizing St. Paul's hope for the salvation of his people at the end of history (Rom 11,25–26).

Chapter 2

The Eschatological Exodus

Situated between the two references to the eschatological opening of the Sanctuary in heaven (Ap 11,19 & 15,5), there is a passage containing a series of seven visions described by St. John[158](Ap 12,1 – 15,4). Mentioned in this passage are the two consecutive time-periods (1,260 days and 42 months) that characterize the prophecy given to St. John in order to 'prophesy again', indicating that this passage forms the main part of that prophecy. Furthermore, since the prophecy will finally be announced by the two witnesses, this passage most probably reveals the content of the prophecy that these two representatives of Moses and Elijah will announce. Some confirmation of this is suggested by the fact that the main theme of this passage evokes a combination of the ministries of Moses and Elijah: the *exodus* of the mother of the male-child to the desert during the 1,260 days (Moses), where she will be *protected from the persecutions of a false and idolatrous religion* during the period of 42 months (Elijah).

The prophetic and eschatological context of this passage is so crucial to its interpretation that when it is not given due importance, the resulting interpretation loses all continuity with the

---

[158] a series of seven visions described by St. John: Ap 12,1–18; 13,1–10; 13,11–18; 14,1–5; 14,6–13; 14,14–20; 15,2–4; (15,1 corresponds to 15,5 and 11,19). Each vision can be distinguished by a change in subject and a characteristic introductory phrase (Beale, *Book of Revelation*, 621): except for the first vision, all start with the phrase 'and I saw' (καὶ εἶδον). The first vision is unique in the entire text of the Apocalypse, because it starts with the passive form of the verb 'to see': 'and a great sign was seen (ὤφθη) in heaven'. The significance of this will be discussed later (see below, n. 162).

rest of the text.[159]

The first vision in the series (Ap 12,1–18) starts with two signs in heaven: a woman in labour and a dragon waiting to eat her child whenever it is born. A male-child is born, who will shepherd all the nations with an iron rod. He is immediately taken up to the Throne of God, before the dragon can devour him. The rest of the vision concerns the consequences of this heavenly birth: there is a war in heaven and the dragon and his angels are thrown down to the earth, whereupon the dragon pursues the woman who gave birth. The woman flees to a place which has been prepared for her in the desert, where she is nourished and protected for 1,260 days (Ap 12,6), and for 'a time, two times and half-a-time'(Ap 12,14). The dragon then goes off to attack the other children of the woman.

The symbolical significance of the main figures of this vision can be interpreted from the many allusions it contains to the Old Testament scriptures. The starting-point for this is the description of the male-child as the one 'who will shepherd the nations with an iron rod' (Ap 12,5), which is a direct reference to the messianic ruler of Psalm 2. The birth and ascension of the male-child presents itself, then, as a much-condensed representation of the earthly life, mission and Ascension of Jesus Christ.

The woman in labour represents the faithful community that, with much suffering and distress, was awaiting the coming of the Messiah. Recalling the temptation of Eve in the story of creation (Gen ch.3) and personifying the wisdom of God (Prov 8,22–31; Wis chs.7–8; Sir 24,1–12), this community is called 'Zion' by the prophets of the Old Testament[160](Is 46,13; 51,16; 52,1; Ps 147,12).

---

[159] The context identifies this passage squarely as an eschatological prophecy. Any interpretation that gives it a different character detaches it, to some extent or other, from the rest of the text of the Apocalypse.

[160] This 'collective' interpretation of the woman in Ap 12,1 is almost universally accepted nowadays. Prigent neatly summarizes the main reasons as follows: "v.17 sees Christians as the other offspring of the woman, who is therefore a community. This image makes use of metaphorical language that is frequent in the Old Testament...." (Prigent, *Apocalypse of St. John*, 377). Referring to the rival tradition of interpreting this woman as Mary, the mother of Jesus, Prigent notes: "The

She is frequently called a mother (Bar chs.4–5; Is 66,7–13; 51,18.20), whose children are the members of the community (Ps 149,2; Lam 1,16; 2,19; 4,2; Lk 19,44), and are referred to collectively as 'daughter of Zion' or 'virgin daughter of Zion' (2Kgs 19,21; Is 1,8; 37,22; 52,2; 62,11; Jer 4,31; 6,2.23; Lam 1,6; Mic 4,8.10.13; Zech 2,14; 9,9)

The identity of the third figure is disclosed unambiguously in the text itself: the dragon represents 'the ancient serpent called the devil and Satan, the one deceiving the entire world' (Ap 12,9).

As a whole, then, the vision represents Zion, the people of God, suffering in expectation of their Messiah, in the face of radical opposition and hostility. Following the birth and glorification of the Messiah, the source of this opposition is partially defeated, and his hostility is transferred to the mother community herself, and then to her large family of followers. In general terms, the vision seems to describe the history of the persecution of the Church, following the Ascension and glorification of Jesus Christ. However, in St. John's vision, the birth of Jesus Christ is not described as a historical event, but as a spiritual event that takes place in heaven immediately after the revelation of the two heavenly signs—the woman and the dragon (Ap 12,1–5).

Particular emphasis should therefore be given to the fact that the vision unfolds from the appearance of these two signs in heaven. Furthermore, there is no clear break between the revelation of the signs in heaven and the rest of the vision: after the heavenly birth, the vision continues by following the fate of the two signs, from heaven to earth. Since these two signs form the subject of the entire vision, it is essential to focus the interpretation on the purpose of these signs. This approach is strongly endorsed by the fact that, in the biblical tradition, the function of a sign is as important, if not

---

mariological interpretation cannot be defended with much seriousness....The exegetes who do not exclude it today generally only retain it in the category of a secondary undertone, cf. J. P. M. Sweet: 'She is Mary, but only insofar as Mary embodies faithful Israel...' (1979, p.195)" (Prigent, *Apocalypse of St. John* , 378, n. 35). Clearly, for many Christians, the Virgin Mary has assumed, and continues to embody, all that 'Zion' previously meant to the community of God's people.

more so, than the sign itself.[161] The interpretation of the vision must therefore concentrate on the function of the signs that are seen, and on the meaning of statements such as "a great sign was seen in heaven" (Ap 12,1) and "another sign was seen in heaven" (Ap 12,3).[162]

In the biblical tradition, a sign has been defined as an object, an occurrence or an event through which a person is to recognize, learn, remember or perceive the credibility of something.[163] Directly or indirectly, the author of a sign is almost always God.[164] Those who witness the sign may experience one or several of the following effects: the gift of new knowledge or understanding, the increase of faith, the assurance of protection, the recollection of an agreement or covenant, or the confirmation of a divine calling or mission.

Applying this definition to St. John's vision (Ap 12,1–18) helps to focus attention on the effect of the signs on those who see them: the event of seeing the signs in heaven causes those who see them 'to recognize, learn, remember or perceive the credibility' of the thing to which the signs refer, namely to the exodus of the woman to the desert, where she will be protected from the dragon and his furious attacks on her children. Why should the people who see the signs need to be assured of the exodus and protection of the woman in the desert, if not because they themselves are called to go

---

[161] This is the underlying theme of Helfmeyer's analysis of the word 'Sign' in the Old Testament, s.v. אות in *Theological Dictionary of the Old Testament*, 1:170–88.

[162] The text states that each of the signs 'was seen' (ὤφθη) in heaven. The use of the passive form 'was seen', in the context of these signs, contrasts with the use of the first person active form (εἶδον) which is found in almost every other part of the text, and indicates, therefore, that these signs are not seen only by St. John, but also by others. The identity of those who see the signs is of the utmost importance and is discussed later.

[163] This is H. Gunkel's definition, quoted by Helfmeyer in his article on 'Signs' in *Theological Dictionary of the Old Testament*, 1:170. Subsequent information is also based on this article.

[164] See *Encyclopaedia Judaica*, s.v. 'Signs and Symbols'. It should not be forgotten, though, that the devil can also be the author of signs, usually performed with the intention of deceiving (Ap 13,13–14; 16,14; 19,20; Mt 24,24; Mk 13,22; 2Thess 2,9).

out to the desert. In those who see them, the signs serve to create what they symbolize, and so re-create a situation, characterized by witnessing and persecution, which is very similar to the one that followed the Resurrection and Ascension of Jesus Christ in the first century AD.

So the vision described by St. John primarily concerns those who see the signs in heaven, and what happens to them afterwards. Seeing signs in heaven suggests a spiritual experience, with a visionary or prophetic character, which is granted to a soul that has been elevated to the heights of mystical contemplation. We suggest that those who see, or contemplate, these signs in heaven actually experience a revelation of Jesus Christ from within their own soul,[165] just as the woman gives birth to the male-child in the vision. In this way, through the 'heavenly birth', the one who sees the signs comes to be identified with Zion, the woman in the vision. So complete is this identification that, just as the woman in St. John's vision, he then flees to a place that has been prepared in the desert,[166] where he

---

[165] This refers to an experience known as the 'heavenly' or 'eternal birth'—a metaphorical expression which was used by Christian mystics to describe an important stage on the path towards union with God, and was developed especially by Origen and Meister Eckhart. Referring to Origen, McGinn writes: "The intimacy of the union [with Jesus] is suggested not only by the dominant image of the Bride and Groom, but also (in a different way) by the procreative symbol of birthing. Thus, Origen can speak of the loving soul as both Bride and Mother: 'And every soul, virgin and uncorrupted, which conceives by the Holy Spirit, so as to give birth to the Will of the Father, is the Mother of Jesus' (*comm. on Matt.* frg. 281 [GCS Origen 12.1:126.10–15]). In his view of the mystic's soul as at once virgin and mother, Origen is an initiator of a potent theme in the history of Christian mysticism, one that displays surprising parallels with later mystics, for example, Meister Eckhart" (McGinn, *Foundations of Mysticism*, 125).

[166] *he then flees to a place which has been prepared in the desert*: just as God protected the Israelites from Pharaoh's army after their exodus from Egypt, so also those who identify with 'Zion' are protected from the diabolical offensive of the serpent, after their exodus from the world. In this 'eschatological exodus', the desert corresponds to that which the Israelites crossed in order to reach the promised land. The waters that the serpent spews from its mouth, to sweep away the woman (Ap 12,15), are later identified with people from many 'races and crowds and nations and tongues' (Ap 17,15), who, even though they do not have a vocation, presume to be called to go out to the desert (cf. Mt 24,24–26). On account of their immorality,

is united with all those who have had a similar experience.[167] There they remain for 1,260 days followed by 'a time, two times and half-a-time'—the two consecutive periods of time which constitute a final week of years.[168] Since the cause of the exodus is the experience of the revelation of Jesus Christ, it is this that determines the start of the period of 1,260 days, at the beginning of the final week of years.

Those who come to be identified with Zion through the 'heavenly birth' can be recognized as the group of 144,000 followers of the Lamb, by the fact that later in the vision, St. John sees them on a mountain called by the same name: Mt. Zion (Ap 14,1–5).

---

these people by no means represent 'Zion', but the Abyss (see n. 79). As a result, the earth opens up and buries them (Ap 12,16), recalling what happened to Korah and his company of Levites, when they presumed to be as holy as Moses and Aaron (Num ch. 16).

[167] One important corollary to this interpretation is that, as a sign, the woman in the vision only partly represents the mother community which produced the Messiah. On another level, she represents the holy and blessed soul raised to the heights of contemplation and granted a revelation of Jesus Christ from within. Confusion between these two levels of significance has fuelled the long debate between the collective and individual interpretations of this passage (see n. 160; also Le Frois, *The Woman Clothed with the Sun*, 3–9). In a similar way the sign of the dragon only partially represents the devil, the origin of all evil, the defeated enemy of Jesus Christ presently locked and chained in the Abyss (Ap 20,2–3). As a sign in this vision, the dragon actually represents the spirit of evil which opposes the revelation of Jesus Christ (the 'heavenly birth'). Not limiting himself to this, however, he proceeds to oppose all those who receive the revelation and then act on it (the woman), as well as those who simply maintain this witness of Jesus Christ (the rest of her descendants). In this context, the battle which takes place in heaven between Michael and his angels, and the dragon and his angels, only partially reflects the battle which took place following the historical Resurrection and Ascension of our Lord. More specifically it is a battle over the truth of the revelation of Jesus Christ, and over the prophetic word in the Apocalypse which confirms it. The sign of the devil—the spirit which opposes this revelation—is defeated through faith in the Word of God, just as the devil was defeated following the historical Ascension of Jesus Christ. The problem of how the devil came to have a sign in heaven, after being defeated and imprisoned in the Abyss, is explained in the vision of Babylon (Ap ch. 17), and constitutes what St. Paul has called the 'mystery of iniquity' (see III. 4: 'The Mystery of Iniquity').

[168] For a full explanation, see n. 132.

Furthermore, just as Zion is traditionally linked with the people of Israel, so also are the 144,000 since they are chosen from the 12 tribes of Israel, and therefore make up 'the remnant' of that people (cf. Ap 7,2–8).[169]

Looking retrospectively at those parts of the text which concern the 144,000 followers of the Lamb, it becomes clear that a characteristic feature of this group is indeed their deep identification with the history of Zion, a feature that appears to be established in them by means of spiritual, or mystical, experiences:

a) The sealing of the 144,000 on their foreheads with the name of the living God (Ap 7,2–8; 14,1) recalls the Presence of God among the people of Israel, before the coming of the Messiah, Jesus Christ. The name of God that dwelt in the former Temple was placed on the people by means of the priestly blessing.[170]

b) The revelation of Jesus Christ from within the soul, which has been raised to the heights of contemplation (Ap 12,1–5), corresponds to the historical coming of the Messiah among the Jewish people: the birth, ministry, Passion, Resurrection, Ascension and glorification of Jesus Christ.

c) The exodus of the 144,000 followers of Jesus Christ, to a mountain in the desert where they are assembled in his Presence (Ap 12,6.14; 14,1–5) represents the betrothal of the virgin

---

[169] 'the remnant' of that people: the theme of the 'remnant' is used by many prophets of the Old Testament. The unfaithfulness of Israel is punished, but on account of the God's love for his people, a purified remnant survives (e.g., Am 9,8–10; Is 4,2–3; 10,16–22; 37,30–32; Mic 4,7; Zeph 3,11–13; Jer 5,18; Joel 3,5). The term is applied in a special way to the Jews who remained faithful during the Babylonian exile and then returned across the desert to live in Jerusalem (Ezra 1,3–4; Neh 1,2; Hag 1,12; Is 40,1–11), to await the coming of their Lord (Jer 23,3; 31,7; 50,20; Ezek 20,37; Mic 2,12–13; Is 11,11.17). The number of this 'remnant' in the Apocalypse is often said to be symbolic (144,000 = 12 x 12 x 1000; see Vanni, *L'Apocalisse*, 54), but there are good reasons for supposing it is not *purely* symbolic, and should also be understood literally (see Bauckham, *Climax of Prophecy*, 218–19). Since the precise number of this group is divinely ordained through the granting of spiritual experiences (see n. 171), it should not concern us unduly.

[170] This point was discussed above at I. 9, vii.

daughter of Zion with the Lamb, and the final preparations for her spiritual wedding. This reflects the historical pilgrimage of the Church in this world, while she awaits the glorious return of her Lord.

It is by means of these spiritual experiences,[171] passively granted by God, that the 144,000 identify themselves strongly with 'Zion', embodying her history, and fulfilling the purpose of her mission in the final 'week of years'.

It is clear from the present context, though, that the 144,000 who represent 'Zion', are not the only group making up God's people in the 'final week of years'. Whilst this group is sheltered at a certain place in the desert, the dragon goes off "to make war against the rest of her children, those who keep the commandments of God and have the witness of Jesus" (Ap 12,17). The 144,000 are therefore a relatively small group of people that have been selected for a special mission, described in later visions of the Apocalypse. Before examining this mission in detail, however, St. John describes the fate of the much larger group of God's people whom the dragon goes off to attack.[172]

---

[171] these spiritual experiences: it should be noted that these experiences, which form the basis of the spiritual development of the 144,000, correspond closely to the Vth, VIth and VIIth 'mansions' described by St. Teresa of Avila in her book *Interior Castle*.

[172] The two groups distinguished in ch. 12 have already been seen and described in ch. 7: a) the numbered group of 144,000 men on earth (Ap 7,2–8) and b) the vast multitude in heaven, whom no one was able to number, after they had passed through the great tribulation (Ap 7,9–17). The distinction between these two groups is nowhere more clearly emphasized than in the present passage (Ap 12,17). The two groups are seen again in close proximity in subsequent visions (Ap 14,2–3; 15,2–4).

Chapter 3

The Pseudo-messianic Reign

The next two visions in this part of St. John's prophecy (Ap 12,1 – 15,4) describe in detail how the dragon, after failing to dislodge the 144,000 from their place in the desert, goes off to make war against the rest of God's people, 'those who keep the commandments of God and have the witness of Jesus'. The dragon does not directly engage in any attacks at this point,[173] but operates through a beast that emerges from the sea, to whom he had previously given 'his power, his throne and great authority' (Ap 13,2). This beast not only inherits the dragon's power but his form as well, since he also has seven heads and ten horns (Ap 12,3; 13,1).

In the biblical tradition, this description evokes Leviathan (sometimes called Rahab), the mythical female monster symbolizing oppressive foreign power (Ps 74,14; 87,4; Is 30,7; Ezek 29,3; 32,2–3; Jer 51,34). More specifically, the beast from the sea is described as a conflation of all four beasts revealed in a vision to the prophet Daniel (Ap 13,1–2; cf. Dan 7,2–8). Just as these represent successive powers or kingdoms in the ancient world, so the beast described by St. John represents a single power in the contemporary world that reflects elements of all these ancient kingdoms. The full manifestation of this evil power is identified with only one of its heads:[174] this head represents a ruler who is fatally wounded, but

---

[173] This is a reminder that the dragon in this vision does not represent the devil specifically, but is only an external 'sign' of his influence on earth at this time. The devil is presently locked and chained in the Abyss (see n. 167).

[174] one of its heads: in ch. 17 additional information is revealed concerning this beast with 7 heads and 10 horns: it is confirmed that the heads of the beast represent successive rulers. The head which is described in ch. 13 is called the beast "that was, and is not, and is about to come up from the Abyss, and goes to destruction" (Ap 17,8); "even he is an eighth head, he is also one of the seven (Ap 17,11). Which

recovers and goes on to receive international authority and admiration for a limited period of 42 months (Ap 13,3–5.7).

The emergence of the beast from the sea, to begin his reign of 42 months (Ap 13,1.5), links this vision with the ascension of the beast from the Abyss[175] at the end of the period of 1,260 days (Ap 11,7), in order to make war against the two witnesses, overcome them and kill them. The link between these two passages not only confirms that the two time-periods are consecutive, as previously demonstrated,[176] but also indicates that the two witnesses are the first victims of the beast from the sea, in this phase of the dragon's war against Zion's children. During the subsequent period of 42 months,

---

of the seven? Since the beast only has 7 heads, the 8th head merely represents the full revelation of the beast which occurs after the previous (i.e., the 7th) head has recovered from his mortal wound (Ap 13,3). The 8th head is therefore the continuation of the 7th and last head, but in a more manifest and powerful way. The text, however, is unusually vague and enigmatic about this, perhaps in order to permit the 8th head to be identified also with the 1st head, in imitation of the risen Lord, who is 'the first and the last' (Ap 1,17; 2,8; 22,13). If, then, the 1st head is taken to be the Roman Emperor Nero (54–68 AD), the 8th head could indeed be understood as an eschatological fulfilment of the Nero Redivivus legend, so popular in the Mediterranean region during the 1st century AD (see Bauckham, *Climax of Prophecy*, 407–23; Aune, *Revelation 6–16*, Excursus 13A, 737–40). As in other contexts in the Apocalypse, the number seven is symbolical (see n. 24), and here represents the total number of heads of the beast, rather than the actual number (Bauckham, *Climax of Prophecy*, 404–407; Aune, *Revelation 17–22*, 948). The information that 'five have fallen, one is, the other has not yet come' (Ap 17,10) places the author's vision during the reign of the sixth head, just before the seventh and final manifestation of the beast. This need not refer to the time of writing, as often proposed in the commentaries (it is even used as a basis for dating the time of writing), but to the timing of the vision relative to the entire sequence of events recorded in the Apocalypse (just as John's eating the little scroll is to be interpreted in relation to other events in the Apocalypse, namely the unsealing of the Lamb's scroll in heaven). The vision recorded in ch. 17 therefore refers to the time immediately preceding the last and greatest manifestation of the beast, a fact which suggests that the contents of the vision may be instrumental in precipitating this event (see III. 4: 'The Mystery of Iniquity').

[175] The 'Abyss' is synonymous with the 'sea' in the visions of the Apocalypse (see n. 79), so the beast ascending from the Abyss refers to the same event as the beast ascending from the sea.

[176] See II. 8 ('The Two Periods of Time')

the beast is allowed to make war against the saints, and overcome them (Ap 13,7). He finally undertakes to make war against the Lamb, but is defeated (Ap 17,14).

The way in which the beast 'makes war against the saints' is disclosed in the next vision (Ap 13,11–18). This concerns a second beast who comes up from the land[177] in a way that corresponds to the rising of the first beast from the sea, and recalls Behemoth, the mythical male monster who, according to Jewish tradition, lived in the desert to the east of Eden.[178]

---

[177] Although there is little or no problem in understanding why the first beast arises from the sea, or Abyss, since this is understood as the home of evil spirits and other agents of destruction, there is no agreement about why the second beast should arise 'ἐκ τῆς γῆς'—from the land or earth (Ladd, *Commentary on Revelation*, 183; Mounce, *Book of Revelation*, 258; Aune, *Revelation 6–16*, 755). More than one meaning appears to be intended. Firstly, as the land is complementary to the sea, it is implied that, in a finite sense, the two beasts together represent the entire globe. Secondly, with his origin in the earth, it is very appropriate that the role of the second beast is specifically directed to the 'inhabitants of the earth'. Thirdly, as the earth is often contrasted with heaven, the beast that arises from the land can not truly identify himself with the prophet Elijah who, in some circles, is still expected to return from heaven. Finally, the phrase 'from the land' can be understood as a reference to a specific region. Swete [*Apocalypse of John*, 168] and Mounce [*Book of Revelation*, 258] both suggest Asia Minor. In the Jewish tradition, however, 'the Land' could only refer to the Land of Israel (הארץ) and this is probably the most significant aspect of its meaning in the present context.

[178] For references to this tradition, see n. 84. The allusion to the mythical monsters, Leviathan and Behemoth, in the Apocalypse is by no means as superficial as it may seem (contra Aune, *Revelation 6–16*, 728–29). Not only do the two beasts represent the role of the two monsters in a Christian re-reading of the eschatological banquet of the righteous (see I. 9, xvi), but they also reflect the symbolism of these monsters, as expressed by an old Chassidic tradition (Brod, *Days of Moshiach*, 153). According to this tradition, the two monsters symbolize two complementary aspects of 'spiritual service': since the sea represents the hidden depths of the spiritual world, the sea monster symbolizes those religious individuals who aspire to profound spiritual knowledge. Since the land represents the lower, visible world, the land monster symbolizes those individuals whose religious activity is focused on preparing the lower, physical world for the spiritual revelations of the former class of service. The main difference is that in the Apocalypse the 'sea', or 'Abyss', represents the *unredeemed* spiritual world (see n. 79), with the result that whereas, in the Chassidic tradition, the service symbolized by the two monsters is directed

In St. John's vision, the second beast "exercises all the authority of the first beast in front of him, and makes the earth and its inhabitants worship the first beast" (Ap 13,12). All the inhabitants of the earth will worship the first beast—all except for those whose names are inscribed in the scroll of Life (Ap 13,8; 17,8), since they remain faithful to God and to Jesus Christ.[179] The text then goes on to describe precisely how the second beast makes the inhabitants of the earth worship the first beast. As a result of the signs he is able to perform, he deceives them into making and worshipping a speaking image of the first beast.[180]

Those who do not worship this image will be killed (Ap 13,15), and all those people who do not have a mark of loyalty to the beast,[181] on their foreheads or hands, will be prevented from

---

towards Hashem (God), the two beasts that represent these monsters in the Apocalypse are servants of the devil (cf. Ap 2,24).

[179] During the period of the beast's rule, the divine Judgement is in progress: those who become followers of the beast are those whose names are removed by the Lamb from his scroll of Life (Ap 3,5; 3,8; 17,8; 20,15; cf. 14,11; 2Thess 2,9–12). For a detailed account of this subject, see II. 9 ('Conclusions and the Importance of the Little Scroll'.

[180] Literally: "And he was allowed to give breath to the image of the beast, so that the image of the beast might even speak..." (Ap 13,15). In the ancient classical world, the ability to make images move or speak was the task of a specific kind of magician (a 'theurgist', see Aune, *Revelation 6–16*, 762–64). Nowadays, however, it is impossible to read this passage without thinking of televised images displayed on huge screens in public places and at mass gatherings or ceremonial events.

[181] a mark of loyalty to the beast: described as a mark representing the name of the beast, or the number of his name, placed either on the forehead or on the right hand of his followers (Ap 13,16–18). It is understood as a parody of the seal of God placed on the forehead of his servants (Ap 7,3; 9,4; 14,1; 22,4). In connection with commercial activity, the practice was unknown in classical antiquity. R. H. Charles suggested that the practice could be modelled on the Jewish custom of wearing 'tefillin' (i.e, phylacteries, cf. Deut 6,8; 11,18; Ex 13,9.16; Mt 23,5) during prayer (Aune, *Revelation 6–16*, 767–68). The number of the beast (666) is the number of a man (Ap 13,18) and refers to the numerical system called Gematria, in which every letter of the alphabet has a numerical value. The number of the name is therefore the sum of the numerical value of each of its letters. Up to this day, Gematria continues to be an important element in Jewish mystical speculation (Kabbalah), and Hebrew

participating in the commercial life of the society, since they will be forbidden to buy or sell (Ap 13,16–17). As indicated in other parts of the text, this form of persecution leads to the death of multitudes of people, in what is called 'the great tribulation' (Ap 7,9–17; 15,2–4; 20,4).

At the root of this persecution of the people of God is the beast's false claim to divinity,[182] and the enforcement of a kind of false and idolatrous worship of his person during the period of 42 months. There are subtle indications in the text that help to clarify the precise character of the false religion established by the beast from the sea and his partner, the beast from the land.

The first of these concerns the beast from the sea. On one hand, he acts decisively against Christ and his followers: he kills the two witnesses (Ap 11,7), persecutes the saints (Ap 13,7) and goes off to make war against the Lamb (Ap 17,14). On the other hand, many aspects of his rule resemble the mission and imitate the mystery of Jesus Christ: one of the heads of the beast is fatally wounded (Ap 13,3), but his recovery signals the ascension of the beast from the Abyss and the full manifestation of its power in the world (Ap 13,12.14), in ways that appear to imitate the Passion, Resurrection and Ascension of Jesus Christ. Furthermore, this beast is worshipped as God following his ascension from the Abyss to rule for 42 months, in a way that seems to imitate the worship of Jesus Christ following his Ascension to heaven and glorification (cf. Ap 5,9–14). This combination of hostility to Christ and his followers, together with imitation of the true Saviour, suggests only one conclusion: the beast is a false messiah, a challenger to the title of

---

is one of the few modern languages which continues to use the alphabet as a numerical system.

[182] the beast's false claim to divinity: the beast blasphemes God and his dwelling—those dwelling in heaven—and makes war against God's people (Ap 13,5–7). At the same time, he is given authority over people in all the earth (Ap 13,7–8), and is worshipped for his military strength: "Who is like the beast, and who can fight against him?" (Ap 13,4). The fact that this acclamation imitates the way that God himself is worshipped in the Psalms (Ps 113,5; 89,7.9; 86,8; 35,10; Ex 15,11), implies that the diabolical ruler who represents the full manifestation of the beast claims to be God (2Thess 2,4).

Christ, the last and strongest manifestation of the antichristian spirit[183] that has been present in the world since the beginnings of Christianity. This is confirmed by his position in a hierarchy of three figures which are contrasted with God, his Christ and their prophet, St. John. The devil is contrasted with God, the beast from the sea with Christ, and the beast from the land is contrasted with St. John, the author of the Apocalypse.

Having identified the beast from the sea as the ultimate false messiah, it is no surprise to find that later in the text, his partner—the beast from the land—is identified as the 'false prophet', on the basis that the signs he performs are responsible for deceiving people (Ap 16,13; 19,20, 20,10). One of the signs he performs is particularly important, since it reveals the character of his mission: "And he performs great signs such that he even makes fire come down from heaven to earth in the sight of men" (Ap 13,13).

Firstly, since this sign recalls the divine power given to the prophet Elijah (2Kgs 1,9–14; 1Kgs 18,30–40), the imitation of this sign by the false prophet suggests that he wishes to identify himself with Elijah. Secondly, in the history of the ancient sacrificial cult, this sign frequently appeared at the consecration of a new altar, indicating divine confirmation (Lev 9,24; 1Chr 21,26; 2Chr 7,1; 2Macc 1,18–36). Its imitation by the false prophet therefore implies his participation in the dedication of a new altar connected to the ancient Israelite cult.

In view of the central importance of the Temple in Jerusalem for the performance of the ancient cult, the dedication of a new altar by the false prophet, in this impressive but unauthentic way, certainly implies the reconstruction of the Temple in Jerusalem. Furthermore, it is clear from the text that the renewed cult is not directed to the worship of God, but rather to the false messiah and his patron, the devil, even though it is based on the site of the ancient Temple in Jerusalem (cf. 2Thess 2,4; Mt 24,15; Mk 13,14).

---

[183] That is to say, the eschatological antagonist of Christ, called the antichrist in Christian tradition (for a brief synopsis of this tradition, see Excursus 13B in Aune, *Revelation 6–16*, 751–55).

The precise character of the false religion deceitfully established and enforced by the false prophet is therefore discernable: it is an idolatrous form of the ancient Israelite cult, directed towards the worship of a false messiah and the source of his authority, the devil.[184]

The text of the Apocalypse advises the faithful to discern with wisdom and intelligence the realization of this false messianic reign (Ap 13,18) and to oppose it peacefully by refusing to worship the image of the false messiah, or receive the mark of his name. Even though this brings great tribulation (Ap 13,15–17; 7,13–14) to the opponents of the false messiah, the text encourages them to endure like the saints, with constant faith in Jesus Christ (Ap 13,9–10; 14,12–13).

In the fifth of the seven visions (Ap 14,6–13) in this part of the prophecy (12,1 – 15,4), St. John describes a series of three angelic announcements addressed to the people on earth, all of which concern judgement. The first warns of the nearness of the final Judgement and advises people to worship God and give him glory (Ap 14,6–7). The third is a severe warning against worshipping the beast and his image, or receiving his mark on the forehead or hand. Those who participate in these practices will not

---

[184] Modern interpretation of the religious activity described in this passage is almost entirely focused on the idolatrous worship of the ruler, identifying it with the imperial cult—a form of pagan idolatry practised in the first century AD, which made the image of the Emperor an object of worship. Very few commentators seem to notice the messianic overtones in this passage, or the allusions to OT prophetic and ceremonial traditions. Those scholars who do comment on these (e.g., Beale, *Book of Revelation*, 710–15) do not seem to be aware of their incompatibility with first-century pagan practices. In fact, there is only one religion into which the religious activity described in this passage fits, and that is Judaism—especially those branches of Orthodox Judaism which actively maintain OT traditions whilst awaiting the coming of a prophet representing Elijah (Mal 3,23–24) and a political messiah. Furthermore, the single most important Halachic criteria for identifying this messiah is his supervision of the rebuilding of the Temple *in its place* (see Maimonides, *The Code [Mishneh Torah]*, Book 14: Judges. Treatise five: Kings and Wars, chs. 11–12, 238–42). In St. John's prophecy the reign of the beast and his false prophet represents a realization of this false messianic expectation of Orthodox Judaism.

only receive the full force of God's passionate anger, but will also suffer divine and eternal condemnation (Ap 14,9–11). The second angel announces the downfall of an entity called Babylon the great, "who caused all the nations to drink from the wine of the passion of her fornicating" (Ap 14,8). Since Babylon's downfall is caused by the beast and his allies (Ap 17,16) and therefore occurs during the false messianic reign elucidated above, it will be considered next, before returning to the 144,000 followers of the Lamb who, by this time, are securely encamped at their place in the desert.

Chapter 4

The Mystery of Iniquity

Linked to the announcement of the hour of God's Judgement in the fifth vision of this part of St. John's prophecy (Ap 14,6–13), there is the notification, but not the description, of the downfall of Babylon (Ap 14,8). The description of this event, and the reasons for Babylon's judgement, are given later in the text (Ap 17,1 – 19,10), at the end of the account of the eschatological judgements of God represented by the outpouring of the wine of his anger (Ap 15,5 – 16,21). Although described as one of the eschatological judgements of God, the earlier announcement of Babylon's downfall indicates that this event actually precedes the manifestation of these judgements. In other words, the judgement and subsequent downfall of Babylon stand out as important anticipatory signs of the judgements of God on earth at the end of history. In spite of the importance of this event in the Apocalypse, where it occupies more than a tenth of the text (Ap 17,1 – 19,10), it is not described, or even mentioned, in any other part of the New Testament.

The reason why the judgement of Babylon takes place during the 42–month reign of the beast, before all the other eschatological judgements, is explained by the fact that the beast himself, aided by his ten horns representing ten other rulers, is the agent through which God's violent condemnation of Babylon is put into effect (Ap 17,12.16–17).[185] The remarkable fact that divine

---

[185] This agrees with the recognition of the reign of the beast as the realization of the false messianic expectation of Orthodox Judaism. One of the duties of the false messianic leader will be to take revenge against Rome for the destruction of Jerusalem in ancient times and the continuous oppression of the Jewish people during the subsequent exile. Although Rome is called Babylon in the Christian tradition (1Pet 5,13; Ap 17,9), in Jewish tradition it is referred to as Edom, and is therefore to expect the same fate as Edom in the OT prophecies (Is 35,5–6; 63,1–4). The

justice is executed by means of this final manifestation of evil and his allies is expressed in the following way, describing Babylon as a prostitute: "And the ten horns which you saw and the beast, these will hate the prostitute, and will leave her desolate and naked, and will eat her flesh, and will consume her with fire; for God put it into their hearts to serve his purpose and to be of one mind, and to give their kingdom to the beast until the words of God shall be fulfilled" (Ap 17,16–17).[186]

The instructions in the next part of the vision actually seem to be addressed to this coalition of ten rulers with the beast: "Pay her as indeed she paid out, and give her double in proportion to her deeds; mix her double in the cup in which she mixed; as much as she glorified and lived in luxury, by that much give her torment and sorrow. Since she says to herself: 'As queen I sit and am not a widow, and sorrow I certainly do not see', so in one day will come her plagues—pestilence and sorrow and famine—and with fire she will be consumed, for strong is the Lord God, the One condemning her" (Ap 18,6–8).

There follows an account of the mourning of all those who profited, in one way or another, from Babylon's unbridled desire for luxury: they express wonder and amazement at the suddenness and speed of her destruction, and for the immense wealth that was

---

destruction of Edom (= Rome, or the 'evil kingdom') is believed to remove one of the obstacles to global redemption (see Brod, *Days of Moshiach*, 133–35; Klausner, *Messianic Idea in Israel*, 503–504).

[186] This description of Babylon's destruction at the hands of the beast specifically recalls the language used by the ancient prophets to describe the punishment of Jerusalem for her idolatry, at the hands of foreign invaders (cf. Ezek chs. 16, 23; Jer 13,20–27). In other parts of the vision, the language echoes the judgement oracles against a variety of ancient cities in the region: Babylon (Is chs. 13, 21, 47; Jer chs. 50–51), Tyre (Ezek chs. 26–27), Edom (Is ch. 34), Nineveh (Zeph 2,13–15; Nah 3,4) and also Jerusalem (Jer 7,34; 16,9; 25,10). The divine commissioning of the beast and his allies recalls the similar role given to foreign invaders in ancient times: these agents of God's anger tended to exceed the task assigned to them, so earning their own divine condemnation (Is 10,5–26; 14,4–21). In a similar way the beast fatally oversteps his limits by blaspheming God and persecuting the followers of Christ, and so goes on to receive eternal condemnation.

destroyed (Ap 18,9–19). Her destruction and condemnation will not only be swift but also eternal (Ap 18,21–24; 19,3).

In contrast to the sorrow and mourning on earth, there is great rejoicing and celebration in heaven, since Babylon was the cause of corruption on earth, and her judgement answered the prayers of the martyrs for vindication (Ap 19,1–5, cf. 6,10). Her judgement also opens up the way for the fullness of God's Kingdom and the consummation of his mystery (Ap 19,6–10).

Although the judgement of Babylon is such an important theme in the Apocalypse, the problem of her identity remains un-solved. Given that the destruction of Babylon takes place just before the divine judgements at the end of history, and these have not yet occurred, it follows that far from being an ancient city,[187] Babylon is a historical reality that currently exists, but is difficult to identify.

The difficulty in identifying Babylon derives from the fact that she participates in a mystery that involves the beast with seven heads and ten horns, to whom the devil gave 'his power, his throne and great authority' (Ap 17,7; cf. 13,2), that is to say the historical incarnation of evil. Since this mystery is presented in the Apocalypse as the evil counterpart of the mystery of God (cf. Ap 10,7), it should be considered the same as 'the mystery of iniquity' that was mentioned briefly by St. Paul in one of his letters (2Thess 2,1–11).[188]

---

[187] far from being an ancient city: the ancient cities of Rome and Jerusalem are those most commonly identified with Babylon in the commentaries, but both were rebuilt and repopulated after their destruction in ancient times. In contrast, the destruction of Babylon will be complete and eternal, according to what is prophesied in the Apocalypse (Ap 18,2.21–24; 19,3).

[188] Commenting on St. Paul's presentation of the mystery of iniquity (or 'lawlessness') in his second letter to the Thessalonians, Marcus Bockmuehl writes: "What is interesting about the 'mystery of lawlessness' in our text is that Paul envisions a clandestine present activity in the world, even prior to its eschatological manifestation in the antichrist. The idea of a present anticipation of the eschatological evil is not without parallel in the Qumran texts (see 1QH 5:36ff.; 1QM 14:9 with 15:2f.; cf. 1QS 3:20–24)....

"Presumably the mystery of lawlessness, although already active, is at present still hidden from men; it is known to Paul as part of his God-given insight into the eschatological mysteries...."

It is not surprising, therefore, that it is difficult to identify Babylon: the concealment of her identity is indeed an integral part of the mystery that, according to St. Paul, is impeding the eschatological manifestation of evil (2Thess 2,6–7). The definitive identification of Babylon, then, would have the effect of unmasking the 'mystery of iniquity', so preparing the way for the full manifestation of evil that must precede the return of the Lord at the end of history (2Thess 2,1–11). In brief, the identification of Babylon is essential for the initiation of the events that lead to the eschatological fulfilment of the mystery of God.[189]

Contemplating the mystery of Babylon and the beast, St. John was deeply astonished (Ap 17,6–7). It seems that he did not by any means expect to see what was revealed to him. The correct solution to the identity of Babylon, therefore, should explain the prophet's astonishment and may even arouse the same reaction among the faithful.

In order to receive the vision of Babylon, St. John was transported 'in spirit' to the desert (Ap 17,3), but not because Babylon is situated in the desert, since she is seen, in fact, sitting on many waters (Ap 17,1). Instead, it seems that St. John was transported to the desert because the mystery of Babylon can only be revealed to the one who is purified of worldly desires and lives spiritually, as if he were in the desert.[190]

"...the mystery of lawlessness is the destructive masterplan of the prince of darkness, set in terminal hostility against the salvific designs of God. Just as in the ongoing preaching of the gospel the mystery of Christ is being manifested, so also the evil mystery is working itself out. It will ultimately be personified in the revelation of the antichrist, and in this figure in turn the counsels of Satan will be overcome at the final confrontation" (Bockmuehl, *Revelation and Mystery*, 197–98).

[189] This probably explains why the vision is referred to the reign of the sixth head, according to the enigmatic statement: "five have fallen, one is, the other has not yet come" (Ap 17,10). The information presented in this vision helps to identify Babylon, and so prepares the way for the reign of the seventh and last head, during which the beast fully reveals himself (see n. 174).

[190] At the same time, the author is identifying himself with the 144,000, those who have a special vocation to go to the desert (see III. 2: 'The Eschatological Exodus'), indicating that the contents of this vision are particularly relevant to them.

In the vision granted to St. John, Babylon is revealed as a woman who represents a city: "The woman who you saw is the great city, the one which has a kingdom over the rulers of the earth" (Ap 17,18). We know therefore that Babylon is, above all, a great power; she has an international authority which is greater than that of any nation or state, and her base is described as a city.

Further information is derived from the fact that she is not only sitting on many waters (Ap 17,1.15), but also on the seven heads of the beast, which represent seven hills and seven successive rulers (Ap 17,3.9–10). As a whole, then, this vision represents the woman being supported by the heads of the beast, while the body of the beast remains submerged beneath the waters of the sea or Abyss.[191] Although this beast is the same as the one who reigns over the earth for 42 months (Ap ch.13), he is revealed in this vision before he emerges from the sea or Abyss (Ap 11,7; 13,1). Before emerging from the Abyss and fully manifesting himself in order to rule over the earth, he is clandestinely engaged in supporting the city called Babylon, so contributing to her success as an international power with 'a kingdom over the rulers of the earth'. As the historical incarnation of evil, however, the beast not only contributes to her worldly success, but also to her ability to corrupt the earth to such an extent that her sins pile up to heaven (Ap 18,5; 19,2). Operating indirectly in this way, through the beast and the sin of Babylon, the devil continues to have an influence in heaven and on earth, despite being chained in the Abyss.[192]

Returning to the question of Babylon's identity, it is significant that the seven heads on which she sits are also seven hills (Ap 17,9), for this is an ancient and widely-acknowledged allusion to the city of Rome.[193] Babylon, then, is described as a woman who

---

[191] As previously noted on a number of occasions, the waters, the sea and the Abyss are synonymous in the visions of the Apocalypse (see n. 79).

[192] This explains how the devil can have a sign in heaven (Ap 12,3; see n. 167) despite being chained in the Abyss for a thousand years (Ap 20,2–6). For the interpretation of the Millennium, see I. 11, iii.

[193] Aune, *Revelation 17–22*, 944–45.

represents an international authority based in the city of Rome, through which the devil continues to operate in a limited way, despite being chained in the Abyss.

Perhaps the most important clue to the identity of Babylon, however, is that she is described as a great prostitute (Ap 17,1), who makes the inhabitants of the earth drunk with the wine of the passion of her fornication (Ap 14,8; 17,2; 18,3), and seduces the rulers of the earth to fornicate with her (Ap 17,2; 18,3.9).

To determine the metaphorical meaning of Babylon's 'fornication', it is important to note that her passion for 'fornication' is essentially the same as the lust of her soul for riches and luxury (Ap 18,3.7.14). Filled with this 'passion for fornication', then, the inhabitants of the earth preoccupy themselves with the accumulation of riches and articles of luxury. In this way, under the influence of Babylon, the whole world becomes corrupted (Ap 19,2). In the same mindless search for luxury, the rulers of the earth are seduced by Babylon's wealth and power (Ap 17,4) and seek to establish immoral relations with her.

Understood in exactly the same way, the concept of 'fornication' was used frequently in the Old Testament to describe the idolatry of the people of Israel, because it represented the height of infidelity to their Covenant with God (1Chr 5,25; Ps 73,27; Jer 3,6; Ezek 16,17; 23,19; Hos 9,1). The use of the metaphor of fornication with respect to Babylon, therefore, indicates that this international authority is fundamentally a religious, or spiritual, authority that has been unfaithful in its relationship to God, on account of an idolatrous love for riches and luxury (cf. Mt 6,24).[194]

There is even an indication in the text as to the specific religious character of this power: it is written that Babylon is "drunk with the blood of the saints and the blood of the martyrs of Jesus" (Ap 17,6). Since the saints generally die a natural death, and are not

---

[194] Without an established relationship, or Covenant, with God, idolatry per se is not unfaithfulness to God but ignorance of him. For this reason the idolatrous power that is called Babylon, and is described as a great prostitute, should not be identified as an idolatrous pagan power such as Imperial Rome, since the idolatry in that city was performed out of ignorance of the true God and not unfaithfulness.

killed for witnessing their faith like the martyrs, this statement does not mean that Babylon is guilty of shedding the blood of the saints and martyrs of Jesus, as alleged by so many biblical scholars.[195] Neither is there any indication elsewhere in the text that Babylon persecutes or kills the people of God. To be 'drunk' with their blood carries a different meaning: incorporating the lives and deaths of the saints and the martyrs, Babylon appropriates their glory and merit, and exalts herself. This self-exaltation, or spiritual pride, causes her to act in an irresponsible and disordered way, like a woman who is drunk.

Moreover, knowing that the irresponsible and disordered way in which Babylon acts is described as 'fornication', it is not difficult to recognize her state of 'drunkenness' as the necessary condition for her 'fornication'. In fact, it appears that these two negative aspects of her behaviour should be interpreted together: considering the merits of the saints and martyrs as her own (being 'drunk' with their blood), Babylon succeeds in satisfying her lust for riches and luxury (her passion for 'fornication'). In a few words, Babylon 'glorifies herself and lives luxuriously' (Ap 18,7) by exploiting the merits of the saints and martyrs of Jesus.[196] Allying

---

[195] Identifying Babylon with ancient Rome, most commentators start from the assumption that she is drunk with the blood of the saints and martyrs of Jesus because she killed and persecuted them (e.g., Swete, *Apocalypse of John*, 217–18; Aune, *Revelation 17–22*, 937–38; Beale, *Book of Revelation*, 860). They nevertheless recognize the inadequacy of this interpretation, because: (a) the addition of 'the blood of the martyrs' to 'the blood of the saints' seems unnecessarily repetitive, and without reason; (b) the idea of Babylon drinking this blood is inconsistent with the rest of the vision, in which Babylon's cup is full of the filth of her fornication, totally contrasting with the blood of the saints and martyrs of Jesus. It is therefore supposed that the statement must be an editorial interpolation. However, the problem with this interpretation has nothing to do with the editing of the text, but with the initial assumption: neither in the vision nor in the explanation of the interpreting angel is there any indication that Babylon is guilty of shedding the blood of God's people. In the discussion which follows another explanation for her intoxication is proposed.

[196] The practice by means of which Babylon exploits the merits of the saints and martyrs, in order to satisfy her passion for riches, coincides exactly with the 'cult of the saints and martyrs' around which, it must be admitted, many and various abuses,

herself in this way with the saints and the martyrs of Jesus, the religious power that is called Babylon in the Apocalypse can not be anything else but Christian.

Defined as a Christian power with 'a kingdom over the rulers of the earth' (Ap 17,18), and having its base in a city identified as Rome (Ap 17,9), it is difficult to escape the identification of Babylon with the administrative centre of the Catholic Church, or more specifically with the place that is presently called Vatican City. The gravity of the accusation, which is implied by the identification of Babylon with the Vatican, obviously demands further confirmation and clarification from the other details given in St. John's vision.

Babylon has "a name, a mystery: mother of the prostitutes and of the abominations of the earth" (Ap 17,5). Just as 'fornication' is a biblical metaphor to indicate the idolatry of the people of God, so also 'prostitute'[197] is the metaphor used in the Old Testament to describe the community that was unfaithful to God on account of idolatry (e.g., Deut 31,16; Is 1,21; Jer 3,6–10; Ezek 16,15; 23,7.19; Hos 2,7). In the New Testament context, the prostitutes whose mother is said to be Babylon can be identified with all those Christian communities that have indulged in the same passion for riches and luxury. These include communities, or sects, which in the course of history have separated themselves from the central Authority of the Catholic Church. Babylon is by no means the only 'prostitute', but her responsibility is the greatest because she is the mother of all the others.

---

excesses and defects have occurred in the history of the Catholic Church, and have proved to be difficult to eradicate (see Lumen Gentium, 51, *Conciliar and Post Conciliar Documents*, Ed. Flannery, vol. 1). The collection of relics for this cult would explain how "blood of prophets and of saints and of all those slain on the earth was found in her" (Ap 18,24). Although Babylon is not guilty of shedding the blood of the people of God, she profits financially from this crime through the 'cult of the saints and martyrs'. A particularly vivid historical illustration of this is given by St. Bernard in his "Apology to Abbot William", ch. 12, para. 28 (*The Works of Bernard of Clairvaux*, 1: 63–66).

[197] In both Greek and Hebrew, the words for 'fornication' and 'prostitute' are derived from the same root: πορνεία, πόρνη in Greek; and זונה, זנונים in Hebrew.

Babylon has a golden cup in her hand, which is "full of the abominations and the filth of her fornication" (Ap 17,4), another way of describing the wine that makes all the nations drunk (Ap 14,8; 17,2; 18,3). However, as the time for the destruction of Babylon draws near, the role of the cup changes: instead of being instrumental in the corruption of the nations, it becomes an instrument in the condemnation of Babylon. It is said to those who have the task of destroying her: "mix her a double measure in the cup in which she mixed" (Ap 18,6). Finally, Babylon is forced to drink from the same cup, now precisely identified as 'the cup of the anger of God, full of the wine of his passion' (Ap 16,9). Therefore, the golden cup which Babylon holds in her hand is none other than the cup of the anger of God, entrusted to her by the Lord with a single purpose, that of bringing divine justice to the nations (cf. Jer 13,27). However, instead of distributing the 'wine of the passion of God', Babylon filled the cup with the 'wine of the passion of her fornicating'; in giving it to the nations she brought them corruption instead of divine justice.

Babylon says in her heart: "I sit as queen and am not a widow and sorrow I certainly do not see" (Ap 18,7). The fact that she says this 'in her heart', meaning 'to herself', implies that Babylon does not pronounce it publicly. There is therefore likely to be a difference between that which Babylon expresses publicly, and the way in which she thinks and acts privately (cf. Matt 23,1–4).

Believing herself to be queen, it is probable that Babylon wishes to identify herself with the Holy City, the New Jerusalem, which descends from heaven and is gloriously described as the wife, and therefore queen, of the one whose title is Lord of lords and King of kings (Ap 17,14; 19,7; 21,2.9). The fact that Babylon refuses to participate in, or even recognize, situations of affliction and suffering ("I am not a widow and sorrow I certainly do not see"), seems to confirm that she identifies herself with the city in which "there will be no more death, nor mourning, nor crying, nor pain" (Ap 21,4). However, the New Jerusalem, Eternal City, home of the Throne of God and of the Lamb, will not be established on the earth until after the final Judgement has taken place at the end of history.

The mentality of Babylon can therefore be recognized by the fact that she is not expecting the final Judgement. Claiming to be the Holy See in the Eternal City, she thinks the salvific plan of God has already been completely fulfilled, and acts as if she herself represented that fulfilment.

    This survey of the remaining information in the text concerning Babylon does not by any means contradict her identification with the administrative centre of the Catholic Church at Rome, that is to say, with the City of the Vatican.[198] It is extremely significant, therefore, that in reality the condemnation of Babylon falls on the buildings of that institution and not on its personnel. Immediately before she is destroyed, the Lord says: "come out of her, *my people,* so that you do not take part in her sins and share in her plagues, for her sins have piled up to heaven and God has remembered her iniquities" (Ap 18,4–5).

    Since there is no mourning for the loss of human life after the downfall of Babylon, but only for the loss of trade and precious articles (Ap 18,9–20), it is evident that all those who find themselves in that city at the time of her destruction obey the divine command to leave, indicating in this way that they are all God's people. Abandoning their city in obedience to the Lord, these people demonstrate true repentance for the sins that led to Babylon's condemnation—sins that, even though they may have been forgotten with the passing of time, God has remembered.

---

[198] Adhering to the warnings of Christ (Mt 24,24; Mk 13,22), the Early Church seems to have identified the workings of the mystery of iniquity with the activity of false teachers and false prophets within her communities (2Tim 4,3–4; 2Pet ch.2; Jude, 1Jn 2,18–23; 2Jn 7–11; Ap 2,2.14–15.20). Following the institution of Christianity as the religion of the Empire (4th cent. AD), and the formulation of the creeds and doctrines of the Church, the threat from false teaching receded. According to this vision in the Apocalypse, however, the mystery of iniquity did not cease, but continued to operate by tempting the leadership of the Church with riches and wealth. It should not be forgotten however, that in the same text the Church is seen retrospectively as the millennial Kingdom of Christ, with the bishops sitting on thrones and reigning amongst the priests of God and of Christ (Ap 20,2–6).

Chapter 5

The New Temple of God on Mt. Zion

The three remaining visions in this part of the prophecy (Ap 14,1–5; 14,14–20; 15,2–4) are so closely interrelated that they must be considered together. The first of these visions reveals the group of 144,000 followers of the Lamb assembled on Mt. Zion (Ap 14,1–5), in the immediate vicinity of the heavenly crowd that is described in the third vision (Ap 15,2–4). The second vision (Ap 14,6–20) concerns the eschatological harvest (Ap 14,14–16), whose first fruits are the 144,000 appearing in the first vision (Ap 14,4). It also heralds the start of God's judgements (Ap 14,6–7), which are celebrated by the heavenly chorus described in the third vision (Ap 15,2–4). Taken as a whole, then, these three visions regard the gathering of the 144,000 with the Lamb, in close relation to the assembly before the Throne in heaven, at the time of God's eschatological judgements on earth, and at the place that is called Mt. Zion.

The place of this gathering not only acts as a starting-point for the three visions as a whole, but also links them with the vision of the woman identified with Zion, and described at the beginning of the 'central prophecy' of the Apocalypse[199](Ap 12,1–18). After coming to identify with 'Zion' by experiencing a revelation of Jesus Christ,[200] the 144,000 followers of the Lamb flee to the desert to take shelter at the place prepared for them, here described as a mountain called 'Zion': "And I looked and behold, the Lamb standing on

---

[199] the 'central prophecy' of the Apocalypse: denotes the prophecy that was given to St. John so that he could 'prophesy again', and consists of an introduction (Ap 11,3–13), and a series of seven visions (Ap 12,1–18; 13,1–10; 13,11–18; 14,1–5; 14,6–13; 14,14–20; 15,2–4). It can be identified as a message that stands on its own within the prophecy of the Apocalypse—a prophecy within a prophecy (for a brief explanation, see the Appendix at the end of this book).

[200] See III. 2, ('The Eschatological Exodus').

Mount Zion, and with him a hundred and forty-four thousand having his name and the name of his Father written on their foreheads" (Ap 14,1).

Assembled on Mt. Zion, the community of the 144,000 represents the city in the midst of which God lives. In the Old Testament, this city was called Jerusalem, and also 'Zion'. As a synonym of Jerusalem, the name 'Zion' acquired a transcendental, or spiritual, meaning because of its association with the name of the mount where God had established his Dwelling. One could say, in fact, that Jerusalem was 'spiritually' called Zion, because this name implied the Presence of God in the midst of the city. It is probably for this reason that the name 'Zion' is most frequently used in the OT in order to refer to the eschatological city of God's people.[201]

The allusion to 'Zion' in this vision of the 144,000 on 'Mt. Zion' differs, in one important point, from references in the Old Testament: during the final, or eschatological, period of 42 months, 'Zion' is no longer synonymous with the contemporary city of Jerusalem, and is no longer associated with her. When the two witnesses are killed at the start of the 42-month period, the city where their Lord was crucified, namely Jerusalem, will no longer be 'spiritually' called Zion, but Sodom and Egypt. Jerusalem will no longer be the Holy City, but the 'great city'(Ap 11,8).[202] From that time onwards, 'Zion' is firmly identified with the assembly of the 144,000 with the Lamb, on Mt. Zion.[203]

---

[201] the eschatological city of God's people: it is in this sense that the name 'Zion' was used mainly by the OT prophets (Is, Jer, Joel, Mic, Zech), see *Theological Dictionary of the New Testament*, s.v. 'Σιών', 7: 292–338.

[202] See also n. 156.

[203] on Mt. Zion: although the location of this mountain is not openly stated in the text, two points are clear: (a) it is not in the historical city of Jerusalem (see n. 156); (b) it is a mountain in a desert that corresponds to the one through which God led the Israelites after their exodus from Egypt (Ap 12,6.14). Only two mountains are held to be 'holy' according to the Old Testament: Mt. Zion, which is the place of the Dwelling or Sanctuary of God, and Mt. Sinai (Horeb), which is the place of the Revelation of God (de Vaux, *Ancient Israel*, IV 1.3, 281). As explained later in this study, Mt. Zion in the Apocalypse is a mountain which integrates both these locations, since it is the site of the Revelation of the Sanctuary of God.

Given that 'Mt. Zion' refers especially to the place of God's Temple, its appearance in this vision (Ap 14,1) suggests that the assembly of 144,000 men, in the Presence of the Lamb, represents the new Temple of God. Confirmation of this is the fact that the 144,000 have the name of God on their foreheads (Ap 7,2–8; 14,1). Just as the ancient Temple of the Jews was considered the place that God had chosen 'as a dwelling for his name' (Deut 12,11), so also the 144,000 men, individually and as a community, constitute a home for the name of the living God—the site of his new Temple on earth.

In this vision of Zion and of the new Temple, the Lamb represents the Presence of God in the midst of the community, just as the Messiah, or anointed king, represented the Presence of God in the midst of Zion, in ancient times (Pss 2 & 110). However, even though the Lamb stands at the centre of the Throne as the Messiah of God (Ap 5,6; 7,17), neither the Throne nor its radiant glory (Ap 4,2–3) are revealed or described in this vision. Since the Throne is situated within the heavenly Sanctuary, it is implied that the inside of this Sanctuary, though present in a mysterious way, is not visible in this vision of the new Temple.[204]

Despite the Presence of the Lamb in their midst, the 144,000 do not yet have a constant vision of the Throne within the heavenly Sanctuary.[205] Instead, their proximity to the Throne is described as follows: "And I heard a sound from heaven like the sound of many waters, and like the sound of loud thunder, and the sound which I heard was like harpists playing their harps. And they sing a new song before the Throne and before the four living creatures and the elders, and no one was able to learn the song except the hundred and forty-four thousand, those that were bought from the earth. These are

---

[204] This mysterious situation recalls the introductory vision (Ap 1,10–20) in which the author, St. John, found himself near the heavenly Sanctuary and, although not able to see the Throne, was faced by the 'one like a son of man' (see I. 1), who is later identified with the Lamb (see I. 3).

[205] a constant vision of the Throne: which refers to the 'beatific vision'—the means by which "the blessed are brought to fruition in such a union with God in knowledge and love that they share forever in God's own happiness" (*New Catholic Encyclopaedia*, s.v. 'Beatific Vision', 2:186).

the ones who have not defiled themselves with women, for they are virgins; these follow the Lamb wherever he may go. These were bought from among men, first fruits to God and to the Lamb, and no lie was found in their mouth—they are immaculate" (Ap 14,2–5).

The fact that the 144,000 learn the heavenly song confirms that these are men of flesh and blood living on the earth, because only souls united to their bodies have the faculty and the need to learn. Their nearness to the Lord identifies them in some way with the priests of the former Temple. In fact, several other features of the 144,000 tend to confirm the correspondence between them and the priests of the former Temple:

a) The 144,000 "follow the Lamb wherever he may go" (Ap 14,4). This links them to the priesthood because the Lamb has already been identified as the high priest of the heavenly Sanctuary.[206]

b) The 144,000 are of the male sex and absolutely pure in their relations with women[207] (Ap 14,4); such conduct actually goes well beyond the prescribed norms on these matters, for the priests of the ancient Temple (Lev 21,7.13–14; 22,1–7).

c) The 144,000 are immaculate and "no lie was found in their mouth" (Ap 14,5). The absence of blemish, defect or deformity was an indispensable qualification for the priestly ministry in the

---

[206] See I. 3 ('The Priest')

[207] absolutely pure in their relations with women: this can be deduced from the description "these are they who have not defiled themselves with women, for they are virgins" (Ap 14,4). Among the ancient Israelites, even lawful sexual relations were believed to be a cause of impurity for both partners (Lev 15,18). Finding himself in this temporary state of impurity, a man had to excuse himself from his duties in the Temple (Lev 15,31; 22,37) or from his military service (Deut 23,10–12; 1Sam 21,56). In the light of Christ, the cause of the impurity is not the sexual act in itself, but the disordered and selfish desires associated with this act (Mk 7,20–23), which then give birth to sin (Mt 5,27–28). So in the Christian sense, those "who have not defiled themselves with women" refers to men whose heart has never been corrupted by disordered sexual desires for women, that is to say, they are perfect in the virtue of chastity. The addition of the statement "they are virgins" indicates that these men are not only perfectly chaste, but are also virgins, i.e., they are not married and have never had sexual relations. Given that sexual conduct is that aspect of human nature most affected by original sin (Gen 3,7), such purity can be understood as a sign of the most perfect reconciliation with God.

former Temple (Lev 21,17–24).

The musicians who play harps and sing the song that is
learnt by the 144,000 (Ap 14,2–3) correspond to the invisible part of
the new Temple, and are identified later in the prophecy as those
who are standing on the glassy sea mixed with fire, within the
heavenly Sanctuary: "And what I saw was like a glassy sea mixed
with fire, and those who conquered the beast and his image and the
number of his name, standing on the glassy sea holding harps of
God. And they sing the song of Moses, the servant of God, and the
song of the Lamb saying:
>Great and wonderful are your deeds, Lord God Almighty;
>
>Just and true are your ways, King of the nations;
>
>Who will not fear and glorify your name, Lord?
>
>It is because you alone are holy,
>
>That all the nations will come and worship before you,
>
>For your acts of judgement have been revealed" (Ap 15,2–4).

By means of certain details in this vision (Ap 14,2–3; 15,2–4), those
who conquered the beast can be identified with groups described
elsewhere in the text of the Apocalypse:
a) the new song that the conquerors sing in front of the Throne (Ap
    14,3) associates them with the 24 elders around the Throne, who
    sing a new song in praise and adoration of the Lamb (Ap 5,8–9).
b) The acts of God's judgement,[208] which the conquerors celebrate
    by singing the songs of Moses and of the Lamb (Ap 15,3), can
    be interpreted as the divine justice impatiently awaited by the
    martyrs under the altar (Ap 6,10), and implies that these
    conquerors of the beast are the people they were told to wait for,
    "their fellow servants and brothers…those about to be killed just
    as themselves" (Ap 6,11).
c) The roaring sound of voices and music that is produced by the

---

[208] The acts of God's judgement: these acts of judgement refer to the consequences,
on earth, of the outpouring of the bowls that contain the wine of God's passionate
anger (Ap ch. 16).

conquerors (Ap 14,2–3) identifies them with the heavenly choir in a later vision, who emit the same sound when they give thanks to God,[209] sing hallelujah and announce the forthcoming marriage of the Lamb (Ap 19,1–8).

d) The conquerors of the beast refused to worship his image or to receive his mark, and as a result they were killed during his short 42-month reign—a period of severe and widespread persecution (Ap 13,7.15–17); in this way they can be identified with the innumerable multitude of martyrs who celebrate their salvation in heaven, after passing through the 'great tribulation' (Ap 7,9–17).

Tracing the interrelation of all these groups permits a glimpse of the origin and growth of the enormous multitude of souls that fill the heavenly Sanctuary. It begins with the 24 elders (Ap 5,8–10), increases with the arrival of the first martyrs under the altar (Ap 6,9–11) and becomes an innumerable multitude with those who are killed in the 'great tribulation' (Ap 7,9–17), all singing songs of salvation (Ap 14,2–3; 15,2–4) and praise (Ap 19,1–8).

There is a close correspondence between the musical activity of this multitude of martyrs and the ministry of the Levitical choirs and musicians of the former Temple in Jerusalem. Like the martyrs in the visions of the heavenly Sanctuary, the Levites used to accompany the liturgy with singing and instruments, as well as being organized in 24 divisions and supervised by 24 elders (1Chr ch.25), in the same way as the priests (1Chr ch.24).

Just as the four living creatures take no rest, day or night, in order to praise God (Ap 4,8), so also the martyrs serve God "day and night in his Sanctuary" (Ap 7,15). A great act of liturgical adoration appears to be taking place in heaven, which begins with the four living creatures, is taken up by the 24 elders, spreads out through the

---

[209] when they give thanks to God: here the martyrs give thanks to God for having condemned the great prostitute, Babylon, and for having avenged their blood in this way (Ap 19,12). The words of their celebration confirm the association (noted in (b) above) between these martyrs and those under the altar who ask the Lord how much longer before he will judge and avenge their blood (Ap 6,10).

innumerable multitude of martyrs and, from time to time, embraces myriads and myriads of angels (Ap 5,11–12; 7,11) and all the creatures on earth, in heaven and under the sea (Ap 5,13).

The interpretation of these three visions altogether gives an impression of the new Temple in the eschatological period of history. At a specific time, 144,000 men of extraordinary virtue and purity gather together in the desert, on a mountain called Mt. Zion, in order to form a community of priests. This community on earth is the visible part of the new Temple of God. The invisible part is indicated by their communion with the assembly of souls, singing in front of the Throne, like the Levites used to sing in the former Temple in Jerusalem. Mysteriously united by the Presence of the Lamb in their midst, these two parts can be identified as the superior and inferior parts of the Sanctuary of God, seen and described in the earlier visions of the Apocalypse.[210]

In this vision of the Sanctuary of God at the end of time, all the elements that St. John was asked to measure—'*the Sanctuary of God, the altar and those worshipping there*'(Ap 11,1–2)—can be recognized: the *Sanctuary of God* is God's Dwelling in its final and most perfect form; the glassy sea mixed with fire, on which the conquerors of the beast are standing, corresponds to the hearth of the *altar* blazing with fire (Ap 15,2);[211] and the 144,000 are the only ones on earth who are able to participate in the heavenly *worship* (Ap 14,3). This is the Temple, then, in whose construction St. John participates by witnessing the prophecy given to him in order to 'prophesy again' (Ap 10,11).[212]

---

[210] See I. 1('The Sanctuary of God').

[211] The identification of the martyrs with 'the altar' is strengthened by the fact that the author hears the altar praising God (Ap 16,7). The altar in the Apocalypse, which corresponds to the outer altar in the ancient Temple, is not a structure made of earthly materials; it is a spiritual force and presence that continues to work for salvation.

[212] See II. 6 ('The Command to Measure').

Chapter 6

The Culmination of the Heavenly Liturgy

In the vision of the Sanctuary of God, the resemblance of the 'glassy sea mixed with fire' (Ap 15,2) to the flaming hearth of an altar introduces a specific liturgical feature into the interpretation of the vision, since it recalls the event which brought the daily service in the ancient Temple to an end. This event was called the presentation of the offerings before God, and it represented the culmination of all the preceding liturgical activity.[213]

From this point of view, the assembly of the 144,000 men and the multitude of martyrs not only correspond to the priests and Levites of the former Temple, but also to the offerings that used to be presented before God. In the Old Testament, the offerings that were presented on the altar in the daily service (Ex 29,38–42; Ezek 46,13–15) were of three types:

a)   the continual whole offering, or holocaust (a lamb);
b)   the cereal offering, or oblation (wheat flour mixed with oil);
c)   the drink offering, or libation of wine.

While the continual whole offering and the cereal offering were presented before God in the fire of the altar, the libation of wine was poured out at its base. In these concluding visions of the heavenly liturgy, the corresponding offerings were presented in the same order, as follows:

a)   *The continual whole offering*
As shown previously, the Lamb in the visions of the Apocalypse corresponds to the lamb sacrificed as the continual whole offering in the daily service that was performed in the former

---

[213] See also I. 9, x.

Temple.[214] Therefore, in these visions of the culmination of the liturgy in heaven, the continual whole offering is clearly represented by the Lamb in the midst of the 144,000 (Ap 14,1–5). The 144,000 men who accompany the Lamb have his name written on their foreheads and follow him wherever he may go (Ap 14,1.4); furthermore "no lie was found in their mouth, as they are immaculate" (Ap 14,5). Two aspects of this description indicate that, together with the Lamb, the 144,000 correspond to the continual whole offering in the daily service: their inseparable relationship with the Lamb and their perfect nature, which is described in terms analogous to the legal requirements for whole offerings in the ancient sacrificial cult (Lev 1,3; 22,18–25).

However, complementary to their identification with the continual whole offering, the 144,000 are described in terms that refer to the subsequent vision of the eschatological harvest (Ap 14,14–20): "these were bought from among men, first fruits to God and to the Lamb" (Ap 14,4; cf. 5,9). The description of the 144,000 men as 'first fruits' not only identifies them as the first of the produce from the eschatological harvest, but also recalls two eternal laws of the Old Testament, concerning the first fruits of the grain harvest (Lev 23,9–21).

According to these laws, a sheaf of the first fruits of the grain harvest (of barley) had to be brought to the priests of the Temple on the day after the Feast of the Passover, in order to be 'waved' before the Lord. After seven weeks, a second offering of the first fruits (of wheat, this time) had to be presented to God in the Temple, and waved as part of the liturgical celebration on the annual Feast of Weeks ('Shavuot'), which, up to the present day, is held at the beginning of the summer and commemorates the giving of the Torah to Israel on Mt. Sinai (Ex 23,19; 34,26; Deut 16,9–12; 26,1–11).

Following their exodus to the desert, then, the 144,000

---

[214] …on a very special day, the Day of Atonement, see I. 10 ('Summary and Conclusions'). For the identification of other members of the continual whole offering, see I. 9, v.

present themselves before the Lamb, in the place that represents the Sanctuary of God, in a way analogous to the presentation of the first fruits of the grain harvest. In practice, they are the first of the offerings to be presented to God in his Sanctuary, at the culmination of the liturgy that is being performed there.[215]

b) *The cereal offering*

Given that the 144,000 followers of the Lamb are the first fruits, the bulk of the grain harvest is represented by the rest of the faithful, "those who keep the commandments of God and have the witness of Jesus" (Ap 12,17), against whom the dragon goes off to make war by means of the beast (Ap 13,5.15–17). These are the martyrs who are seen and described in various ways in the text: they conquer the beast by refusing to worship its image or to receive its mark (Ap 15,2–4), and so they are killed in the great tribulation (Ap 7,13–17).

These martyrs appear in heaven as "a vast multitude which no one was able to count, from all nations and tribes and races and tongues, clothed in white robes and with palms in their hands, standing before the Throne and before the Lamb" (Ap 7,9–10).

Their celebration in heaven recalls the ancient Israelite Feast of Tabernacles ('Sukkot'), when palm branches were 'waved', 'hosannas' were sung and the people of Israel lived in tabernacles for seven days (Lev 23,39–43; Ps 118,15–29). This Feast was, and continues to be, celebrated in autumn, at the time when the farmers had just finished gathering in the produce of the 'threshing floor and the winepress' (Ex 23,16; Deut 16,13).

This reference to the Feast of Tabernacles further clarifies the identification of the martyrs with the bulk of the eschatological grain harvest. In a context that recalls the Feast of Tabernacles, in

---

[215] Their precedence in the order of offerings also conforms to their identification with the continual whole offering. In relation to the Lamb, the 144,000 correspond to the members of the continual whole offering, whereas in relation to the rest of the faithful they are identified as the offering of the first fruits. As offerings presented before God at the culmination of the heavenly liturgy, the 144,000 therefore appear to combine important features of these two different classes of offering.

fact, the martyrs can be identified more specifically with the produce of the threshing floor (the grain). Their martyrdom in the great tribulation, and their gathering into the heavenly Tent (Ap 7,9–17), therefore correspond to the ingathering of the produce from the threshing floor.[216]

As offerings presented to God on the altar at the culmination of the heavenly liturgy, the martyrs seen standing on the glassy sea mixed with fire (Ap 15,2) are analogous to the cereal offering in the ancient sacrificial ritual.

Furthermore, since the Feast of Tabernacles takes place several months after the Feast of Weeks in the ritual calendar, it is implied that the 'gathering of martyrs' into heaven occurs after the 144,000 have arrived as first fruits, at the place representing the Sanctuary of God. This order in the presentation of the offerings follows that of the daily service, in which the cereal offering was presented on the altar after the members of the continual whole offering.

c) *The libation of wine*

Immediately after the members of the continual whole offering and its corresponding cereal offering were presented on the altar in the daily service, the libation of wine was poured out at its base (cf. Sir 50,15–17).

Just as the cereal offering is represented in the Apocalypse as the product of the eschatological harvest (Ap 14,14–16), so also the libation of wine is represented as the product of the vintage (Ap 14,17–20). After being cut from the vine, the grape clusters are thrown into the great winepress of God that is outside the city. When the clusters of grapes are trodden in this winepress, two liquids come out: the wine of the passion of God (Ap 14,10) and blood "up to the

---

[216] The association between the 'threshing' of the grain and the great 'tribulation' is not evident in the English language. In the classical languages, however, these two ideas are closely related. In Latin, the word for tribulation (noun: tribulatio; verb: tribulare) is etymologically related to the name of the instrument that was used for threshing (tribulum), which in turn appears to be related to the Greek word for tribulation and affliction (noun: θλίψις; verb: θλίβειν).

bridles of the horses, for one thousand six hundred stadia" (Ap 14,20).

In Old Testament times, the celebration of the Feast of Tabernacles indicated not only the end of the threshing of the grain, but also the completion of the treading of the grape. In the Apocalypse, therefore, the celebration in which the martyrs in heaven participate also indicates the end of the vintage and the conclusion of the pressing process (Ap 14,17–20). However, in contrast to the grain, the wine is not stored up in the heavenly Sanctuary, but is poured on the earth from the seven bowls full of the passion of God (Ap ch.16), in a way that clearly corresponds to the libation of wine at the end of the daily service in the ancient Temple. The catastrophic effects of the seven bowls represent the judgements of God on the unredeemed world (Ap 16,5–7) during "the hour of his judgement" (Ap 14,6–7).[217]

In the daily service it is significant that the libation of wine is poured out at the base of the altar of holocausts, in the same place that the blood of the lamb, sacrificed as a whole offering, had previously been poured out.[218] In the context of the heavenly liturgy, this can be interpreted to mean that those in the world who are not redeemed by the blood of the Lamb will, in the end, receive the wine of the passion of God's anger[219] (Ap 14,9–11).

---

[217] Interpreting the vision of the eschatological harvest together with that of the presentation of the offerings in the Sanctuary of God helps to resolve a long debate over the significance of the harvest of the grain (Ap 14,14–16) and of the grape (14,17–20). There are two kinds of interpretation: those that explain both the grain and grape harvests as the negative judgement of God upon the wicked (for example: Aune, Beasley-Murray, Beale, Charles, Wikenhauser) and those which explain the harvest of the grain in a positive sense (for example: Swete, Bauckham, Ladd). The identification of the harvest of the grain with the gathering of the 144,000, and with the assembly of martyrs in the Sanctuary of God, leaves no doubt that it should be interpreted in a positive sense. On the other hand, the harvest and treading of the grape continue to have the same negative significance that was intended by the prophet Joel, in the original context of this image of judgement (Joel 3,13).

[218] For the order of these liturgical elements in the daily service, see I. 7, 2 & 11.

[219] In the heavenly liturgy described in the Apocalypse, the base of the altar is represented by almost all the created world, see n. 62 above.

However, the Feast of Tabernacles was not only an agricultural feast. It was, in fact, mainly a religious feast, which commemorated the Presence of God and the protection of the Israelites during their journey through the desert, a time when they used to live in tents (Ps 118; Lev 23,43). According to one of the ancient prophets, the celebration of this Feast will also express the joy of the eschatological Presence of God (Zech 14,16–19). Furthermore, the procedure of this feast was adopted later in order to commemorate the re-consecration of the former Temple by the Maccabees, after its profanation in the days of the Syrian king, Antiochus Epiphanes.

The reference to the Feast of Tabernacles in the visions of the Apocalypse, then, confers a double meaning to the celebration in which the martyrs participate in heaven. On the one hand, it is the way in which they celebrate their own salvation and protection in the heavenly Sanctuary at the end of time (Ap 7,9–17); on the other hand, the celebration of this feast indicates the completion and the consecration of the new Temple (Ap 15,1.5–8), in whose construction St. John participates by witnessing the prophecy he was given in order to 'prophesy again' (Ap 10,11).

Chapter 7

The Sign of the Presence of God

The vision of the martyrs performing their Levitical ministry in the heavenly Sanctuary (Ap 15,2–4) coincides with an event of decisive importance: "And I saw another sign in heaven, great and wonderful: seven angels with seven plagues—the last, because with them the passion of God was finished" (Ap 15,1). A few verses later, this brief report is elaborated as follows: "And after this I looked, and the Sanctuary of the Tent of testimony in heaven was opened, and out of the Sanctuary came the seven angels with the seven plagues, dressed in clean bright linen and bound around the breast with golden belts. And one of the four living creatures had given to the seven angels seven golden bowls full of the passion of God, the One living for ever and ever" (Ap 15,5–7).

The meaning of the opening of the heavenly Sanctuary can be explained by comparing the heavenly Dwelling with the Tent that Moses built. In fact, the reference to the heavenly Sanctuary as 'the Sanctuary of the Tent of the testimony' (Ap 15,5) is an invitation to do this.

The 'opening' of the Sanctuary in heaven does not only refer to the opening of a door, since the door has already been opened (Ap 4,1). Instead, the 'opening' points to the removal of the existing separation between the inside of the heavenly Sanctuary and the surrounding area—the separation that corresponds to the curtain which used to hang at the entrance of the Tent which Moses ordained (Ex 26,36; 40,28). Also in the Temple, which succeeded the Tent, there was a curtain that covered the entrance of the

Sanctuary (1Macc 4,51).[220] This curtain was opened at the start of the great feasts, so that the pilgrims standing in the inner court could see inside the Sanctuary, right up to the veil that impeded the view of the 'Holy of Holies'.[221]

In an analogous fashion the opening of the Sanctuary in the visions of the Apocalypse has a liturgical significance, and indicates the start of a great feast: "blessed are they that are invited to the wedding-feast of the Lamb" (Ap 19,9).

However, in contrast to the Sanctuary in the former Temple, there is no veil within the heavenly Sanctuary, so a view of its interior corresponds to a direct view into the 'Holy of Holies' and includes the revelation of God on his heavenly Throne. It follows that the part of the Temple that was previously invisible—the interior of the heavenly Sanctuary—becomes visible to those who are near but outside, that is to say, to the 144,000 men assembled on Mt. Zion. After this event, the part of the Sanctuary that is on earth becomes identical to the part that is in heaven, since there is no longer any separation between them.[222]

In another part of the text, the opening of the heavenly Sanctuary is described in a way that explains its significance more fully: "And the Sanctuary of God in heaven was opened, and the Ark of his Covenant was seen in his Sanctuary, and there were lightnings and noises and thunders, an earthquake and a great hail" (Ap 11,19).

In the Old Testament the Ark was considered to be the inferior part of the heavenly Throne, 'the footstool of our God' (1Chr 28,2; Ps 99,5; 132,7; Lam 2,1; Ezek 43,7).[223] Since it

---

[220] For the 'topography' of this separation, and its correspondence to the curtain that used to hang at the entrance of Tent, and then the Temple, see I. 1 ('The Sanctuary of God') at the start of this study.

[221] For a summary of the procedure at the start of the pilgrim festivals, see *Encyclopaedia Judaica*, s.vv. 'Sacrifice' (col. 610) and 'Temple' (col. 978). For references to this in ancient sources, see n. 83 above.

[222] For the absence of a veil in the Sanctuary described in the Apocalypse, see I. 1 ('The Sanctuary of God'). For the situation before the 'opening of the Sanctuary', see III. 5 ('The New Temple of God on Mt. Zion').

[223] See also de Vaux, *Ancient Israel*, IV 2.3, 299–300.

contained the tablets of God's Law, the tablets of the testimony,[224] the Ark also served as a testimony against those who transgressed the Law and rebelled against God (cf. Deut 31,24–27). For the same reason, the Tent that Moses built for the Ark was also called the Tent of the testimony.

Just as the Law, the Ark and the Tent served as a testimony against those who rebelled against God, so also the revelation of the Ark at the opening of the Sanctuary of the Tent of the testimony in heaven (Ap 15,5) will serve as a testimony against those inhabitants of the earth who continue to rebel against God, shortly before his judgements come down on top of them, in the form of the outpouring of the bowls of God's anger (Ap 15,5–8; ch.16).

Simultaneously with the opening of the heavenly Sanctuary, a phenomenon with a very particular significance is observed: "And the Sanctuary was filled with the smoke of the glory of God and of his power, and no one was able to enter the Sanctuary until the seven plagues of the seven angels were finished" (Ap 15,8). This phenomenon vividly recalls the way that God revealed himself to the Israelites on Mt. Sinai, when smoke and cloud appeared over the mountain (Ex 19,16–25). Since both smoke and cloud appeared on that occasion, it follows that both smoke (Ex 19,16) and cloud (Ex 19,18) should be understood as visible signs of God's Presence.[225]

Moses had only just completed the Tent that God wanted as his Dwelling (Ex 25,8–9), when the Lord manifested his Presence in a very similar way: "Then the cloud covered the Tent of Meeting, and the glory of the Lord filled the tabernacle. And Moses was not able to enter the Tent of Meeting because the cloud remained above it, and the glory of the Lord filled the Dwelling" (Ex 40,34–35). The same phenomenon occurred at the completion of the Temple built by King Solomon, immediately after the Ark of the Covenant was installed there (1Kgs 8,10–13).

---

[224] 'testimony': see n. 27.

[225] In the vision of the Throne of God described both by Isaiah (Is 6,1–6) and by St. John (Ap 15,8), the Presence of God is represented by smoke.

In the context of the Apocalypse, therefore, the filling of the Sanctuary with the smoke of the glory of God and of his power signals the completion of the new Temple, in whose construction St. John had been participating with the prophecy he was given.

At this point nobody else will be able to enter the Sanctuary (Ap 15,8), a fact that indicates that the great tribulation will have come to an end (Ap 13,15–17) and no more martyrs will be added to the innumerable multitude already united before the Throne in heaven, in the midst of the 144,000 on Mt. Zion (Ap 7,9–17; 14,1–5).

Nevertheless, it is important to clarify what is meant by 'the completion' of the new Temple. One should not think that there is limited space in the heavenly Sanctuary for the martyrs who enter, as if it were made of earthly materials; neither is it justifiable to believe that a predetermined number of witnesses of Jesus Christ must be killed[226] before the new Temple reaches completion. The fact that no one was able to count the number of the multitude of souls in the heavenly Sanctuary (Ap 7,9) confirms that the precise number is not important, in contrast to the exact number of the 144,000 men sealed with the seal of the living God (Ap 7,4).

Instead, the 'completion' of the new Temple is determined by the opening of the heavenly Sanctuary and the outpouring of the bowls of God's passionate anger, in the hour of his judgement (cf. Ap 14,6–13). The 'completion' is therefore destined to occur at a time that has been established by God (cf. Mk 13,20 & par.) and coincides with the end of the period of 42 months, during which the beast was permitted to reign (Ap 13,5.7). From this time onwards, it

---

[226] a predetermined number of witnesses of Jesus Christ must be killed: this is an erroneous idea transmitted by most of the modern translations of Ap 6,11. After asking how much longer until the divine judgements, the martyrs under the altar were told to wait for a short time more "until the number would be complete both of their fellow servants and of their brothers and sisters, who were soon to be killed as they themselves had been killed" (Ap 6,11 according to the NRSV). However, the word 'number' does not appear in the Greek text and its inclusion implies, wrongly, that a predetermined number of witnesses must be killed before the judgements of God will be revealed. Our suggestion for the translation of this verse is explained later (n. 236).

will no longer be possible to receive protection in the heavenly Sanctuary (Ap 7,15–16) from the plagues of judgement, which will fall during the hour of the test "that is to come upon the whole world, to test the inhabitants of the earth" (Ap 3,10).

Another interpretation of the filling of the Sanctuary of the new Temple, with the smoke of the glory of God and of his power (Ap 15,8), derives from a description of the same phenomenon in the prophecy of Ezekiel concerning the return of the glory of God to the Temple. During the Babylonian exile, the prophet Ezekiel had a vision of the departure of the glory of God from the Temple and from the city of Jerusalem (Ezek ch.10; 11,22–25). A short while later, the city and Temple were destroyed by King Nebuchadnezzar of Babylon (Ezek ch.24). Finally, Ezekiel prophesies the return of the glory of God to the renewed Temple described in his final vision (Ezek 43,1–12).

Ezekiel's prophecy of the return of God's glory can be subdivided into four stages, as follows:
a)   the glory of God approaches from the East (Ezek 43,1–2);
b)   the earth shines with his glory (Ezek 43,2);
c)   the glory reaches (Ezek 43,2) and then enters by the eastern gate of the new Temple (Ezek 44,2);
d)   the glory of the Lord fills the Sanctuary, and a voice says to the prophet: "Son of man, this is the place of my Throne and the place for the soles of my feet, where I will dwell among the people of Israel forever" (Ezek 43,7).

Since the construction of the new Temple, to which the visions in the Apocalypse allude (Ap 11,1–2), fulfils Ezekiel's vision of the Temple in the messianic era,[227] it is not a coincidence that Ezekiel's prophecy of the return of the glory of God should also be represented, in all its stages, in the following passages of the Apocalypse:
a)   the angel with the seal of the living God comes up from the East

---

[227] See n. 115 above.

(Ap 7,2) in order to seal the 144,000 on their foreheads;

b) the angel that proclaims the downfall of Babylon enlightens the earth with his glory (Ap 18,1–2);
c) the Sanctuary in heaven opens (Ap 11,19; 15,5);
d) the smoke of the glory of God and of his power fills the Sanctuary (Ap 15,8).

The main differences between the two prophecies is that while Ezekiel describes the return of the glory of God from outside the Temple, in the Apocalypse this 'return' is described as a revelation of the glory of God and of his Throne from within the innermost part of the new Temple, the Sanctuary in heaven. Since Jesus Christ, the Lamb, is at the centre of the Throne (Ap 3,21; 5,6; 7,17; 12,5), this revelation corresponds to the Christian expectation of the coming of Christ in the glory of God at the end of time—the event which has been called the 'Parousia'.

Chapter 8

The Consecration of the New Temple

The filling of the Sanctuary with the smoke of the glory of God has a specific purpose and effect, which are explained by the words of the Lord in the following passage of the Old Testament: "And there I will meet with the children of Israel, and the Tent shall be consecrated by my glory. I will consecrate the Tent of the meeting and the altar; also I will consecrate Aaron and his sons to serve me as priests. I will dwell among the children of Israel, and I will be their God" (Ex 29,43–45).

Contact with the glory of God brought about the consecration of the place that God had chosen as his Dwelling among the Israelites. In the Apocalypse, therefore, the filling of the Sanctuary with the smoke of the glory of God and of his power can be understood as the act that brings about the consecration of the new Temple. To fully understand this reference to 'consecration' in the prophecy of the Apocalypse, it is necessary to compare it with the original event described in the Old Testament.

The consecration of the Tent that Moses built, which included the altar and the priests, was a procedure that lasted 8 days and consisted of an elaborate ritual with two principle stages: Moses performed certain ritual acts of consecration and then God confirmed and completed them with the manifestation of his glory. Here follows a summary of the procedure:

For the Tent and its furnishings (Ex 40,9; Lev 8,10), Moses performed the rite of consecration by sprinkling them with sacred oil (Ex 30,22–33). After he had done this, God consecrated them with his glory (Ex 40,34–35).

In order to consecrate the altar, Moses sprinkled it in the same way, with sacred oil (Ex 40,10; Lev 8,11). However, the altar had first been purified with the offering of an expiatory sacrifice on each of the seven preceding days, during which the rite of the consecration of the priests was carried out (Ex 29,36–37).

The rite of the consecration, or investiture, of the priests began with several sacrifices, of which the most important was a special kind of communion sacrifice (מלאים). Summarized from the account in the Old Testament (Ex ch.29; 40,12–14; Lev ch.8), the rite consisted of the following steps:

a) Aaron, as the high priest, and the candidates for the priesthood were ritually washed and clothed with ceremonial garments of fine linen. As a sign of their forthcoming consecration, Aaron placed on his forehead a golden plate inscribed "like the engraving on a seal, 'Holy to the Lord'" (Ex 28,36; Lev 8,9).

b) Aaron and his sons were then anointed[228] by pouring sacred oil on their heads.

c) The lobe of the right ear, the thumb of the right hand and the great toe of the right foot of every candidate, were smeared with the blood of the special sacrifice for the rite of consecration. Parts of this sacrifice were then 'waved before the Lord' as a ritual gesture of presentation, before being burnt on the altar.

d) The candidates, wearing their ceremonial garments, were sprinkled with sacred oil mixed with the blood of the sacrifice.

e) They then ate their portion of the sacrifice as a sacred meal.

f) Finally the candidates remained for a period of seven days inside the Tent, and at the end of that time their consecration was complete.

At the end of the seven days, on the eighth day, the newly

---

[228] Aaron and his sons were then anointed: the priests in these three passages (Lev ch. 8; Ex ch. 29; 40,12–14) are called 'sons of Aaron'; in the first two it is only Aaron, the high priest, who was anointed (Lev 8,12; Ex 29,7), while in the third all the priests were anointed (Ex 40,15). This difference reappears in other parts of the Pentateuch and reflects a change in the practice of anointing after the exile: initially only the high priest was anointed, but later the practice was extended to all the priests. Before the exile only the King was anointed (this is the meaning of the word 'Messiah') and in the times of the Romans the practice of anointing had fallen out of use (de Vaux, *Ancient Israel*, II 5.2, 105).

consecrated priests performed their first rite in front of the community (Lev ch.9). This rite was arranged by Moses, so that the Lord could reveal his glory to the people of Israel (Lev 9,6). At the moment of the presentation of the continual whole offering, the glory of God was manifested as a flame that came out from his Presence, inside the Dwelling, and consumed the offering on the altar (Lev 9,23–24), thus completing the entire procedure for the consecration of the priests and the altar.

Even though the procedure is greatly simplified with the sacrifice of the Lamb, who substitutes every kind of animal sacrifice, certain aspects of the ancient rite of consecration are reflected in the events prophesied in the Apocalypse, and help in their interpretation. In fact, the three parts which Moses was asked to consecrate, namely the Tent, the altar and the priests, correspond to the three elements that St. John was asked to measure, 'the Sanctuary, the altar and those who worship there' (Ap 11,1–2). It is therefore understood that the role of Moses in the rite of consecration is reflected in the task of measuring the three elements of the new Temple undertaken by St. John during its construction.[229] In fact, on this analogy, St. John's role in the construction of the new Temple can be more specifically defined as providing the necessary preparation for its consecration at the end of time.

In the prophecy of the Apocalypse, the filling of the heavenly Sanctuary with the smoke of the glory and power of God (Ap 15,8) corresponds to the confirmation and conclusion of the ancient rite of consecration, which was realized by the manifestation of God's glory (cf. Ex 40,34–35). Nevertheless the situation in the Apocalypse is different from that of Moses, because the heavenly Sanctuary is already consecrated by the glorious Presence of God. Therefore, the filling of the Sanctuary with smoke has the effect of consecrating those elements of the new Temple that, before the opening of the heavenly Sanctuary, were near but outside—in other

---

[229] This conclusion is completely consistent with the fact that the author of the Apocalypse, St. John, represents the 'prophet like Moses' who was expected in those days (see n. 105).

words, the 144,000 men gathered together on Mt. Zion.

It has already been proposed that the 144,000 correspond in some way to the priests of the former Temple.[230] So it is no coincidence that the instructions given to Moses for the consecration of the priests are particularly relevant to this group of men. Just as the high priest wore on his forehead, on behalf of all the priests, a sign of consecration bearing the name of God, so also each of the 144,000 men is sealed on his forehead with the name of the Lamb and of his Father (Ap 7,2–8; 14,1).

While the candidates for the priesthood were clothed in their ceremonial garments as part of the ancient rite of consecration, the 144,000 will be clothed with the glory and power of God, following the revelation of his Throne at the opening of the heavenly Sanctuary (Ap 15,8).

The candidates for the priesthood remained inside the Tent, in the desert, for a whole week (seven days) before their consecration was complete. This period corresponds to the final week of years (seven years) described in the Apocalypse, during which the 144,000 are protected at their place in the desert, on Mt. Zion.[231]

The correspondence between the two periods indicates the great importance of the final period of seven years. The period of seven days during which the priests had to remain in the Tent (Lev 8,35) recalls the creation of the world in seven days (Gen 1,1 – 2,4), and implies that the consecration of the Tent, the altar and the priests was understood as a recapitulation of the whole work of creation.[232] How much more reason there is for considering the period of seven years at the end of history, which is the time of preparation for the consecration of the new Temple, as a recapitulation of the entire work of creation, so fulfilling the plan of God for the fullness of

---

[230] See III. 5 ('The New Temple of God on Mt Zion')

[231] See III. 2 ('The Eschatological Exodus') and also n. 132.

[232] For further information on the verbal-thematic links between the account of the creation and that of the construction of the Tent, see Blenkinsopp, "The Structure of P", *Catholic Biblical Quarterly*, 38(1976), 275–92. For a brief summary, see Blenkinsopp, *The Pentateuch*, 218.

time, "to sum up all things in Christ, things in heaven and things on earth" (Eph 1,9–10).

The first rite performed by the priests after their consecration is vividly represented in the Apocalypse by an event that occurs when 'the camp of the saints'—the 'beloved city'—is surrounded by armies from the four corners of the earth, from 'Gog and Magog' (Ap 20,7–10). Just as the flame of fire consumed the holocaust presented to God in the sight of the whole community of Israel, so also fire descends from heaven and consumes the hostile forces that surround the camp of the saints.

The filling of the Sanctuary with the smoke of the power and glory of God not only completes the consecration of the 144,000 as priests in the new Temple, but also consecrates the place where they reside—Mount Zion. On reflection, this phenomenon strongly recalls the event in which cloud and smoke descended on Mt. Sinai (Horeb), when God revealed himself to Moses and to all the Israelites (Ex 19,16–20). In fact, the holy mountain called 'Zion' in the Apocalypse seems to unite in one single place, the only two holy mountains recognized by the biblical tradition: the mountain of the Dwelling of God (Mt. Zion) and the mountain of his Revelation (Mt. Sinai).[233]

In the description of the consecration of the new Temple, no mention has yet been made of the place that corresponds to the outer altar. In the Sanctuary of God, however, this altar is represented by the multitude of martyrs standing before the Throne, accompanying the heavenly liturgy with music and singing of psalms (Ap 15,2–4).[234] So the martyrs are not only identified with the altar, but also with the Levitical ministers in the former Temple. The consecration of the altar in the Apocalypse, therefore, cannot be considered apart from the liturgical procedure for the dedication of the Levitical ministers in the former Temple.

As Levites, then, the martyrs fulfil a role that is complementary to that of the 144,000, who correspond to the priests in the cult

---

[233] See n. 203.
[234] See the end of III. 5 ('The New Temple of God on Mt Zion')

instituted by Moses. Nevertheless, in the Old Testament there is a clear difference in the status of Levitical ministers and priests, and it is important to know if this distinction is maintained in the prophecy of the Apocalypse, where the martyrs in heaven represent the Levites and the 144,000 on Mt. Zion represent the priests.

The difference in rank between the priests and the Levites of the former Temple can be demonstrated by comparing the procedures for installing members of each class: the investiture of the priests (Ex ch.29; 40,12–15; Lev ch.8) and the inauguration of the Levitical ministry (Num 8,5–22). In the first place, a different expression is used to describe the procedure in each group: the priests were 'consecrated'(מלא יד) while the Levites were 'dedicated' (נתן נתנים). In the second place, the Levites did not have to remain for one week in the Tent, nor did they participate in a special sacrificial ritual, in which certain parts of the victim were 'waved before the Lord'. Instead the Levites themselves, as if they were parts of a sacrifice, were 'waved before the Lord' by the high priest, and in this way started their service in the Tent under the direction of the priests: "And the Levites purified themselves and washed their clothes; then Aaron presented them as a wave offering before the Lord, and Aaron made atonement for them to cleanse them. After that, the Levites went into the Tent of Meeting to do their service, in the presence of Aaron and his sons" (Num 8,21–22).

In Ezekiel's regulations for the Temple, this distinction in rank between the Levites and the priests is even more emphatic. Only the descendants of Zadok[235] were allowed to serve as priests at

---

[235] only the descendants of Zadok: in some parts of the Old Testament (those written before or during the exile), the priests are called 'sons of Zadok', while in other passages (those written after the exile), they are called 'sons of Aaron'. This difference goes back to the two priests whom King David appointed to administer the Ark (2Sam 15,24–29), Abiathar and Zadok. The son and successor of King David, Solomon, dismissed Abiathar on account of his disloyalty (1Kgs 1,25–26; 2,26–27) and nominated Zadok as the priest in the Temple (2Kgs 2,35). From that time, up until the exile, all the priests of the Temple were descendants or 'sons' of Zadok (1Chr 5,34–41). After the exile, the reforms of Ezra permitted the descendants of Abiathar to serve as priests in the Temple alongside the descendants of Zadok. Since the offspring of both priests could prove their descendance from

the altar and enter the Sanctuary (Ezek 44,15–16). The rest of the tribe of Levi were assigned an explicitly servile role as penitence for their sins of idolatry at the time of the monarchy (Ezek 44,10–14): "And they shall not come near to me, to serve me as priests, nor touch any of my sacred things, nor any of the things that are most sacred; but they shall bear their shame as a result of the abominations that they have committed" (Ezek 44,13).

However, despite their humiliation, the Levites were still considered as members of the priesthood. In fact, in Ezekiel's regulations, these Levites are called the 'priests who keep guard over the Temple' and are allotted a place in the inner court, beside that of the descendants of Zadok (Ezek 40,45–46). By referring to these Levites as priests, Ezekiel hints at the possibility of their purification and the eventual reconciliation between the two groups of priests.

It is clear in the Apocalypse that this reconciliation has taken place: those who correspond to the Levites, that is to say the martyrs standing on the glassy sea in heaven, are not only seen with the harps of God in their hands (Ap 15,2)—sacred things that previously they were not allowed to touch—but also they are before the Throne, inside the heavenly Sanctuary (Ap 7,15–16), exercising a privilege that was exclusively reserved for the priests who were descendants of Zadok (Ezek 44,16).

In a way that vividly recalls the purification and the dedication of the Levites for their ministry (Num 8,5–22), the text of the Apocalypse explains how those who correspond to the Levites (the martyrs) come to be able to serve openly as priests in the heavenly Sanctuary: "These are the ones coming from the great tribulation, and they have washed their robes and bleached them in the blood of the Lamb" (Ap 7,14).

The priestly dignity of the martyrs is also indicated in the Apocalypse, by applying to them a word that alludes to the priestly consecration. After the breaking of the fifth seal, the martyrs under the altar were told to wait "a short time more, until also their fellow

---

Aaron, they came to be known as 'sons of Aaron' (de Vaux, *Ancient Israel*, IV 7.12, 372–76; and IV 8.3, 394–97).

servants and their brothers had been *consecrated*, those about to be killed just as themselves" (Ap 6,11).[236]

Equality in rank between those who correspond to the Levites in the new Temple (the martyrs) and those who correspond to the priests (the 144,000) is confirmed by the fact that there are only 24 elders in the heavenly Sanctuary. In the Old Testament, it is recounted that King David established that 24 elders should be nominated to head the 24 divisions of the Levites (1Chr ch.25), in addition to the 24 elders nominated to be heads of the 24 divisions of the priests (1Chr ch.24).[237]

Confirming that there is no longer any difference in status between the two groups, the 24 elders in the Apocalypse act as heads of division for both Levites and priests: not only do they fulfil the Levitical function of singing and providing musical accompaniment (Ap 5,8–9), but they also perform the priestly function of holding the golden bowls full of incense (Ap 5,8)—sacred things (cf. Ex 30,34–36)—which they give, at the appropriate time, to the angel who offers the incense on the golden altar before the Throne (Ap 8,3).

---

[236] (Ap 6,11): literally translated, the martyrs under the altar must wait "for a short time more, until also their fellow-servants and their brothers have been *filled* (πληρωθῶσιν), those about to be killed just as themselves" (Ap 6,11). The allusion to the priestly consecration consists in the use of the Greek verb that means 'to fill' (πληροῦν), since 'to fill the hand' is the literal translation of the ancient Hebrew expression for the consecration of the priests (יד מלא: the etymology is obscure, see de Vaux, *Ancient Israel*, IV 5.2, 346–47). Furthermore, this Hebrew expression is translated literally in the Greek version of the Old Testament (the Septuagint) using the same verb or its cognate forms (πληροῦν, πίμπλημι, ἐπιπίμπλημι τὴν χεῖρα). In this context (Ap 6,11), then, the use of the Greek verb that means 'to fill' not only evokes the priestly consecration, but also suggests an act of consecration that involves the whole soul and not just the 'the hand'. It is not stated in the text precisely what fills the souls of these martyrs, but it seems to be the vision of the Throne itself, after their martyrdom, that entirely fills their souls and so completes their consecration (cf. Acts 7,55–56; 2,28; n. 205).

[237] For the identification of the elders of the Apocalypse with the 24 heads of the priests and Levites, see Aune, *Revelation 1–5*, 287–92; Thompson, *Apocalypse and Empire*, 70. In the first centuries of this era, it was quite common to refer to these heads as elders (see the *Mishnah*: m.Yoma 1:5; m.Tamid 1:1; m.Middoth 1:8).

Chapter 9

The Holy War

The judgement of evil and its eradication from the creation are inevitable consequences of God's love for his people. In the Apocalypse, this is represented by the emptying of a series of bowls over the earth, which contain the wine of God's passionate anger (Ap ch.16) and result in the war of the great Day of God Almighty (Ap 16,14; 17,14; 19,19–21), followed by the final Judgement (Ap 20,11–15).

In the text, the final war is described in two parts (Ap 19,19–21 and 20,7–10), with one thousand years (the 'Millennium') in between (Ap 20,1–6). However, in the eyes of God this period of a thousand years is "like a yesterday that has passed" (Ps 90,4) and corresponds to the Day in heaven, whose liturgy for atonement coincides with the present age of salvation.[238] The two parts of the

---

[238] See I. 11, iii. There are many other reasons for identifying the millennial reign of Christ with the present age of salvation: (a) those who reign with Christ in the first resurrection ('the Millennium') have authority to judge and are called priests of God and Christ (Ap 20,4–6). They can be identified as the people from every tribe, tongue, race and nation whom Christ has acquired for God with his blood, and formed into a kingdom of priests that reign over the earth (Ap 5,10). These people, redeemed by the blood of Jesus Christ, constitute the Church in the present age of salvation (Ap 1,6). (b) According to Ap 11,15–18, the second coming of the Lord and the completion of the God's Kingdom coincide with the sound of the seventh trumpet. The fact that these also coincide with the time to judge the dead (Ap 11,18) indicates that there will **not** be an interval of one thousand years between the second coming (Ap 17,14; 19,11–21) and the final Judgement (Ap 20,11–15). Since the millennial reign of Christ describes the Church *before* the second coming, one should ask why the vision of this period (Ap 20,2–6) is described *after* the vision of the second coming (Ap 19,11–21). Because of its humility, the millennial reign of Christ is very different from any other kingdom in the world (Mk 10,42–45), and is therefore appropriately described after the kingdom of this world has ended with the second coming of the Lord. Being *in* the world, but not *of* this world (Jn 18,36), it

final war, therefore, represent two successive phases in the same ultimate attempt of evil to oppose the Will of God and his love. These two phases can be summarized as follows:

a)   There is a concentration of forces originating from the East (Ap 16,12) and from the rest of the world (Ap 16,13–14), in a place called 'Harmagedon'[239](Ap 16,16). The heavens open and the Lord appears with his army in order to defeat his enemies (Ap 17,14; 19,11–21).

---

can only be recognized by those whose Faith is in Christ. So, to place the vision of Christ's reign after that of his second coming implies that many people will not have recognized Christ's reign before he comes in glory, at which time his thousand-year reign will be revealed (cf. Ap 1,7) as 'a yesterday already passed', according to the words of Psalm 90,4. It is understood that the Lord will come in glory before all men will have entered under his rule, a fact concisely confirmed by the Church in the following words: "The kingdom will be fulfilled, then, not by a historic triumph of the Church through a progressive ascendancy, but only by God's victory over the final unleashing of evil…" (*Catechism of the Catholic Church*, no. 677). For other arguments in support of this 'preconsummationist' interpretation, see Fowler White, "Reexamining the Evidence for Recapitulation in Rev 20:1–3, *Westminster Theological Journal*, 51(1989), 319–44.

[239] Harmagedon is a Hebrew name meaning 'mount of Megiddo'. Megiddo was an ancient city situated on a mound or 'Tel', at the edge of a great plain, which has been the site of many historical battles. Since it is situated on a plain, Tel Megiddo cannot be identified precisely with the place that is called the 'mount of Megiddo' in the Apocalypse. The mountain that dominates the plain is, in fact, Mount Carmel, where Elijah challenged the false prophets of Baal, in front of the people of Israel (1Kgs ch.18). In the Apocalypse, the mount of Megiddo is presented in contrast to Mount Zion (Ap 14,1), which is the place from where 'the Lord will send out the rod of his strength' (Ps 110,2; 2,6–9). Taken in this way, the mount of Megiddo represents the place where the false messiah (the beast) will seek to demonstrate his military strength after his throne has been struck by the 5th plague (Ap 16,10–11). It is in this context, therefore, that there will be a gathering of forces for the final battle. However, in a way which recalls the decisive event in the conflict between Elijah and the false prophets on Mt. Carmel, the Lord will come with his armies and be victorious at the battle of Harmagedon (Ap 19,19–21). In that day the mourning will be like that of Hadad-rimmon (Baal) when his prophets were defeated by the God of Israel, and then slaughtered in the plain of Megiddo (1Kgs 18,40; cf. Zech 12,10–14; Jn 19,37; Mt 24,30; Ap 1,7).

b) An expedition of international forces called 'Gog and Magog'[240]
    cross 'the land' to reach the 'camp of the saints', which is also
    called 'the beloved city', and then they surround it. They are
    defeated by fire that comes down from heaven[241](Ap 20,7–10)
    and the final Judgement follows immediately (Ap 20,11–15).

   According to the Old Testament, the 'beloved city' is Zion
(Ps 87,1–3). In the Apocalypse it is also called the 'camp of the
saints' (Ap 20,9) and is represented by the assembly of the 144,000
followers of the Lamb. The fact that this place is surrounded by the
forces of 'Gog and Magog' is further confirmation that the 144,000
are called to assemble at a particular location on the earth, more
specifically, one that can be physically surrounded. The expression
'camp of the saints',[242] and its use in the context of war, recalls the
condition of the Israelites while wandering in the desert, during their
migration from Egypt to the Promised Land. Furthermore, the Old
Testament account of the advance of the Israelites in the desert can
be understood as the advance of an army engaged in holy war, up to
and including their arrival in, and conquest of, the Promised Land.[243]
   The determining characteristic of holy war is that God fights in
favour of his people (Deut 1,30). Since it used to be conducted in a
ritual and systematic way, the main phases in the unfolding of a holy
war can be identified from accounts in the Old Testament. The

---

[240] called 'Gog and Magog': these terms correspond to the names of the tribal forces
hostile to Israel in Ezekiel's prophecy of the final battle (Ezek chs. 38–39). The
allusion to the prophecy at this point indicates its fulfilment in the final battle
prophesied in the Apocalypse.

[241] by fire which comes down from heaven: the way in which the Lord will 'manifest his glory among the nations' in the final war (Ezek 39,21) corresponds to the
way in which he manifested his glory to the Israelites at the conclusion of the
consecration of the Tent in the desert (Lev 9,6.23–24) and of the Temple of
Solomon (2Chr 7,1). This was previously discussed at III. 8 ('The Consecration of
the New Temple').

[242] The expression 'camp of the saints': the Greek term for 'camp' (παρεμβολή) is
frequently used in a military sense (e.g., Deut 23,10–15 in the Septuagint).

[243] See de Vaux, *Ancient Israel*, III 5.1, 259.

following phases in holy war have been identified by R. de Vaux,[244] and form a suitable basis for comparison with the final war described in the Apocalypse:[245]

a)   The assembly of the combatants (2Chr 20,4; Judg 20,1–2) was followed by their consecration (Josh 3,5) and the consecration of the encampment (Deut 23,10–15).

b)   The Lord was consulted about the plan of attack (2Chr 20,5–17), and then sacrifices were offered before battle was engaged (1Sam 7,9).

c)   Their faith in the power of God made the combatants sure of victory (Josh 6,2; 8,1.18; Judg 3,28; 4,7; 7,9.15; 1Sam 23,4; 24,5). They were to have faith and not fear (Josh 8,1; 10,8.25).

d)   The Ark of the Covenant was exposed and carried in solemn procession as a visible sign of the Presence of God (Josh 6,6).

e)   When the battle was about to begin, the sounding of the trumpet (or horn) was the signal to raise the battle-cry (Josh 6,5–21; Judg 7,16–22; Num 10,9; 2Chr 13,12–15).[246]

f)   During the battle, it was God who fought for Israel (Josh 10,14.42; Judg 20,35), throwing the enemy into confusion (Judg

---

[244] See de Vaux, *Ancient Israel*, III 5.1–5, 258–67.

[245] The idea of making a comparison with OT accounts of holy war was inspired by *The Book of Revelation: The Open Book of Prophecy* by Giblin. In that book, however, the emphasis on the theme of holy war in the Apocalypse seems excessive. So in this study the scope of the comparison has been limited to the final battle and its preparations. In contrast to Bauckham (*Climax of Prophecy*, 211–37, especially n. 12 on 216) our work indicates that the role of the 144,000 men in this battle is very different from that of the martyrs, and because of this they must not be killed in the eschatological tribulation (see also n. 172).

[246] R. de Vaux writes: "This battle-cry…was originally a savage shout meant to inspire the ranks and to strike fear into the enemy. But it was also a religious cry, closely bound up with the role of the Ark in fighting (cf. 1Sam 4,5f); it then became part of the ritual surrounding the Ark (2Sam 6,15), and finally passed into the Temple liturgy (Lev 23,24; Num 29,1) and certain Psalms" (de Vaux, *Ancient Israel*, III 4.2, 254). It appears that with the passage of this ancient battle tactic into the liturgy, the meaning of the word (תרועה) broadened: in addition to the battle-cry itself, it came to signify a particular quality of sound delivered by the horn or trumpet (for a brief discussion on the quality of this sound see *Encyclopaedia Judaica*, s.v. 'Shofar').

4,15; 7,22; 1Sam 14,20), provoking divine terror (1Sam 7,10; 14,15) and summoning the forces of nature to assist (Josh 10,11; 24,7; Judg 5,20).

g) The holy war culminated in the 'anathema' (חרם), or extermination, of the defeated enemy and his possessions. In Old Testament times, the defeated enemies and their possessions were all dedicated to God (Deut 7,1–5; Josh 8,2; 1Sam 15,13–15). In theory every human being and all their livestock should have been killed, and their houses and property burnt; objects made of precious stones and metals were to be taken to the priests to be purified, consecrated to the Lord and stored in the Temple treasury (Josh 6,19; Num 18,14; 31,21–23.50–54). In practice, the anathema was usually not fully implemented: it was often limited to the killing of human beings (Deut 2,34–35; 3,6–7) or males only (Num 31,7; Judg 21,11; Deut 20,14).

Returning to the Apocalypse and identifying the 144,000 as the combatants, it is possible to demonstrate, in a list parallel to the preceding one, how the characteristics of holy war described in the Old Testament are reflected in the new situation of war, and help to explain it.

a) *The combatants assembled and this was followed by their consecration and that of their encampment.*
The first four trumpets (Ap 8,6–13) are the signal for assembling the combatants, since it is written: "And when the assembly is to be gathered together, you shall blow the trumpet, but not raise the battle-cry" (Num 10,7).

Before the sound of the fifth trumpet, the 144,000 men will be sheltered (Ap 14,1) in such a way that they will not be tormented by the plagues that follow this trumpet (Ap 9,4).

The preparation for the consecration can be understood as the period of seven years in which the combatants remain at their place in the desert, and at the end of this period the consecration of the combatants and their camp is brought about by contact with the smoke of the glory of God and of his power (Ap 15,8).[247]

b) ***God was consulted about the plan of attack and then sacrifices were offered.***

The Word of God that guides the combatants in the imminent battle is the prophecy given to John in the Apocalypse. The offering of sacrifices refers to the martyrdom of the faithful during the great tribulation (Ap 13,15.17). This takes place during the period of 42 months, in which the beast reigns with his false prophet (Ap 13,5–7).

c) ***Faith in the power of God makes the combatants sure of victory.***

The faith of the 144,000 combatants derives from their intimate and inseparable association with Jesus Christ (Ap 14,1–5), after having experienced a revelation of him as "the one who will shepherd the nations with a rod of iron" (Ap 12,5). Before the final battle, the combatants are endowed with divine power by means of their contact with the smoke of the glory and power of God (Ap 15,8).[248]

d) ***The Ark of the Covenant was exposed as a visible sign of the Presence of God.***

This action is clearly reflected in the Apocalypse, when "the Sanctuary of God in heaven was opened, and the Ark of his Covenant was seen in his Sanctuary" (Ap 11,19). The event of the opening of the Sanctuary links the revelation of the Ark with the revelation of the glorious Presence of God within his Sanctuary (Ap 15,5–8), described by the author as a great and wonderful sign (Ap 15,1). As noted previously, this event takes place among the 144,000 assembled with the Lamb on Mount Zion.[249]

---

[247] As explained in III. 8 ('The Consecration of the New Temple').

[248] As explained in III. 2 ('The Eschatological Exodus') and in III. 8 ('The Consecration of the New Temple').

[249] See III. 7 ('The Sign of the Presence of God')

e) ***The sounding of the trumpet was the signal to raise the battle-cry.***

The sounding of the trumpet followed by the shouting of the battle-cry announced that the battle was about to begin: "When you go to war in your land against the enemy that is oppressing you, raise the battle-cry with the trumpets and you will be remembered before the Lord your God and saved from your enemies" (Num 10,9).

In the Apocalypse, this combination of the sound of the trumpet and the shouting of the battle-cry is represented as follows: "And the seventh angel blew, and there were loud voices in heaven saying: "the kingdom of the world has become our Lord's and his Christ's, and he shall reign for ever and ever" (Ap 11,15).

This battle-cry is extraordinary because it proclaims the result of the battle, whose beginning has only just been signalled by the sounding of the seventh trumpet. Furthermore, the result is described as the all-powerful Presence of the Lord in the world, and is indicated by the appearance of the Ark in his Sanctuary, among the 144,000 on Mt. Zion.

As it is described in the Apocalypse, this aspect of the battle recalls the account of a war between Jehoshaphat's army and the forces of an alliance between the Moabites, the Ammonites and the Edomites (2Chr 20,1–30). In this 'holy war', the enemy was defeated at the moment when the Levitical singers started their clamour of praise: "Give thanks to the Lord, for his mercy endures forever" (2Chr 20,21).

In the Apocalypse, the elders express their thanks in a very similar way, after the sounding of the seventh trumpet and the battle-cry: "We thank you Lord God Almighty, the One who is and who was, because you have taken up your great power and have come to reign" (Ap 11,17).

This is then echoed by the great chorus of martyrs in heaven "Hallelujah, because the Lord our God, the Almighty, has come to reign! Let us rejoice and be glad and give him the glory" (Ap 19,6–7).

It has already been noted how the martyrs in heaven correspond to the Levites in the ancient Temple,[250] and how the 24 elders represent the heads of the 24 divisions of the Levites and priests.[251] It is not a coincidence, therefore, that the praise of the elders and martyrs in heaven should resemble that of the Levites in the account of Jehoshaphat's war.

f) *God fought for his people during the war.*

During the preparations for Jehoshaphat's war, the Word of the Lord was directed to the Israelites as follows: "You will not have to fight in this battle; take your position, stand still, and see the salvation of the Lord who is with you, O Judah and Jerusalem. Do not fear or be dismayed; go out against them tomorrow, and the Lord will be with you" (2Chr 20,17).

According to his Word, the Lord took Israel's enemies by surprise and they began to kill one another, so when Jehoshaphat's army approached they found only the corpses of their enemies, without a single survivor.

The situation is very similar in the Apocalypse: in the first phase of the battle, the 144,000 combatants have no need to fight because the heavens open and the King of kings appears with his army in order to defeat the forces coming from the East and from the rest of the world, and they are completely destroyed (Ap 19,11–21).

So also in the second and final phase of the battle: when the hostile forces of 'Gog and Magog' surround the camp of the 144,000, fire comes down from heaven, consumes the enemy and gives victory to the people of God (Ap 20,9).

g) *The holy war culminated in the 'anathema', or extermination, of the defeated enemy and his possessions.*

In the Apocalypse, the 'anathema' can be recognized in the final destiny of the enemies of God: the armies are totally consumed by the birds of the sky (Ap 19,21) or by fire (Ap 20,9) and their

---

[250] See III. 5 ('The New Temple of God on Mt. Zion').

[251] See III. 8 ('The Consecration of the New Temple').

leaders, namely Satan, the beast and the false prophet, are all removed to their eternal condemnation in the lake of fire (Ap 19,20; 20,10). After the Judgement, the same end awaits 'death and Hades', Babylon and whoever was not found to be inscribed in the Lamb's scroll of Life (Ap 20,11–15). By contrast, the precious stones and metals that belonged to these enemies will be taken to the Holy City and used in its construction (Ap 21,24–26).[252]

---

[252] and used in its construction: according to St. John's vision in the Apocalypse, the main street of the Holy City is covered with pure gold (Ap 21,18.21), the wall is incrusted with jasper (Ap 21,18) and the foundations of the wall are adorned with every kind of precious stone (Ap 21,19–20).

Chapter 10

The New Heaven and the New Earth

The prophecy of the Apocalypse concludes with a vision of the fulfilment of the mystery of God, which he had made known to his servants the prophets (Ap 10,7). Every prophecy will vanish when this perfection is realized, as explained by St. Paul: "Love never ends. As for prophecies, they will not be needed; as for tongues, they will cease; as for knowledge, it will be replaced. For our knowledge and our prophecy are imperfect, but when the perfect comes, the imperfect will pass away" (1Cor 13,8–10).

In the Apocalypse, the perfection that we await is described as 'a new heaven and a new earth' (Ap 21,1), which is a biblical expression that is often mistakenly understood to involve the destruction of this planet and the transfer of all life to a place in some other part of the universe (a 'new earth').[253] This 'literalistic' interpretation clearly fosters a negligent attitude towards the environmental and ecological conditions which prevail on this planet.

However, there is no indication in the Bible that the planet 'earth' will be less pleasing to God at any time in the future, than it was when he created it (Gen 1,9–10) and neither is there any explicit

---

[253] In fact, with regard to the expression 'the new heaven and the new earth' there are two types of misunderstanding, which are expressed in a very concise way by the former Archbishop of Milan, Carlo Maria Martini: "The Christian hope is at risk of being reduced in two ways: either to longings of a purely celestial kind for the other life, or (...) to completely earthly expectations (the Kingdom of God is already here in its fullness!), as in some propositions of political theology. In practice, it is difficult for us to comprehend the entire human horizon in one go. We have to adjust our thoughts and our language continually in order to grasp the unity that combines earthly hopes—of which the Bible often speaks—with those which are invisible and definitive, but give flavour to all the rest" (Martini, *Sto alla Porta*, Pastoral Letter, 1992–1994, para.18; our translation).

warning that God would want to destroy the planet, or even allow it to be destroyed.[254] On the contrary, it is written that the time will come when those who are destroying the earth will, themselves, be destroyed (Ap 11,18).

Moreover, the eternal Covenant that God established with Noah and all the creatures, when he swore he would never again destroy every living creature as he had done (Gen 8,21; 9,11–17), is not ignored in the prophecy of the Apocalypse; it is, in fact, recalled with the appearance of the rainbow in the vision of the angel that announces the imminent fulfilment of the mystery of God: "And I saw another mighty angel coming down from heaven, clothed with a cloud and with the rainbow over his head" (Ap 10,1).

In the Apocalypse, the transformation of 'the first heaven and the first earth' into 'the new heaven and the new earth' is described in such a way that an examination of this transformation can help to clarify the meaning of the expression 'new heaven and new earth' in its biblical context (Is 51,6; 65,17–25; 66,22; Mk 13,31; 2Pet 3,13).

After the Lamb broke the sixth seal of the scroll in heaven, St. John describes a vision that represents the disappearance of 'the first heaven and the first earth': "And I saw when he opened the sixth seal, and a great earthquake occurred and the sun became black

---

[254] The passage which probably comes closest to describing a total distruction of the planet is to be found in the Second Letter of St. Peter: "then the heavens will pass away with a loud noise, and the elements will be dissolved with fire, and the earth and the works that are upon it will be *burned up*" (2Pet 3,10 according to the RSV). Several details in this description, however, suggest that the transformation of the present world by means of fire does not involve the total distruction of the planet. In the first place, the word for '*burned up*' is not found in the most reliable Greek manuscripts (א, B, K, P, et al.); instead, these simply state that "the earth and everything that is done on it will be *disclosed* (εὑρεθήσεται)" (NRSV), a prediction that is entirely consistent with the fact that the final Judgement is taking place at the same time (2Pet 3,7). In the second place, the transformation of the present world is compared to the destruction of the preceding world by the Flood (2Pet 3,6–7). The Flood, however, did not destroy the planet, but transformed it into the present heaven and earth. It is implied, then, that the transforming fire is not destructive, but purificatory, and can therefore be identified with the fire of the Spirit (1Cor 3,10–17; 1Pet 4,12; Mt 3,11; Lk 12,49; Ap 8,5).

as sackcloth made of hair, and the whole moon became like blood, and the stars of heaven fell to the earth as a fig-tree drops its unripe figs when shaken by a great wind, and the heaven departed like a scroll being rolled up, and every mountain and island was moved from its place" (Ap 6,12–14).

However, the realization of the events described after the sixth seal is delayed (Ap 7,1) in order to prepare those who will be able to survive the great Day of God's anger (Ap 6,17; 7,2–8).

Following the breaking of the seventh seal, a series of events occur that are announced by the sound of trumpets and cause considerable environmental damage to the earth (Ap ch.8). The fact that this series of happenings is described as the falling of heavenly bodies on to the earth, suggests that it represents the disappearance of the 'first heaven'.

The disappearance of the 'first earth' is represented as the consequence of a tremendous earthquake (Ap 6,12; 11,19; 16,18), which occurs after the outpouring of the contents of the seventh bowl: "And there were lightnings and noises and thunders and a great earthquake occurred, such as never had happened since man had been on earth, such an earthquake—so great....And every island fled and mountains were not found" (Ap 16,18.20).

When the time for the final Judgement arrives, 'the first heaven and the first earth' disappear completely: "And I saw a great white Throne and the one seated on it, from whose face the earth and heaven fled, and no place was found for them" (Ap 20,11).

When "the first heaven and the first earth had passed away, and the sea is no more" (Ap 21,1), John saw and described a vision of 'the new heaven and the new earth'. Since many features of the present way of life are recognizable in his description of 'the new heaven and the new earth', it must not be concluded that the disappearance of 'the first heaven and the first earth' will involve the destruction of this planet. St. John recounts how, after the final Judgement, there will be 'nations' that will need to receive healing from the leaves of the trees of Life (Ap 22,2), so that they may then be able to walk by the light of the Holy City (Ap 21,24). There will also be 'rulers of the earth', who bring the glory and the honour of the nations into this City (Ap 21,24–26).

Furthermore, when it is stated in the text that the Holy City "has no need for the sun or the moon to shine upon her, for the glory of the Lord gives her light, and her lamp is the Lamb" (Ap 21,23; 22,5), it does not mean that there will be neither sun nor moon in the 'new heaven and the new earth'; it means, instead, that there will be a source of light which is divine and even more essential for Life. What has been promised to the faithful servants of God, and is presently in course of preparation, is not an immaterial fantasy. There are solid indications in the prophecy of the Apocalypse that 'the new heaven and the new earth' represent a continuation of life on this earth, but only after it has been totally transformed, so that it can become a place "in which righteousness dwells" (2Pet 3,13).

After being transported 'in spirit' on to a great and high mountain, St. John saw the Holy City, the New Jerusalem, coming down from heaven[255](Ap 21,10). This vision recalls prophecies in the Old Testament (Is 2,2–3; Mic 4,1–2; Ezek 40,2) that identify the great and high mountain with Mt. Zion, where St. John had previously seen the 144,000 assembled in the Presence of the Lamb (Ap 14,1–5). Since this mountain certainly exists as a real place on earth, it therefore follows that the Holy City will also be established on the earth, in a place that can be seen from 'Mt. Zion'.

A brief examination of St. John's description of 'the new heaven and the new earth' reveals that, far from anticipating the elimination of life from the planet, it foresees the elimination of the former reality ('the first heaven and the first earth') from the life on this planet. As a result of the final Judgement, the following realities of the present age will no longer exist: the sea[256](Ap 21,1); death and Hades (Ap 20,14; 21,4); the devil (Ap 20,10); the beast, the false

---

[255] the New Jerusalem, coming down from heaven: since 'heaven' refers to the invisible realm of divine transcendence, one should not imagine the descent of the Holy City from heaven like the landing of a 'floating island' from outer space. It is sufficient to understand that this City, which is currently spiritual and invisible, will become a material reality in those days.

[256] the sea: in the Apocalypse this word is used as a synonym for the 'Abyss' (see n. 79).

prophet (Ap 19,20) and their followers (Ap 14,9–11); Babylon (Ap 19,2–3); sorrow, mourning, pain (Ap 21,4) and every curse (Ap 22,3).

To emphasize the totality of the transformation, St. John specifically reports the absence of any sanctuary or temple in his vision of the Holy City "because her Sanctuary is the Lord God Almighty and the Lamb" (Ap 21,22). Despite the importance of the Sanctuary and its liturgy throughout the visions of the Apocalypse, all this will disappear at the consummation; as a part of 'the first heaven and the first earth', even the heavenly Sanctuary and its liturgical functions are destined to disappear with the realization of 'the new heaven and the new earth'. Freshly completed and consecrated, the new Temple is only an intermediate stage in the maturation and realization of God's plan for all mankind.[257] After the perfect fulfilment of this divine plan, there will no longer be a sanctuary or temple,[258] because there will no longer be a need for people to retire to a separate and sacred place to encounter God. In those days, in fact, everyone will be able to enjoy immediate and direct contact with his divine Presence.

In conclusion, the new reality described as 'the new heaven and the new earth' does not by any means involve the transfer of life from this planet to any other place in the universe, but rather the

---

[257] This situation agrees well with the finding that St. John represents the fulfilment of Ezekiel's vision (chs. 40–48) in two phases: (i) before the Judgement—the construction of the new Temple; (ii) after the Judgement—the realization on earth of the New Jerusalem, in which there will be no temple (cf. n. 114).

[258] Against the background of the Jewish Faith from the first century to the present day, St. John is unique in his conviction that there will not be a Temple in Jerusalem, the city of the eschatological fulfilment (see Aune, *Revelation 17–22*, 1166–68; Briggs, *Jewish Temple Imagery*, 220–23). In the same way, "…the Church, as it exists in the present age, is destined to disappear. It will be transformed into the resplendent heavenly city that will descend to earth. The glorified Church will not act as an intermediary between God and people, as a sacrament of the divine presence because the inhabitants of the New Jerusalem will enjoy the immediate knowledge of God. They will see him as he is and his presence will fill completely the Church that will encompass the totality of the new creation" (Spatafora, *From the Temple of God*, 247).

total transformation of the life on this planet, through the confrontation of every soul that ever lived on earth, with the One who sits on the Throne (Ap 20,11). The result of this perfect union between the Creator and his creatures is a new creation (Ap 21,5), 'new' because every trace of the old way of life has been removed: "For behold, I am creating a new heaven and a new earth and the former things shall not be remembered or come to mind" (Is 65,17).

Chapter 11

The Eternal Marriage

The perfect union of God with his creatures is represented in the Apocalypse as a consequence of the marriage of the Lamb with his bride (Ap 19,7–9) and is described in the following way: "And I saw the Holy City, the New Jerusalem, coming down out of heaven from God, prepared as a bride adorned for her husband. And I heard a loud voice from the Throne saying:

Behold the Dwelling of God is with mankind,
and he will dwell with them;
and they will be his peoples,
and God himself will be with them;
and he will wipe away every tear from their eyes,
and there will be no more death;
neither sorrow, nor crying, nor pain will there be any more,
because the former things have passed away" (Ap 21,2–4).

If there is any doubt about whether this union, or marriage, has already been celebrated, a brief look at the suffering prevailing in the world should be sufficient to remove this delusion.[259] The New Jerusalem, the bride of the Lamb, has not yet descended from heaven to earth, but remains in heaven where she prepares for her forthcoming wedding. At the appropriate time, this great event is announced as follows: "the marriage of the Lamb has come and his wife has prepared herself, and fine linen, bright and clean, was given to her to wear—because the fine linen is the righteous work of the

---

[259] to remove this delusion: the refusal or denial of the current suffering in the world suffocates any hope for the realization of the Holy City on earth, and is associated with the attitude embodied and promoted by Babylon—that power in the world which does not expect a final Judgement (see III. 4: 'The Mystery of Iniquity').

saints" (Ap 19,7–8).

When St. John finally sees the bride coming down out of heaven (Ap 21,9 – 22,5), he describes her in terms which evoke the final vision of the prophet Ezekiel (Ezek chs.47–48), as a paradise with a river, a large street, many trees and surrounded by a high wall with twelve gates. As the wife of the Lamb, however, the Holy City is not just a place on the map, but also represents the members of a community. The composition of this community is not specified in the text, but is indicated by the resemblance between the clothes worn by its members and the garment made of fine line, bright and clean, which is given to the bride to wear at her wedding. Comparing the clothing in this way, the following groups can be identified with the wife of the Lamb:

a) ***The armies of heaven who follow the Word of God***
The armies of heaven can easily be identified with the bride because they are dressed in the same way, in fine linen, white and clean (Ap 19,14). Furthermore, the fine linen that they wear identifies them with the saints, because the fine linen represents the righteous deeds they performed (Ap 19,8). The way in which the righteous work of the saints arrives in heaven, in order to clothe these armies, is explained like this: "Blessed are the dead, they that die in the Lord from now on. Yes, says the Spirit, so that they may rest from their labours, but their deeds go with them (Ap 14,13).

The deeds that accompany the saints during their millennial rest in heaven, correspond to the righteous works symbolized by the fine linen, bright white and clean, which clothes the armies of saints in heaven.

In the Old Testament, however, the 'armies of heaven' are always identified with the angels under the command of the Lord (1Kgs 22,19; Ps 148,2; 103,20–21; Neh 9,6) and for this reason God is sometimes called 'the Lord of the armies'[260] and the angels are compared to the stars of the sky (Gen 2,1; Ap 1,20; 12,4.7–9).

Since both the angels and the saints are identified with the

---

[260] 'the Lord of the armies': is the literal translation of יהוה צבאות.

armies of heaven, it can be inferred that, in heaven, the saints are equal to the angels. In fact, Scripture is clear on this point: in the resurrection, men and angels are equal (Ap 19,10; 22,9; 21,17; Lk 20,34–36) and, at the end of time, both saints and angels will come with Jesus Christ in the glory of God, in order to defeat their enemies (Ap 19,14; 1Thess 3,13; Jude 14–15; Mt 25,31).

b) *The martyrs*

The martyrs who come through the great tribulation wash their robes[261] and bleach them in the blood of the Lamb (Ap 7,14–17). Since these robes will be *clean* and *bright* after being *washed* and *bleached*, they can also be identified with the wedding garment of the bride, made with fine linen, bright and clean (Ap 19,8). In this way, the martyrs come to be identified with the bride of the Lamb, and their robes with her fine linen. Given that the fine linen symbolizes the righteous work of the saints, the robes of the martyrs therefore represent their own righteous deeds,[262] which, as in the case of the saints, have accompanied them to heaven (Ap 14,13).

However, the martyrs who are under the altar in heaven did not previously have these robes, but receive them as a gift after their martyrdom (Ap 6,11). Interpreted literally, this means that the martyrs under the altar had not performed the deeds necessary to make their own robes. It seems to refer to the fact that many of the first martyrs were killed for their testimony to Jesus soon after their conversion to the Faith and therefore they did not have the opportunity to perform righteous deeds. It could also refer to martyrs, especially those of the Old Testament, whose deeds had not

---

[261] their robes: in contrast to the other word used in the Greek text to denote white clothing (ἱμάτιον), the word which is here translated by 'robe' (στολή) represents a type of ceremonial dress that was used by people of high society.

[262] their own righteous deeds: why do the martyrs have to wash and bleach their robes? It is implied that the works that they perform are not perfect (Ap 2,4–5; 3,2–4), and that they are stained with self-love. Nevertheless, these witnesses of Jesus Christ persevere along the way of perfection (continually *washing* their robes in the blood of the Lamb), before attaining the greatest perfection by means of their martyrdom (*bleaching* their robes in the blood of the Lamb).

been rendered 'righteous' by faith in Jesus.

The giving of the robes of fine linen to the martyrs under the altar (Ap 6,11) suggests that, by means of performing righteous deeds, the saints are able to produce fine linen not only for themselves, but also for those who are identified with the bride and, for whatever reason, have not been able to perform righteous deeds. This capacity of the saints to make amends for their companions in the Faith recalls the doctrine of the Church concerning the granting of indulgences.[263]

c) *The 144,000 men*

Their virginity (Ap 14,4), the description of their camp as the 'beloved city' (Ap 20,9) and their intimate and faithful relationship with the Lamb (Ap 14,1), all point to the identification of the 144,000 on earth with the bride of the Lamb.[264]

Just as the bride prepares herself, and fine linen is given to her to wear, so also the 144,000 subject themselves to a process of preparation for their consecration. As previously explained, this process closely corresponds to the procedure for the consecration of the priests, according to the instructions that were given to Moses.[265] In particular, the 'clothing' of the 144,000 with the smoke of the glory and power of God[266](Ap 15,8) corresponds to the clothing of the priestly candidates with their ceremonial garments, which were also made of fine linen (Ex 28,4–5; 39,27–29).

This comparison between the preparation of the bride and the consecration of the 144,000 carries two implications: firstly, the fine linen that represents the righteous work of the saints and clothes the bride, corresponds to the smoke of the glory and power of God that envelops and 'clothes' the 144,000 during their consecration.

---

[263] See *Catechism of the Catholic Church*, nos. 1032, 1471.

[264] with the bride of the Lamb: in the field of mystical theology the kind of relationship between the 144,000 and the Lamb is called 'spiritual betrothal'. Before becoming the Lamb's bride and wife, this community is his 'fiancée'.

[265] See III. 8 ('The Consecration of the New Temple').

[266] In the Old Testament, the glory and power of God is frequently compared to a garment (e.g., Is 52,1; Ps 104,1–2; 93,1; Is 51,9).

Secondly, since the 144,000 are given their robes of fine linen, they are in a similar position to those who had not been able to make their own, by performing righteous deeds. Given that the place where they live is called 'the camp of the saints' (Ap 20,9), there is no reason to doubt that they are saints, even though they have not performed the necessary deeds to provide themselves with the proper robes. It is probable that from a young age these men have practised a special vocation 'to follow the Lamb wherever he may go' (Ap 14,4) and are not therefore involved in the active life, but find themselves among those who were called to a life of contemplation.[267] This particular vocation explains their availability and willingness to go off into the desert for a period of preparation before their consecration.

In conclusion, the bride is the personification of the people of God prepared and purified for their lasting union with Jesus Christ, the Lamb of God (cf. 2Cor 11,2–3). This people is not only represented by the saints, angels and martyrs in heaven, but also by the 144,000 men living in a safe place on earth. All these are members of 'Zion', the eschatological city of salvation (cf. Heb 12,22–24).

However, 'Zion' is the name of the mother community whose members are collectively referred to as the 'Daughter of Zion' and also the 'Virgin Daughter of Zion'.[268] It is the 'Daughter of Zion' understood in this way, that is identified as the bride of the Lamb. So the marriage does not simply represent a special relationship between the mother community (Zion) and her God, as was the Old Covenant between Israel and God (cf. Hos 1,4 – 2,25; Gen 2,1–2; Is 1,21). Instead the marriage signifies the full and eternal union between God and every member of the community, as a result of his or her eternal commitment to the Lamb (Ap 22,3–4).

---

[267] called to a life of contemplation: the fact that the 144,000 are contemplatives is important because it emphasizes that this extraordinary vocation is not obtained through personal strength or volition.

[268] See III. 2 ('The Eschatological Exodus').

This marriage is the mystery of God in Jesus Christ and the consummation of this mystery (Ap 10,7) or marriage, is the realization of the Holy City on earth (Is 54,11–17; Is chs.60 & 62; Ezek chs.40–48; Dan 7,27; Joel 4,17–21).

Chapter 12

Conclusions

Comparing the liturgical activity instituted by Moses and practised at the former Temple in Jerusalem with analogous features described in the visions of the Apocalypse, it is possible to discern in its prophecy the outlines of the entire project for the salvation of mankind. This can be summarized as follows: in the heavenly Sanctuary a liturgy for the reconciliation of men with God is being celebrated. Those who are reconciled while the liturgy is in progress come to represent the new Temple that is being built on earth, whose Sanctuary is the heavenly Sanctuary.

The new Temple is being built with the participation of St. John and the prophecy that was revealed to him. The central part of this prophecy describes events that will take place during the final seven years of history, and will be announced at the start of this period by the two witnesses of the Lord. Their testimony initiates the fulfilment of the prophecy and brings to completion the task that was entrusted to St. John, to measure the new Temple so that it can attain its final and most perfect form on Mt. Zion, in the midst of the 144,000 followers of the Lamb. First, however, the rest of the faithful must pass through the great tribulation, so purifying themselves to serve before the Throne of God in the heavenly Sanctuary.

Understood as a time of preparation for the consecration of the new Temple, the eschatological period of seven years involves a summing up, or recapitulation, of the whole work of creation and its submission to Christ.

At the culmination of the liturgy in the heavenly Sanctuary, at a time established by God, the consecration of the new Temple and its 144,000 priests will be brought about by the manifestation of the power and glory of the Lord. There follow the judgements of

God on the unredeemed world, the defeat of his enemies in the battle of the great Day, and then the final Judgement, when all wickedness will be removed from the creation and every trace of the past will disappear ('the first heaven and the first earth'). Finally, the Holy City will be established on earth: God will live there and his Presence among mankind will renew the creation ('a new heaven and a new earth').

Despite the profusion of symbols and images in the Apocalypse, all of which derive from the Old Testament and other ancient religious traditions of the Jews, the clarification of the theme of the Temple is uniquely valuable because it embraces and unites all the other images into a single and coherent vision, which is centred on the Sanctuary, or new Temple, of God. Interpreting the Apocalypse 'in the light of the Temple' therefore provides a way of understanding the text in its entirety, and not just as the sum of its parts.[269]

Nevertheless, the interpretation that issues from this research is quite surprising and unexpected. Since the new Temple is identified with the Church,[270] the interpretation presented in this study confirms that the Church has a crucial role to play in the fulfilment of the entire project of salvation—a role that, in its final stages at least, is mainly informed and directed by the prophecy of the Apocalypse.

Far from describing the history of the Early Church, the greater part of the text of the Apocalypse is actually a prophecy for the Church at the end of her historical mission—a prophecy that will be realized in the eschatological period, shortly before the ultimate

---

[269] In technical, exegetical, terms the study presented in this book is synchronic: by means of a typological analysis of the Temple symbolism in the Apocalypse, we have been able to identify and describe the 'deep structure' of the Book—the basic framework on which its various parts depend, and through which its meaning as a whole can be discerned (see Schussler-Fiorenza, "Revelation", ch. 15 in *New Testament and its Modern Interpreters*, especially 416–17).

[270] Adhering to the Christian tradition, the Church also identifies herself as the new Temple (see *Catechism of the Catholic Church*, no. 756).

fulfilment of the divine plan for mankind.[271] For this reason the Apocalypse has a much greater importance than that which has hitherto been attributed to this sacred Scripture. Understood in this way, in fact, one could say that, for the people of God, the Apocalypse is one of the most important documents ever written in the history of mankind. For others, though, and especially for those who are not concerned about the Will of God, or even oppose it, this assessment would seem to be a gross exaggeration. Indeed, the Apocalypse has a well-known reputation in the Church for provoking extremes of opinion.

However, perhaps there are others, even within the Church, whose attitude toward this reading of the Apocalypse is suspicious and diffident, because it proposes a literal interpretation of many aspects of the text (for example: the final week of years, the two witnesses, the 144,000 chaste men, the final war, the Holy City established on this planet). It may therefore appear to them like a 'fundamentalist' interpretation.

A fundamentalist interpretation, however, "presents itself as a form of private interpretation which does not acknowledge that the Church is founded on the Bible and draws its life and inspiration from Scripture " (Pontifical Biblical Commission, *The Interpretation of the Bible in the Church*, I, F). A sign that the interpretation of the Apocalypse 'in the light of the Temple' avoids the errors of the fundamentalists[272] is that this interpretation not only recognizes the

---

[271] The idea that the greater part of the Apocalypse describes the history of the Early Church is the result of the interpretation which currently prevails in the Church and is called 'preterist'. The most significant conclusion from interpreting the Apocalypse 'in the light of the Temple' is the confirmation that the greater part of the text refers to the eschatological period of history (see I. 11, ii).

[272] the errors of the fundamentalists: the principal error of fundamentalism is the dogmatic insistence on the 'inerrancy' of the biblical text, with the result that words and expressions used in the text come to be understood uncritically as they are written, in a superficial and 'literalistic' way. In the Apocalypse, this approach leads to really fantastic explanations (for example: horses which appear in the sky, chimeric monsters which attack people, 'floating islands' landing on the earth...). The situation is made more complex by the fact that the same principle of inerrancy permits equal weight to be given to texts of the OT as to those of the NT (cf. n. 94). In

Church's dependence on the text of the Apocalypse, but also explains precisely how the Church will be perfected and the world regenerated through the fulfilment of its prophecy.

Instead, the literal character of this interpretation 'in the light of the Temple' is an indication that it expresses the literal sense of the text.

No other sense of Scripture is as important as the literal sense, since "all other senses of Sacred Scripture are based on the literal" (*Catechism of the Catholic Church*, no. 116, quoting St. Thomas Aquinas). It is the essential task of exegesis, then, to clarify this sense (Pius XII, Divino Afflante Spirito, 11), which is defined as "the sense which the human author directly intended and which the written words conveyed" (*New Jerome Biblical Commentary*, 71:9). "Since it is the fruit of inspiration, this sense is also intended by God, as principal author" (Pontifical Biblical Commission, *The Interpretation of the Bible in the Church*, II, B.1).

If the literal sense of a historical text is what the divine and human authors wished to say about events that happened in the past, then the literal sense of a text of eschatological prophecy is what the divine and human authors wish to say about events that are expected to happen in the future.[273] In other words, the literal sense of a text containing an eschatological prophecy (such as the greater part of the Apocalypse) is nothing other than the prophecy itself conveyed by its words. The clarification of this prophecy, then, is the essential task of exegetical research, and is certainly not a fundamentalist error.

Neither is it a fundamentalist error to expect this prophecy to be literally fulfilled, since this is a basic principle of the biblical tradition. In this tradition, in fact, the literal fulfilment of a prophecy is the main guarantee of its divine origin and authenticity (Deut 18,21–22). Given that the Apocalypse enters fully into this tradition,

---

the interpretation of the Apocalypse, the supposed parity between the OT and the NT leads to the conflation of prophecies from both Testaments, and forms the basis for the millenarian 'dispensationalist' interpretation adopted by the fundamentalists.

[273] It is understood that, up to the time of writing, we have not yet entered this period of history, although we may be very, very close.

it is clear that the plain fulfilment of its prophecy is the main evidence for its authenticity. Furthermore, the fact that the authenticity of the Apocalypse is closely related to the conviction that Jesus is the true Messiah implies that the literal fulfilment of this prophecy ought to be considered an integral part of Faith in Jesus Christ.

Confirmation of the importance of the literal fulfilment of divine prophecies can be traced back to Jesus Christ himself, who spared no effort in literally fulfilling a number of Old Testament prophecies, including the triumphant entry into Jerusalem on a donkey (Zech 9,9), the cleansing of the Temple (Mal 3,1) and the suffering of the servant (Is ch.53). If during his mission on earth Jesus insisted on fulfilling these prophecies literally, how much more will he not insist on the literal fulfilment of the prophecy in the Apocalypse, since it is in this way that he is bringing to completion his messianic task for the whole of mankind.

"Amen, come Lord Jesus. The grace of the Lord Jesus be with you all" (Ap 22,20–21).

APPENDIX

The following article could serve as a guide for the reading and comprehension of the Apocalypse as a whole, and as a clarification of those parts of the text that, in this study, have been referred to as the 'central prophecy'.[274]

The literary structure of the Apocalypse and its implications for the interpretation of the text

Most commentators of the Apocalypse agree that the main body of the text is preceded by a prologue (Ap 1,1–8) and followed by an epilogue (Ap 22,6–21). There is, however, a considerable difference of opinion concerning the fundamental subdivisions within the main part of the text (Ap 1,9 – 22,5). Since the prophecy of the Apocalypse does not closely follow the order in which the visions are described, an awareness of the superficial structure of the text can help a great deal in its interpretation. We would therefore like to propose the following approach, and indicate its main implications.

It is evident from the text, that this report of St. John's visions should be understood as a narration of successive events. In the original Greek text, there is a continuous repetition of the conjunction 'and', which reflects the use of the 'vav consecutive', so characteristic of the narrative style of biblical Hebrew.

The frequent use of the expression 'after these things' (Ap 7,1.9; 15,5; 18,1; 19,1) to join larger sections of text, also has the effect of emphasizing the sequential character of the events that are described in the vision narrative. Furthermore, the visions

---

[274] See n. 199 above.

themselves are structured in four consecutive series: the one who dictates a series of 7 letters reveals the opening of a sealed scroll after the breaking of a series of 7 seals, which leads in turn to the sounding of a series of 7 trumpets, which concludes with the outpouring of a series of 7 bowls.

On the basis of these observations, not only is the narrative intention of the text indisputable, but also through the use of other expressions of time ('what must happen after these things' Ap 1,19; 4,1; 'what must happen soon' Ap 1,1; 22,6) it is clear that the narration is aimed directly towards a point in the future.

In this way, it is possible to define in the text a 'baseline prophetic narrative', which describes, with ever increasing detail, the events which lead up to the fulfilment of the mystery of God at the end of time. This 'baseline prophetic narrative' clearly starts with the words: "Come up here and I will show you what must happen after these things" (Ap 4,1) and can be outlined in the following way:

4,1 – 22,5	"what must happen after these things":
4,1–11	Initial vision of the Throne in heaven
5,1–14	Preparations for breaking the 7 seals of the scroll
6,1–2	Breaking of the 1st seal
6,3–4	Breaking of the 2nd seal
6,5–6	Breaking of the 3rd seal
6,7–8	Breaking of the 4th seal
6,9–11	Breaking of the 5th seal
6,12–17	Breaking of the 6th seal
7,1–17	**Interruption**
8,1	Breaking of the 7th seal
8,2–6	Preparations for the sounding of the 7 trumpets
8,7	Sounding of the 1st trumpet
8,8–9	Sounding of the 2nd trumpet
8,10–11	Sounding of the 3rd trumpet
8,12–13	Sounding of the 4th trumpet
9,1–12	Sounding of the 5th trumpet

9,13–21	Sounding of the 6th trumpet
10,1 – 11,14	**Interruption**
11,15–19	Sounding of the 7th trumpet
12,1 – 15,4	**Interruption**
15,5–8	Preparations for pouring out of the 7 libation bowls
16,1–2	Outpouring of the 1st bowl
16,3	Outpouring of the 2nd bowl
16,4–7	Outpouring of the 3rd bowl
16,8–9	Outpouring of the 4th bowl
16,10–11	Outpouring of the 5th bowl
16,12–16	Outpouring of the 6th bowl
16,17–21	Outpouring of the 7th bowl
17,1 – 19,5	**Interruption**
19,6 – 22,5	The fulfilment of the mystery of God.

This outline of the 'baseline prophetic narrative' displays several large interruptions in the sequence of events narrated by St. John. The largest of these interruptions (12,1 – 15,4) breaks the continuity of the 'baseline prophetic narrative' at the midpoint of the text, thus dividing it into two, more or less equal, halves: 'Part I' denotes the first half (Ap chs.1–11) and 'Part II' the second half (Ap chs.12–22).

The resumption of continuity between the end of Part I (Ap 11,19) and Part II is indicated by the repetition of a statement referring to a single event—the opening of the Sanctuary in heaven:
" the Sanctuary of God in heaven was opened" (Ap 11,19)
" the Sanctuary of the Tent of testimony in heaven was opened" (Ap 15,5).

Furthermore, the interrupting passage (12,1 – 15,4) contains verbal-thematic links to the final chapter of Part I: the use of the two expressions of time, 1,260 days and 42 months (Ap 12,6; 13,5), recalls the mention of the same expressions at the beginning of chapter 11 (Ap 11,2–3).

The implication of these observations is that there is a section of overlap between the end of Part I (Ap 11,1–19) and the

beginning of Part II (Ap 12,1 – 15,4),[275] which can be diagrammati-
cally represented in the following way:

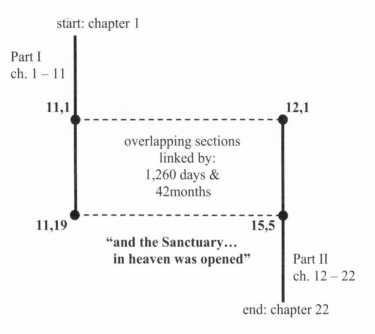

Two characteristics of these overlapping sections suggest
that they have considerable importance for the interpretation of the
text.

In the first place, the overlap is situated at the very centre of
the Apocalypse (Ap ch.11). In ancient documents, the central part
was often reserved for the most important information; for example,
the passage at the centre of the Pentateuch contains the background
to the greatest event in the ancient liturgical calendar of the Jews—
the Day of Atonement (Lev ch.16).

---

[275] In fact, these expressions indicate a connection between 11,2 and 13,5, and also
between 11,3 and 12,6. However, since 11,2 and 12,6 develop themes which were
initiated at 11,1 and 12,1 respectively, and can not be separated from these verses, it
follows that the overlapping begins at 11,1 and 12,1.

In the second place, the overlapping of two parallel passages allows the transmission of a greater amount of information than in only one passage, although it may be expressed in a less obvious way.

To determine the meaning of these overlapping sections, it is necessary to examine their context and content (Ap 11,1 – 15,4).

These sections follow the account of the consequences of the sounding of the 6th trumpet[276](Ap 9,13–21), and announce the sounding of the 7th trumpet (Ap 11,15–19), which also forms an integral part of the 'baseline prophetic narrative'. The overlapping sections, therefore, convey an eschatological prophecy, which describes events that immediately precede the 7th and last trumpet at the end of time.

More specifically, these sections follow immediately after the author was told he must "prophesy again about many peoples and nations and tongues and kings" (Ap 10,11). St. John's response constitutes all the rest of the Apocalypse (Ap 11,1 – the end), which can be understood as the prophecy he was given with the purpose of 'prophesying again'. The overlapping sections therefore represent the first part of the prophecy that St. John wrote in response to what he was told to do.

The meaning of the prophecy in these sections is indicated by the way they begin and end. After the author is told that he must 'prophesy again', the overlapping sections begin with the command to "get up and measure the Sanctuary of God, the altar and those who worship there" (Ap 11,1–2). In order to carry out this command, St. John was given a measuring rod (Ap 11,1). It has just been noted, though, that he was given a prophecy. The prophecy that follows can therefore be identified with the 'measuring rod' that was

---

[276] Only from the literary point of view. A verbal-thematic link indicates that in reality the start of the overlapping sections coincides with the start of the trumpet series—the fall of a third of the stars during the war in heaven (Ap 12,4.7–8) corresponds to the fall of the heavenly bodies after the sounds of the trumpets and even reflects the degree of devastation that follows them (a third).

given to St. John to measure the new Temple of God during its construction.

The overlapping sections finish with the vision of the opening of the heavenly Sanctuary (Ap 11,19; 15,5) and its filling with the smoke of the glory and power of God (Ap 15,8). In the Scriptures of the Old Testament, this event is associated with the completion of the divine Dwelling or Temple (Ex 40,34–35; 1Kgs 8,10–13) and therefore, in the present context, signifies the completion of the new Temple, in whose construction the author and his prophecy have been participating.

In conclusion, the part of the prophecy identified with the overlapping sections (Ap 11,1 – 15,4) can be called either the 'central prophecy' by virtue of its central situation in the text of the Apocalypse, or 'the prophecy for the completion of the new Temple' by virtue of its significance. Since the new Temple represents the Church (Eph 2,19–22; 1Pet 2,4–10; Heb 12,22–24; Ap 3,12), it can be inferred that the overlapping sections contain a prophecy for the perfecting of the Church and the completion of her historical mission.

Furthermore, the contents of this prophecy explain how and when it will be publicly announced. The command given to St. John (Ap 11,1–2) leads directly to the description of the prophetic ministry of the two witnesses (Ap 11,3–13). Since this is the first activity mentioned in the prophecy that was given to St. John, the start of this prophetic ministry also signals the realization of the prophecy, and so brings to an end the task of measuring requested from St. John. Since the appearance of the beast at the start his 42–month reign (Ap 13,5) coincides with the conclusion of the prophetic ministry of the two witnesses during the period of 1,260 days (Ap 11,7), it can be deduced that these two periods of time are consecutive. The total time represented by these two periods is therefore seven years (1,260 days plus 42 months).

Furthermore, the final half of this seven-year period, the 42–month reign, terminates with the completion of God's Kingdom at the sound of the 7th trumpet (Ap 11,15–19). It is evident, then, that the two time-periods (1,260 days and 42 months), which structure the information given in the overlapping sections (the 'central prophecy'), refer to the final seven years of history—a final 'week of years'.

In summary, the overlapping sections represent a prophecy for the perfecting of the Church during the final seven years of history, which will be publicly announced during the first half of this period by the two witnesses. It is not surprising to find that this information, replete with an abundance of detail, forms the central message of the Apocalypse.

Even though 'the prophecy for the Church in the last seven years' can be clearly identified with the overlapping section, it is not by any means limited to this (Ap 11,1 – 15,4). Through verbal-thematic links, the prophecy of the overlapping sections is found to be associated with all the other passages that interrupt the 'baseline prophetic narrative'.

The first interruption to the 'baseline prophetic narrative' is chapter 7 (Ap 7,1–17), in which two crowds are described in close succession: the numbered multitude of 144,000 servants of God (Ap 7,1–8) and the innumerable multitude of martyrs who serve God before his heavenly Throne (Ap 7,9–17). These passages are connected, by verbal-thematic links, to those parts of the overlapping sections that describe the 144,000 followers of the Lamb (Ap 14,1–5) and the conquerors of the beast (Ap 15,2–4).

The second interruption is chapter 10 (Ap 10,1–11), which recounts the preparation of St. John to 'prophesy again'. The entire chapter forms an introduction to the prophecy of the overlapping sections.

The last interruption comprises chapters 17, 18 and 19,1–5 (Ap 17,1 – 19,5) and describes in detail the condemnation and destruction of Babylon. The fact that these events had been previously announced in the overlapping sections (Ap 14,8; cf.18,2) indicates their connection to this part of the text. In this way, it is clear that all three interruptions are linked to the prophecy of the overlapping section (Ap 11,1 – 15,4), which is the central message of the Apocalypse and the prophecy for the perfecting of the Church during the final seven years of history.[277]

At the beginning of his revelation, St. John was asked to write three things: 'what you see', 'what is now', and 'what must happen after these things' (Ap 1,19). On the basis of these three components of his work, the approach that has been proposed in this inquiry leads to the following conclusions about the structure of the Apocalypse:

1,1–8	Prologue
1,9–20	"what you see": introductory vision of the risen Lord
2,1 – 3,22	"what is now": the 7 letters to the churches
4,1 – 22,5	"what must happen after these things":

    4,1–11 — initial vision of the Throne in heaven

    5,1–14 — preparations for breaking the 7 seals of the scroll

    6,1–17 — breaking of 1st, 2nd, 3rd, 4th, 5th and 6th seals

    7,1–17 — **linked to the 'central prophecy'**

    8,1 — breaking of the 7th seal

    8,2–6 — preparations for sounding the 7 trumpets

    8,7 – 9,21 — sounding of 1st, 2nd, 3rd, 4th, 5th, and 6th trumpets

    10,1–11 — **linked to the 'central prophecy'**

    11,1–13

    11,14–19 — sounding of 7th trumpet $\Big\}$ **'the central prophecy'**

    12,1 – 15,4   = overlapping sections

    15,5–8 — preparations for pouring out the 7 libation bowls

    16,1–21 — outpouring of 1st, 2nd, 3rd, 4th, 5th, 6th and 7th bowls

    17,1 – 19,5 — **linked to the 'central prophecy'**

    19,6–10 — the announcement of the marriage of the Lamb

---

[277] Since this prophecy forms a distinct, but integral, part of the Apocalypse, the temporal references in the prophecy must be interpreted according to their context (the eschatological period of history) and not according to the time in which the text is thought to have been written (at the end of the first century AD).

BIBLIOGRAPHY

Augustine of Hippo, St. *The City of God.* Translated by G. Walsh, D. Zema, G. Monahan and D. Honan. Vols. 8, 14 and 24 of the Fathers of the Church series. Washington: Catholic University of America Press, 1950–1954.

Allen, Leslie C. *Ezekiel 20–48.* Vol. 29 of the Word Biblical Commentary. Waco, Texas: Word Books, 1990.

Aune, David E. *Revelation 1–5.* Vol. 52A of the Word Biblical Commentary. Dallas, Texas: Word Books, 1997.

———. *Revelation 6–16.* Vol. 52B of the Word Biblical Commentary. Nashville: Thomas Nelson Publishers, 1998.

———. *Revelation 17–22.* Vol. 52C of the Word Biblical Commentary. Nashville: Thomas Nelson Publishers, 1998.

The Babylonian Talmud. Hebrew-English Edition, edited by I. Epstein. London: Soncino Press, (1971–1987).

Baker, Margaret. *The Revelation of Jesus Christ.* Edinburgh: T. & T. Clark, 2000.

Bauckham, R. J. *The Climax of Prophecy: Studies on the Book of Revelation.* Edinburgh: T. & T. Clark, 1993.

———. *The Theology of the Book of Revelation.* Cambridge: Cambridge University Press, 1993.

Beagley, Alan James. *The 'Sitz im Leben' of the Apocalypse, with Particular Reference to the Church's Enemies.* Berlin: Walter de Gruyter, 1987.

Beale, G. K. *The Book of Revelation.* NIGTC series. Grand Rapids: Eerdmans, 1999.

———. *The Use of Daniel in Jewish Apocalyptic Literature and in the Revelation of St. John.* Lanham: University Press of America, 1984.

Beasley-Murray, G. R. *The Book of Revelation.* London: Oliphants, 1978.

Bernard of Clairvaux, St. "Apology to Abbot William". Translated by M. Casey. *The Works of Bernard of Clairvaux.* Vol. 1 of the Cistercian Fathers series, Treatises I. Shannon: Irish University Press, 1970.

Biguzzi, G. "La donna, il drago e il Messia in Ap 12." In *Theotokos–Ricerche Interdisciplinari di Mariologia,* Anno VIII, 2000, no. 1, 17–66.

Bissoli, Giovanni. *Il Tempio nella Letteratura Giudaica e Neotestamentaria.* Studium Biblicum Franciscanum Analecta 37. Jerusalem: Franciscan Printing Press, 1994.

Black, M. "The 'Two Witnesses' of Rev 11:3f in Jewish and Christian Apocalyptic Tradition." In *Donum Gentilicum: New Testament Studies in Honour of David Daube,* edited by E. Bammel, C. K. Barrett & W. D. Davies. Oxford: Clarendon Press, 1978.

Blenkinsopp, Joseph. *The Pentateuch: An Introduction to the First Five Books of the Bible.* Anchor Bible Reference Library. New York: Doubleday, 1992.

———. "The Structure of P." In *Catholic Biblical Quarterly,* vol. 38, 1976, 275–92.

Block, Daniel I. *The Book of Ezekiel Chs. 25–48.* New International Commentary on the Old Testament. Grand Rapids: Eerdmans, 1998.

Bockmuehl, Marcus. *Revelation and Mystery in Ancient Judaism and Pauline Christianity.* Grand Rapids: Eerdmans, 1997.

Bray, Gerald. *Biblical Interpretation Past and Present.* Leicester: InterVarsity Press, 1996.

Briggs, Robert A. *Jewish Temple Imagery in the Book of Revelation.* Vol. 10 of Studies in Biblical Literature. New York: Peter Lang Publishing, 1999.

Brod, Menachem M. *The Days of Moshiach: the Redemption and the Coming of Moshiach in Jewish Sources.* Kfar Chabad, Israel: Chabad Youth Organization, 1993.

The Catechism of the Catholic Church. London: Geoffrey Chapman, 1994.

Castelot, John J. and Aelred Cody. "Religious Institutions of Israel". Ch. 76 in *The New Jerome Biblical Commentary,* edited by R. E. Brown, J. A. Fitzmyer and R. E. Murphy. New Jersey: Prentice Hall, 1990.

Catherine of Siena, St. *The Dialogue.* Translated by S. Noffke. Classics of Western Spirituality Series. New York: Paulist Press, 1980.

Charles, R. H. *The Apocrypha and Pseudepigrapha of the Old Testament in English.* 2 vols. Oxford: Clarendon Press, 1913.

————. *A Critical and Exegetical Commentary on the Revelation of St. John.* International Critical Commentaries (2 vols). Edinburgh: T. & T. Clark, 1920.

————. *Eschatology: The Doctrine of a Future Life in Israel, Judaism and Christianity. A Critical History.* New York: Schocken Books, 1963.

————. *Studies in the Apocalypse: Being Lectures Delivered before the University of London.* Edinburgh: T. & T. Clark, 1913.

Charlesworth, J. H., ed. *The Old Testament Pseudepigrapha.* 2 vols. Garden City, NY: Doubleday, 1983–1985.

Clements, R. E. *God and Temple.* Oxford: Blackwell, 1965.

Collins, Adela Yarbro. "The Apocalypse (Revelation)." Ch. 63 in *The New Jerome Biblical Commentary,* edited by R. E. Brown, J. A. Fitzmyer and R. E. Murphy. New Jersey: Prentice Hall, 1990.

————. *Cosmology and Eschatology in Jewish and Christian Apocalypticism.* Leiden: E. J. Brill, 1996.

Collins, John J. *Daniel: A Commmentary on the Book of Daniel.* Hermeneia Series. Minneapolis: Fortress Press, 1993.

————. "Introduction: Towards the Morphology of a Genre." In *Semeia* 14, 1979, 1–20.

————. *Jerusalem and the Temple in Jewish Apocalyptic Literature of the Second Temple Period.* International Rennert Guest Lecture Series 1(1998). Tel Aviv: Bar Ilan University, 1998.

————, ed. *Encyclopedia of Apocalyptism, vol. 1: The Origins.* New York: Continuum, 1998.

The Conciliar and Post Conciliar Documents. Vol. 1. Edited by Austin Flannery. New York: Costello Publishing Company, 1987.

Conferenza Episcopale Italiana, Ufficio Catechistico Nazionale. *Incontro alla Bibbia.* Vatican City: Libreria Editrice Vaticana, 1996.

Congar, Yves M.-J. *The Mystery of the Temple, or the Manner of God's Presence to His Creatures from Genesis to the Apocalypse.* Translated by R. F. Trevett. Westminster, MD: Newmans Press, 1962.

Court, John M. *Revelation.* Sheffield: Sheffield Academic Press, 1994.

Culpepper, R. A. *John, the Son of Zebedee: The Life of a Legend.* Columbia: University of South Carolina, 1994.

Davies, W. D. *Jewish and Pauline Studies.* Philadelphia: Fortress Press, 1984.

————. *Paul and Rabbinic Judaism.* 4th Edition. Philadelphia: Fortress Press, 1980.

————. *The Setting of the Sermon on the Mount.* Cambridge: Cambridge University Press, 1964.

————. *The Torah in the Messianic Age/Age to Come.* Vol. 7 of the Journal of Biblical Literature Monograph Series, 1952.

de Vaux, Roland. *Ancient Israel: Its Life and Institutions.* Translated by John McHugh. London: Dartman, Longman and Todd, 1973.

Dictionnaire de Spiritualité. Edited by Marcel Viller. Paris, 1937.

Dictionary of Biblical Interpretation. Edited by R. J. Coggins and J. L. Houlden. London: S.C.M. Press, 1990.

Dunn, James D. G. *The Partings of the Ways: Between Christianity and Judaism and their significance for the Character of Christianity.* London: S.C.M. Press; Philadelphia: Trinity Press, 1991.

Eckhart, Meister. *Selected Writings.* Translated by O. Davies. London: Penguin, 1994.

Edersheim, Alfred. *The Temple: Its Ministry and Services.* Updated edition. Peabody, MA: Hendrickson Publishers, 1994.

Early Christian Writings. Translated by M. Staniforth. Harmondsworth, England: Penguin, 1968.

Eichrodt, W. *Ezekiel.* Old Testament Library. London: S.C.M. Press, 1970.

Encyclopaedia Judaica. Jerusalem: Keter Publishing House, 1971.

Epstein, Isidore. *Judaism.* London: Penguin, 1959.

Eusebius of Caesaria. *The Ecclesiastical History.* Translated by K. Lake and J. Oulton. Loeb Classical Library. 2 vols. London: Heinemann, 1932.

Farrer, Austin M. *The Revelation of St. John the Divine.* Oxford: Clarendon Press, 1964.

Ford, J. Massingbyrd. *Commentary on Revelation.* Anchor Bible Series. New York: Doubleday, 1975.

Forsyth, Neil. *The Old Enemy: Satan and the Combat Myth*. Princeton: Princeton University Press, 1987.

Fowler White, R. "Reexamining the Evidence for Recapitulation in Rev 20:1–10." In the *Westminster Theological Journal*, vol. 51, 1989, 319–44.

————. "On the Hermeneutics and Interpretation of Rev 20:1–3: a Preconsummationist Perspective." In the *Journal of the Evangelical Theological Society*, vol. 42/1 (March 1999), 53–66.

Garrow, A. J. P. *Revelation*. New Testament Readings. London: Routledge, 1997.

Giblin, Charles Homer. *The Book of Revelation: The Open Book of Prophecy*. Good News Studies 34. Collegeville, Minnesota: Liturgical Press, 1991.

Ginzberg, Louis. *The Legends of the Jews*. Translated by Henrietta Szold (7 vols.). Philadelphia: Jewish Publication Society of America, 1909–1938

Goldingay, John E. *Daniel*. Vol. 30 of the Word Biblical Commentary. Dallas, Texas: Word Books, 1989.

Hamerton-Kelly, R. G. "The Temple and the Origins of Jewish Apocalyptic." In *Vetus Testamentum*, vol. 20, 1970, 1–15.

Haran, Menahem. *Temples and Temple-Service in Ancient Israel*. Indiana: Eisenbrauns, 1985.

Hebrew-English Bible. Jerusalem: The Bible Society in Israel, 1997.

Hengel, Martin. *Judaism and Hellenism*. English translation in one volume. London: S.C.M. Press, 1981.

Hippolytus, St. "Treatise on Christ and Antichrist". *The Ante-Nicene Fathers* Series. Edited by A. Roberts and J. Donaldson. Vol. 5. American Reprint of the Edinburgh Edition. Edinburgh: T. & T. Clarke; Grand Rapids: Eerdmans,1990, 204–19.

Himmelfarb, Martha. *Ascent to Heaven in Jewish and Christian Apocalypses*. Oxford: Oxford University Press, 1993.

The Holy Bible. New Revised Standard Version. London: Harper Collins Religious, 1998.

The Holy Bible. Revised Standard Version. New York: Thomas Nelson & Sons, 1953.

The Jerusalem Bible. Standard Edition. London: Dartman, Longman & Todd Ltd, 1996

The Jewish Encyclopaedia. New York: Ktav Publishing House, 1901.

John of the Cross, St. *Complete Works*. Translated by E. Allison Peers. Wheathampstead, England: Anthony Clarke, 1978.

John Paul II. *The Splendour of Truth*. Encyclical Letter. Vatican City: Libreria Editrice Vaticana, 1993.

Josephus, Flavius. *Jewish Antiquities*. Translated by H. Thackeray, R. Marcus, A Wikgren, and H. Feldman. Vols. 4–9 in the Loeb Classical Library series: Josephus in Nine Volumes, London: Heinemann, 1926–1965.

Kiddle, M and M. K. Ross. *The Revelation of St. John*. Moffatt New Testament Commentary, 17. London: Hodder & Stoughton, 1940.

Klausner, Joseph. *The Messianic Idea in Israel*. New York: Macmillan, 1955.

The Koran. Translated by N. J. Dawood. Penguin Classics series, revised edition. London: Penguin, 1997.

Ladd, G. E. *A Commentary on the Revelation of John*. Grand Rapids: Eerdmans, 1972.

Le Frois, B. J. *The Woman Clothed with the Sun (Ap 12): Individual or Collective? An Exegetical Study*. Roma, 1954.

Ling, Trevor. *The Significance of Satan*. London, 1961.

Maimonides. *The Code of Maimonides (Mishneh Torah)*. Book 14, The Book of Judges. Translated by A. Hershman. Vol. 3 in the Yale Judaica Series. New Haven: Yale University Press, 1949.

Martini, Carlo Maria. *Sto alla Porta*. Pastoral Letter 1992–1994. Milan: Centro Ambrosiano, 1992.

McGinn, Bernard. *The Foundations of Mysticism: Origins to the Fifth Century*. Vol. 1 of The Presence of God: A History of Western Christian Mysticism. New York: Crossroad, 1992.

McKelvey, R. J. *The New Temple: The Church in the New Testament*. Oxford: Oxford University Press, 1969.

Meyers, C., and E. Meyers. *Haggai, Zechariah 1–8*. Vol. 25B of the Anchor Bible Commentaries. New York: Doubleday, 1987.

Midrash Rabbah, edited by H. Freedman and M. Simon, 10 volumes (Pentateuch and Megilloth). London: Soncino, 1939.

The Mishnah. Translated by Herbert Danby. Oxford: Clarendon Press, 1933.

Mitchell, Smith and Bewer. *Haggai, Zechariah, Malachi, and Jonah*. International Critical Commentary Series. Edinburgh: T. & T. Clark, 1912.

Morris, Leon. *Revelation*. 2nd Edition. Leicester: InterVarsity Press, 1987.

Moore, George F. *Judaism in the First Centuries of The Christian Era: The Age of the Tannaim*. 3 vols. Cambridge, Mass. 1927–30.

Mounce, R.H. *The Book of Revelation*. Revised edition. New International Commentary on the New Testament. Grand Rapids: Eerdmans, 1998.

Nestle-Aland. *Novum Testamentum Graece*. 26th Edition. Stuttgart: Deutsche Bibelgesellschaft, 1979.

Neusner, Jacob. *The Torah: From Scroll to Symbol in Formative Judaism*. Atlanta: Scholars Press, 1988.

The New Catholic Encyclopaedia. Produced by the editorial staff at the Catholic University of America. New York: McGraw-Hill, 1967.

The New International Dictionary of New Testament Theology. Edited by Colin Brown. Exeter: Paternoster Press, 1978.

The New Jerome Biblical Commentary. Edited by R. E. Brown, J. A. Fitzmyer and R. E. Murphy. New Jersey: Prentice Hall, 1990.

The New Testament and its Modern Interpreters. Edited by Eldon Jay Epp and George W. McRae. Atlanta: Scholars Press, 1989.

Nicklesburg, George. *Jewish Literature between the Bible and the Mishnah*. Philadelphia: Fortress Press, 1981.

Pagels, Elaine. *The Origin of Satan*. New York: Random House, 1995.

Patte, Daniel. *What is Structural Exegesis?* Philadelphia: Fortress Press, 1976.

Petersen, D. L. *Haggai and Zechariah 1–6*. Old Testament Library. London: S.C.M. Press, 1985.

Pedersen, Johannes. *Israel: Its Life and Culture*. 2 vols, (Parts I-IV). London: Oxford University Press, reprinted 1946–1953.

Pio XII. "Lettera Enciclica: Divino Afflante Spiritu." In *La Divina Ispirazione*. Roma: Edizioni Paoline, 1964.

Pontifical Biblical Commission. *The Interpretation of the Bible in the Church.* Vatican City: Libreria Editrice Vaticana, 1993.

————. *The Jewish People and their Sacred Scriptures in the Christian Bible.* Vatican City: Libreria Editrice Vaticana, 2002

Prigent, Pierre. *Apocalypse 12: Histoire de l'exégèse.* Tübingen: J. C. B. Mohr (Paul Siebeck), 1959.

————. *Commentary on the Apocalypse of St. John.* Translated by W. Pradels. Tübingen: J. C. B. Mohr (Paul Siebeck), 2001.

Rahner, Hugo. *Maria e la Chiesa.* Già e non ancora series. Milan: Jaca Books, 1977.

Ravitsky, Aviezer. *Messianism, Zionism and Jewish Religious Radicalism.* Chicago: Chicago University Press, 1996.

Rossi de Gasperis, Francesco. *Maria de Nazaret: Icona di Israele e della Chiesa.* Magnano: Edizioni Qiqajon, 1997.

Rowland, Christopher. *The Open Heaven.* New York: Crossroad, 1982.

Ruiz, J.-P. *Ezekiel in the Apocalypse: The Transformation of Prophetic Language in Revelation 16:17 – 19:10.* Frankfurt: Lang, 1989.

Russell, D. S. *The Method and Message of Jewish Apocalyptic.* London: S.C.M. Press, 1964.

Russell, J. B. *The Devil: Perceptions of Evil from Antiquity to Primitive Christianity.* Ithaca, New York: Cornell University Press, 1970.

Sanders, E. P. *Jesus and Judaism.* Philadelphia: Fortress Press, 1985.

Sanders, James. *Torah and Canon.* Philadelphia: Fortress Press, 1972.

Sbaffoni, Fausto, ed. *Testi sull'Anticristo, secoli I-II.* Biblioteca Patristica. Firenze: Nardini Editore, 1992.

————, ed. *Testi sull'Anticristo, secolo III.* Biblioteca Patristica. Firenze: Nardini Editore, 1992.

Schauss, Hayyim. *The Jewish Festivals: History and Observance.* New York: Schocken Books, 1962.

Schlink, Basilea. *Patmos: When the Heavens Opened.* London: Lakeland Marshall, Morgan and Scott, 1976.

Scholem, Gershom. *The Messianic Idea in Judaism and Other Essays.* New York: Schocken Books, 1971.

————. *On the Kabbalah and its Symbolism.* New York: Schocken Books, 1965.

Schürer, Emil. *History of the Jewish People in the Age of Jesus Christ.* New English Version (3 vols.). Edinburgh: T. & T. Clark, 1973.

Smith, Ralph L. *Micah-Malachi.* Vol. 32 of the Word Biblical Commentary. Waco, Texas: Word Books, 1984.

Spatafora, Andrea. *From the Temple of God to God as the Temple: A Biblical Theological Study of the Temple in the Book of Revelation.* Tesi Gregoriana Serie Teologia, 27. Rome: Editrice Pontificia Università Gregoriana, 1997.

Stefanovic, Ranko. *The Background and Meaning of the Sealed Scroll of Rev 5.* Barren Springs, Michigan: Andrews University Press, 1996.

Sweet, J. P. M. *Revelation.* S.C.M. Pelican Commentaries. London: S.C.M. Press, 1979.

Swete, H. B. *The Apocalypse of John: The Greek Text with Introduction, Notes and Indeces.* 3rd edition. London: Macmillan, 1917.

Teresa of Avila, St. *The Interior Castle.* Translated by R. Van de Weyer. London: Harper Collins Religious, Fount Paperbooks, 1975.

Theological Dictionary of the New Testament. Edited by G. Kittel and G. Friedrich, Translated by Geoffrey Bromiley. Grand Rapids: Eerdmans, 1964–1974.

Theological Dictionary of the Old Testament. Edited by G. J. Botterweck and H. Ringgren, Translated by John T. Willis. 1st reprint. Grand Rapids: Eerdmans, 1979.

Thompson, L. L. *The Book of Revelation: Apocalypse and Empire.* Oxford: Oxford University Press, 1990.

Ulfgard, H. *Feast and Future: Revelation 7:9–17 and the Feast of Tabernacles.* Stockholm: Almqvist and Wiksell, 1989.

Urbach, Ephraim E. *The Sages: The World and Wisdom of the Rabbis of the Talmud.* Cambridge, MA: Harvard University Press, 1987.

Vanni, Ugo. *L'Apocalisse: Ermeneutica, Esegesi, Teologia.* Bologna: Centro Editoriale Dehoniano, 1988.

———. "Liturgical Dialogue as a Literary Form in the Book of Revelation". In *New Testament Studies*, vol. 31, 1991, 348–72.

Walker, P. W. L. *Jesus and the Holy City: New Testament Perspectives on Jerusalem.* Grand Rapids: Eerdmans, 1996.

Wikenhauser, Alfred. *L'Apocalisse di Giovanni.* Italian translation by G. Rinaldi and F. Montagnini. Milano: Rizzoli Editore, 1983.

INDEX OF REFERENCES
to the Bible and other Ancient Sources

OLD TESTAMENT

237

NEW TESTAMENT

OTHER ANCIENT SOURCES

INDEX OF SUBJECTS

Hallelujah!